Tourism in China

Tourism in China

Geographic, Political, and Economic Perspectives

EDITED BY

Alan A. Lew
and Lawrence Yu

Westview Press

BOULDER • SAN FRANCISCO • OXFORD

Copyright © 1995 by Westview Press, Inc.

Published in 1995 in the United States of America by Westview Press, Inc., 5500 Central Avenue, Boulder, Colorado 80301-2877, and in the United Kingdom by Westview Press, 36 Lonsdale Road, Summertown, Oxford OX2 7EW

Library of Congress Cataloging-in-Publication Data
Lew, Alan A.
   Tourism in China : geographic, political, and economic
perspectives / Alan A. Lew and Lawrence Yu.
      p.   cm.
   Includes bibliographical references and index.
   ISBN 0-8133-8874-0
   1. Tourist trade—China.   I. Yu, Lawrence.   II. Title.
G155.C5L49   1995
338.4'791504429—dc20

94-29615
CIP

Printed and bound in the United States of America

∞ The paper used in this publication meets the requirements
   of the American National Standard for Permanence of Paper
   for Printed Library Materials Z39.48-1984.

10   9   8   7   6   5   4   3   2   1

To our wives
Mable Wong Lew
and
Sarah Chen Yu
for their support
and understanding

Contents

Preface

China has one of the oldest continuous civilizations in the world. It is a land of mystery and ambiguity that has long attracted the more adventurous of international travelers. Travel in China before 1949 was well documented and described in both Chinese history books and the travel writings by foreign adventurers. However, China did not develop a modern, international travel and tourism industry until 1978 when the new leadership instituted an open door policy for international tourists as part of a revolutionary economic development program. Since then China has enjoyed the success of rapid development and suffered the pains of unbridled growth. Today, the travel and tourism in China is a major industry with a modern, albeit over-burdened, transportation network, world-class lodging facilities, comprehensive travel services, and numerous training centers. Much more needs to be done, however, if China hopes to reach its goal of becoming the most visited tourist destination in Asia by the end of this century.

The scale and speed of tourism development in China since 1978 has made the country a major player in the global network of international travel and tourism. However, its impressive growth, and the numerous lessons it presents, have not been systematically and collectively presented to interested academics and industry professionals. This book attempts to make such a contribution. We have invited some of the most eminent scholars currently writing on tourism in China to analyze the country's tourism development. The collection of original contributions in the book presents an objective and interdisciplinary view of the evolution, organization, and social, cultural, and environmental impact of both international and domestic tourism development in China since 1978.

The book is organized into five parts and fourteen essays. The three essays in Part One discuss the evolution of China's international and domestic tourism industry. This includes the formulation of tourism development policies and the sometimes precarious relationship between tourism and politics in China. Part One concludes with an overview of tourism resources in China today.

Part Two deals with the organization and administration of China's tourism industry. The first essay includes an examination of the functional aspects of the travel and tourism industry, such as how travel and lodging service management and operations are performed in China. The second essay discusses the formation of tourist hotel landscapes in China and how the tourist hotel reflects the transformation of the economic, social, and cultural life of the Chinese people. The third essay in Part Two presents a detailed discussion of tourism education in China.

Part Three is entitled "Chinese Tourists" and includes four essays that present tourism from specifically Chinese perspectives. Two essays examine domestic tourism in China from policy and geographic perspectives, while a third looks at how Chinese cultural history has shaped the perception and development of tourist sites in the country. The final essay focuses on ethnic Chinese who reside outside of the People's Republic of China and assesses their role in the country's tourism development.

China is a vast country of many landscapes and peoples. The three original essays in Part Four analyze, in detail, tourism development in three minority ethnic regions of China. These are areas where the dominant Han Chinese majority go to experience "exotic" cultures. These studies demonstrate the impact of tourism development on the socioeconomic systems, cultures, and environments of these "other Chinas."

Part Five is a concluding essay in which we, with the assistance of Professor Zhang Guangrui, integrate and summarize the issues discussed in the previous essays in order to ponder the future prospects of tourism in China. Recommendations are presented, based upon these conjectures.

This book is well suited to the needs of tourism scholars and students. It is of interest to scholars and individuals who specialize in Asian studies and will be a valuable resource to government tourism agencies and the travel and tourism industry. In particular, the development path and lessons learned through the Chinese experience can serve as an example to many developing countries in their pursuit of tourism development.

This book would not have been completed without the help of many people. We would like to thank our families for their tolerance during our long hours of translation and editing. We would also like to thank the many individuals without whose assistance we would not have achieved as much as we did. These include all of the contributing authors, and especially Professor Zhang Guangrui, Mr. Tim Gibson and Ms. Lauren Asia Hall Lew for proofreading assistance, and anonymous reviewers for their editorial recommendations.

Alan A. Lew
Lawrence Yu

About the Contributors

Erdmann Gormsen is the director of the Department of Geography at the University of Mainz in Germany. He previously held positions at the University of Heidelberg, where he received his Ph.D., and at UNESCO. He has conducted extensive research on tourism in Central America, where he was awarded the Aguila Azteca Distinguished Service Medal by the President of Mexico in 1986. In recent years he has begun to focus his research interests on tourism in the People's Republic of China.

Alan A. Lew is an associate professor in the Department of Geography and Public Planning at Northern Arizona University, where he teaches courses in geography, planning, and recreation/tourism. He holds graduate degrees in geography and urban planning from the University of Oregon. He was a Fulbright Scholar to Singapore where he conducted research on tourist attraction development. In 1989 he was a member of one of the first groups of American tourism scholars to be invited to China following the Tiananmen Square incident. He also conducts research and consults on tourism in rural areas and Indian reservations in the western United States. He is a member of the American Institute of Certified Planners and has published in several journals including the *Annals of Tourism Research* and the *Journal of Travel Research*.

Liu Zhijiang received a master degree in economics from Nankai University in Tianjin. As the director of the Division of Tourism Colleges and School Management in China's National Tourism Administration, he is responsible for China's policies for tourism education and coordinates academic and professional tourism education programs at all levels in the country. He has published numerous articles on tourism education in China.

Timothy S. Oakes is a Ph.D. candidate in the Department of Geography at the University of Washington. His research focus has been on ethnic tourism in Southwest China, particularly Guizhou Province. In addition to his contribution to this volume, he has published on this topic in *The Journal of Cultural Geography* and *Environment and Planning D: Society and Space*. Research for his contribution to this book was supported by the National

Science Foundation and the National Academy of Sciences' Committee on Scholarly Communication with China.

Ying Yang Petersen received a Ph.D. in cultural geography from the University of California at Berkeley and is currently an independent scholar and teacher residing in the Los Angeles area. Her interests include the Chinese landscape and its relationship to tourism, both foreign and domestic. She conducted field research in China in 1991 for the chapter included in this volume.

Qiao Yuxia is an associate fellow in the Institute of Finance and Trade Economics of the Chinese Academy of Social Sciences. A graduate of the Chinese People's University, she has been a full-time researcher in tourism studies since the late 1970s. She also serves as a standing council member of the Chinese Tourism Association.

Wesley S. Roehl is an associate professor in the Department of Tourism and Convention Administration in the William F. Harrah College of Hotel Administration, University of Nevada, Las Vegas. His academic background includes degrees in geography at Trenton State College and Southern Illinois University and a Ph.D. in Recreation Resource Development from Texas A&M University. His work has been published in the *Annals of Tourism Research*, the *Journal of Travel Research*, *Tourism Management*, *Coastal Management*, the *Hospitality and Tourism Educator*, and the *Journal of Cultural Geography*. He is chairman of the paper review committee for the Convention/Expo Summit, for which he also serves as the *Proceedings* editor. Professor Roehl also serves as the book review editor for the *Journal of Travel and Tourism Marketing*. His current research interests involve tourism development, travelers' risk perception, the role disasters play in tourism, and gambling-related tourism.

Margaret Byrne Swain holds a Ph.D. in anthropology from the University of Washington and is currently a research anthropologist at the University of California, Davis, where she has taught courses on ethnic diversity in China, gender and sexuality, and indigenous development. Tourism was one focus of her initial fieldwork in Panama with the Kuna Indians. Her recent research in Yunnan, China, with the Sani Yi minority group on gender, ethnic relations, and cultural hegemony issues was supported for 1993 by the National Academy of Sciences Committee on Scholarly Communication with China. She is on the editorial board of the *Annals of Tourism Research* and is guest editor of a special issue on gender in tourism for 1995.

Stanley W. Toops is an assistant professor in the Geography and International Studies Department at Miami University, Oxford, Ohio, where he offers courses for the East Asian Studies minor. After receiving a B.A. in geography from Drake University, he obtained the M.A. and Ph.D.

in geography from the University of Washington. Dr. Toops has taught classes on East Asian geography, politics, and history. His research interest focuses on development and ethnicity issues in China. Since his first research visit to Northwest China in 1985, he has spent a total of two years of fieldwork on tourism, handicrafts, and trade of the area. He has published in the *Journal of Cultural Geography, Focus, Central Asian Survey, Annals of Tourism Research,* and *Journal of Social and Economic Intelligence.* In 1993, he led a Silk Road Study Tour for the Smithsonian Institution.

Xiao Qianhui holds a masters degree in economics from the Chinese Academy of Social Sciences. He is the deputy director of the Department of Personnel, Labor, and Education in the National Tourism Administration of China and is involved in developing national policies on human resource development for China's travel and tourism industry. He is also a guest professor of the Beijing Tourism Institute and has published numerous books and articles on tourism in both Chinese and English. Among his English publications are *Thoughts on Tourism Economy, A Strategy for Tourism Development in China,* and *Involvement of Foreign Investment in China's Hotel Industry.*

Lawrence Yu is an assistant professor in the School of Hotel and Restaurant Management at Northern Arizona University. He has been involved in the China tourism industry since 1979. He first worked as an English-speaking interpreter in Hangzhou, a popular tourist city in China. Later he was the director of the Promotion and Education Department of the Zhejiang Provincial Tourism Bureau. This experience has made him intimately familiar with tourism in China. He has a Ph.D. in geography from the University of Oregon and has published several articles on tourism in China in Chinese publications and in several international journals including the *Cornell Hotel and Restaurant Administration Quarterly,* the *Journal of Travel Research,* and the *International Journal of Hospitality Management.*

Zhang Guangrui is an associate fellow and deputy director of the Tourism Studies Department in the Institute of Finance and Trade Economics, Chinese Academy of Social Sciences. He worked in the tourism business for a decade or so before he joined the Academy as a full-time researcher of tourism in 1981. From 1984 to 1986 he was a visiting scholar in the Department of Management Studies for Hotel and Tourism Industries, University of Surrey, UK. He also is a consultant of the China Tourism Association Consultants, Inc., as well as a standing council member of China Domestic Tourism Association, a guest professor of China Tourism Management Institute, and a member of the international editorial board of the journal, *Tourism Management.* He is the author of *World Hotel, Hotel World* and co-author of *China's Tourism Development Strategy* (both in Chinese).

Yongwei Zhang is the coordinator of the Tourism and Travel Program in the Department of Geography, Geology, and Planning at Southwest Missouri State University. He received his Ph.D. degree in geography from Southern Illinois University with a concentration in tourism resource planning. He previously taught courses in international tourism and marketing and tourism and travel planning at Valparaiso University.

PART ONE

Evolution

This part of the book offers an overview of the evolution and development of tourism in China since 1978. It focuses on the formation of tourism policy, the politics of tourism at the national level, and some hard-learned lessons. Also discussed is an overview of the great variety of tourism resources that a country as large and complex as China has. Some of these resources are better developed than others, and there is considerable potential, given the right policies, for tourism expanding into more areas of China in the future.

In the first essay, Zhang Guangrui traces the historical development of tourism in China. He outlines the historical background in which China's tourism was conceived and developed, and defines the nature of the tourism development in China. Mr. Zhang thoroughly analyzes development experiences and lessons learned in this essay.

The Tiananmen Square Incident of 1989 had a devastating effect on China's booming international tourism industry. In the second essay, Wesley Roehl uses this particular example to investigate a destination's response to political shocks. He analyzes the U.S. tourist and travel trade's reaction to this political event in China and discusses the implications for China if future shocks occur.

In the final essay of Part One, Yongwei Zhang provides an overview of the varied tourism resources that China possesses and how they have been developed. In doing so, he assesses the current situation of more developed versus less developed areas, and speculates on future opportunities for expanding and creating new tourist destinations in China.

1

China's Tourism Since 1978: Policies, Experiences, and Lessons Learned

Zhang Guangrui

Leisure travel in China dates back thousands of years. Emperors, scholars, and monks were frequent travelers in ancient times, due to their positions of power, intellectual interests, or free time. International travel to China was once controlled by wealthy or adventurous foreigners. They dominated the travel industry, both as participants and business operators. Thomas Cook and Sons, among other world renown travel companies, opened an office in China during the 1920s (Hibbort 1990). Initially located in Shanghai, they later moved to the old Hotel de Pekin in the country's capital. These offices handled ground services for international and domestic tours in China. However, wars from the late 1930s to the late 1940s put an end to all pleasure travel in the country.

After the People's Republic was born in 1949, the travel business became a form of special political activity. Travel services (travel agents or tour operators) were set up right after the new government formed, but only provided services for visiting overseas Chinese residents and for foreigners with special permission to visit China. Hence for a long time, tourism in China was essentially a "diplomatic activity," serving political goals rather than economic ones. Domestic tourism hardly existed, and outbound travel was limited almost exclusively to diplomats and government officials. The Great Cultural Revolution (begun in 1966 and lasting over a decade) forced the infant travel business to be almost entirely suspended. In the early 1970s, however, Mao Zedong did begin to permit "a few rightists (i.e., non-communists foreigners)" to visit China.[1] However, until 1978, tourism in China remained an insignificant economic activity.

1978 was a year of great significance for China. In that year, the Chinese Communist Party (CCP) held the Third Plenary Session of its 11th Congress, at which an epoch-making decision was made to shift emphasis from political struggle to economic reconstruction. This was based on the so-called "Four Modernizations" of industry, agriculture, science and technology, and the national defense. In addition, the CCP decided to open its door to the outside world. These decisions are often referred to as China's "second revolution" (the first revolution being the Communist victory in 1949). Tourism in China could never have been what it is today without these historical policy changes.

The following discussion outlines the context of China's tourism development and the evolution of related tourism policies, including analyses of experiences gained, lessons learned, and future prospects of the tourist industry in China.

A Decade of Rapid Growth: Facts and Figures

Owing to global economic recessions, conflicts and wars in the Persian Gulf, political crises in the former Soviet Union, and various environmental catastrophes, worldwide tourism growth has remained marginal since the turn of the 1980s. The average annual growth of international visitor arrivals has only been approximately 4 percent, while international tourism receipts from 1980 to 1992 increased by a total of only 10 percent.[2] In sharp contrast to the world situation, China's tourism over the past decade has experienced rapid growth in arrivals and expenditures.

Tourist Arrivals

Inbound Tourism. From 1978 to 1991, China's inbound visitor arrivals averaged an annual growth of 25 percent, while foreign exchange earnings from visitors averaged a 20 percent annual increase (Tables 1.1 and 1.2).[3] In 1992, China received 38 million international visitor arrivals, among which some four million were foreigners. Total foreign exchange earnings from visitors for 1992 were close to US$4 billion. From an almost insignificant beginning only a dozen years ago, China now ranks among the top Asian tourist destinations.

TABLE 1.1 Tourist Arrivals in China, 1978-1993

Year	Total	Overseas Foreigner	Chinese Nationals	H.K. & Macao Compatriots	Taiwan
1978	1809200	229600	18100	1561500	
1979	4203901	362389	20910	3820602	
1980	5702536	529124	34413	5138999	
1981	7767096	675153	38856	7053087	
1982	7924261	764497	42745	7117019	
1983	9477005	872511	40352	8564142	
1984	12852185	1134267	47498	11670420	
1985	17833097	1370462	84827	16377808	
1986	22819450	1482276	68133	21269041	
1987	26902267	1727821	87031	25087415	n/a
1988	31694804	1842206	79348	29773250	437700
1989	24501394	1460970	68556	22971868	541000
1990	27461821	1747315	91090	25623416	947600
1991	33349761	2710103	133427	30506231	946632
1992	38115000	4006400	165100	33943500	1317800
1993	41530000	4500000	n/a	n/a	n/a

Source: Ministry of Public Security.

TABLE 1.2 Tourism Receipts in China, 1978-1993

Year	Receipts (Mn. RMB¥)	Indices (1978=100)	Change (%)
1978	262.9	100.0	
1979	449.3	170.9	70.9
1980	616.7	234.6	37.3
1981	784.9	298.6	27.3
1982	843.2	320.7	7.4
1983	941.2	358.0	11.6
1984	1131.3	430.3	20.2
1985	1250.0	475.5	10.5
1986	1530.9	582.3	22.5
1987	1861.5	708.1	21.6
1988	2246.8	854.6	20.7
1989	1860.5	707.7	-17.2
1990	2217.6	843.5	19.2
1991	2845.0	1082.1	28.3
1992	3947.0	1501.3	38.7
1993	4680.0	1780.1	18.7

Source: State Statistical Bureau.

Domestic Tourism. For most of the period since 1949, leisure travel had been considered a bourgeois lifestyle and contrary to communist ethics. Therefore it was considered socially and politically taboo for the Chinese people. As a result of the Four Modernizations and the emancipation of people's liberties, domestic tourism has increased significantly in the past decade. Conservative estimates by the National Tourism Administration (NTA) indicate that the number of domestic trips jumped from some 240 million in 1985 (the earliest data available) to 330 million in 1992. In the same period, travel expenditures grew from RMB¥8 billion to over RMB¥25 billion. Domestic tourism, therefore, is clearly contributing to the local economic development of many Chinese cities and regions.

Outbound Tourism. Outbound tourism of Chinese citizens is a more recent phenomenon. With deepening reforms, rapidly increasing wealth, and greater openness to the outside world, more and more people in China are expressing interest in temporary travel outside the country. Cross-border day tours in the frontier areas with Russia, Korea, and Mongolia in the north, and to Vietnam, Laos, and Myanmar (Burma) in the south, have been rapidly increasing. Control over Chinese outbound tours has been gradually and cautiously relaxed since 1990.

A handful of travel agencies are now authorized to make travel arrangements to a limited number of countries and regions, including Singapore, Malaysia, Thailand, Hong Kong, and Macao. Unfortunately, there are currently no official statistics for departures of Chinese people across the borders for self-paid pleasure trips. According to the Ministry of Public Security, over 590,073 people visited Hong Kong and Macao for private affairs in 1991 (*People's Daily*, June 22, 1992). Among these, 144,834 were visiting friends and relatives (VFRs) and 416,620 were group inclusive tours (GIT). In 1992, the northernmost province of Heilongjiang reported some 1.2 million departures of non-official businessmen crossing the borders to neighboring countries, among which 550,000 were made through the small border city of Heihe alone (Xu 1992). These numbers do not include passengers on transnational trains between Beijing and Moscow. The majority of these border-crossings are made by small tradesmen.

Tourism Infrastructure

China boasts a long history and rich culture, and there is indeed no lack of tourist attractions of all descriptions. Unfortunately the tourist infrastructure and service facilities were not ready when the country decided to promote tourism in the late 1970s. Both quantity and quality were lacking. Arduous nation-wide efforts over the past decade, however, have resulted in great improvements to China's tourism infrastructure.

Accommodations. In 1978 there were only 76,192 bedspaces in 203 hotels throughout the entire country, of which only about 60 percent were suitable to accommodate overseas visitors (Sun 1992). Most of these were built in the early post-liberation days for foreign experts and state leaders. However, they did not really fit the needs of modern tourists. By the end of 1992, there were 737,700 bedspaces in 2,354 hotels. Among these, 928 were NTA starred hotels up to world standards. More hotels will be added in the newly established tourist resorts and economic development zones in the years to come.

Transportation. China's population of over 1.1 billion accounts for a fifth of the world's people. Transportation has been a long-standing problem in the country, and at the beginning of China's tourism development this proved to be an acute headache for the hospitality industry. International airline services were inadequate and the domestic air transport was even worse. Problems included poor connections and a shortage of airplanes and airports. Railways were the principal means of passenger transport for long-distance travel. Deluxe rail coaches for international tourists, however, were rarely seen.

In the 10-year period from 1978 to 1988, the total passenger traffic on long-distance mass transit increased from 2.5 billion to 9.3 billion. Rail traffic grew from 815 million to 1.2 billion, while air traffic grew from 2.3 million to 14.4 million. In terms of civil aviation, by the end of 1991 China's national airline (CAAC or Air China) had a fleet of 221 airplanes with a seating capacity of 25,574. Air China flew 49 international air-routes to 46 cities in 33 countries world-wide. In addition, over 400 domestic air routes linked up over 100 cities, while direct flights and charters flew between Hong Kong and some 20 cities in the mainland. In terms of road transport, there were over 63,000 vehicles used by the tourist sector in 1990 compared to less than 3500 in 1980. Although transport still remains a bottle-neck for further tourism development (as well as the entire economy), the growth has been tremendous.

Tourist Attractions. In the early days of opening to the outside world, only a select number of Chinese cities were accessible to foreign tourists. By the end of 1978, only 107 cities or regions were open to foreign visitors, and the principal attractions being offered were model factories, schools, neighborhoods, and communes. These made up the majority of a tour group visit, regardless of the interests of the tourists. Although more historical and cultural sites opened to foreign visitors, most were largely imitations of each other, such as the many history museums found in Beijing as well as every provincial capital. Later, visits to local factories, schools, communes, and other working units were decreased, yet the similarity of sights everywhere still made for a dull itinerary. A popular sentiment among incoming tourists was that China consisted of "visiting one temple after another in the day with nothing to do and nowhere to go at night."

The situation is totally different today. There are numerous special interest tours nationwide, and local tourist organizations vie with each other in offering more unique and innovative tours to attract incoming tourists. Among many others, favorite tours include the Silk Road in the northwest, Tibet's "Roof of the World" Tour, the Three Gorges cruise along the Changjiang (Yangtze) River, the Grand Canal Tour, the Tour of Seven Ancient Capitals, the Southwest Minorities Folklore Tour, the Ice and Snow Tour in the northeast, and special interest tours focusing on the arts, religion, and health. Added to these are festivals, shopping, people watching, live entertainment, and other amusements and recreations that sometimes prove to be too many for tired tourists to pack into their limited time. According to the NTA, by the end of 1992 there were 888 cities and counties open to overseas visitors and over 500 points of entry and exit in the country (*People's Daily*, Dec. 18, 1992).

The Context of China's Tourism Policies

In the course of political reform and greater openness, great changes have taken place in China's economic policies. The government has discarded its long-standing closed-door policy and become more open to the outside world. The highly centralized and planned economy has gradually given way to the "invisible hand" of market forces. Under the leadership of the CCP, the government of China has shifted its emphasis from endless ideological campaigns to concrete economic reconstruction as a way to make the country more successful and powerful. The Chinese people, with their minds emancipated, are more realistic and are trying to feed and clothe themselves through their own efforts.

As a component of the country's social and economic development, tourism policies have been adopted in line with the general orientation of the entire nation. These policies have transformed tourism in China in the following ways:

From a Diplomatic Activity to an Industry of Importance

Over the past decade or so, the official purpose of tourism in China has undergone three major changes:

Politics only. From the early establishment of travel services shortly after 1949, until the eve of present reform in 1978, tourist activities were nothing more than an activity serving the foreign affairs of China. It typically centered around "people-to-people diplomacy," seeking no economic benefits for the country in any way. Tourists were either overseas Chinese or "foreign friends and guests." Tourism was a means for the young People's Republic to cultivate friends, understanding, and sympathy from the world. Overseas tourists, though small in number, were treated as VIPs, with endless banquets, meetings with leaders, courtesy calls, and visits to working units. These were all arranged by the host regardless of the real interests of the visitors. In China, it was the destination which selected the tourists rather than the tourists who chose the destination.

Politics plus economics. During the early stages of reform (from 1978 to 1985), tourism was considered both a part of foreign affairs and an economic activity. However, tourism policies and practices still put politics before economic gains. One example of this was the use of a discriminatory pricing policy. Overseas Chinese and compatriot residents from Hong Kong, Macao, and Taiwan paid much less than non-Chinese foreign tourists, even if they received the same services. Consequently, prices and services varied according to the race of the person rather than the willingness to pay. Very often, overseas Chinese or compatriots were refused by hotels or transport ticket offices, or given less than proper services, because they paid less than foreign visitors. Foreign visitors, on the other hand, complained of being embarrassed and annoyed by their preferential treatment.

Economics over politics. In 1986, the national government declared tourism to be a comprehensive economic activity with the direct purpose of earning foreign exchange for China's modernization. For the first time ever, tourism was included in China's national plan for social and economic development (Zhang 1990). In recent years, the national government has continued to stress the importance of tourism as an important service industry which is seen to "require less investment, yet have quicker results, better efficiency, larger employment potential, and a greater potential to improve people's livelihood than many other tertiary service sectors."[4] The development of tourism has been made a key industrial policy for the years to come, placing the economic impact foremost, as opposed to the political emphasis of years past.

From Micro-management and Control to Macro-management and Service

From 1949 to the mid-1960s, there was no single state organ responsible for tourism due to its small scale. The Bureau for Travel and Tourism

(BTT) was set up in the mid-1960s under the jurisdiction of the Foreign Ministry. Travel to China by overseas ethnic Chinese was treated as a foreign affairs activity and was controlled by the Office of Overseas Chinese Affairs, under the State Council. A basic principle proclaimed by the late Premier Zhou Enlai was that "nothing is minor in the handling of foreign affairs, and everything done requires asking for instructions." Therefore, all aspects of tourism were tightly controlled by the national government, including visas, travel permits, tour pricing, places to visit, and tour guides. Local foreign affairs offices or overseas Chinese affairs offices were responsible for the local arrangements of incoming tours, based upon instructions given by their superior administrations.

With the rapid growth of tourism in the late 1970s, and a deeper understanding of its significance in the course of reform, the National Tourism Administration of the People's Republic of China (NTA) was set up in 1981 to replace the BTT. The NTA became China's principal national tourism organization (NTO) under the direct jurisdiction of the country's State Council. As such, it became entirely independent from the Foreign Ministry. The function of the NTA was different from that of its predecessor. It concentrated on the macro-management of the tourism industry through the development of tourism plans for the whole nation. The NTA was also involved in the formulation of rules and regulations governing tourism, conducting major overseas travel promotions, facilitating state-to-state cooperation, and providing tourism information, education, and training services. Like all other government departments in China, the NTA has not entirely cast off the traditional ways of administration, but as a new state organ born in the course of reform, it has paid much more attention to the economic and legal aspects of administration, and to market demands and international practices in business management. Since the mid-1980s, the business operations (travel services) of the NTA have gradually been separated from its governmental functions. For the most part, travel services in China today have become corporate entities with their own decision-making power.

From Monopoly to Decentralization in Tourism Business Operations

At the time when China was still under a strong, centrally-planned economic system with tourism being treated as a political activity, tourism business operations were, as mentioned above, tightly held in the hands of state organizations. All travel business was monopolized by a handful centrally-controlled travel services. The first were the China International Travel Service (CITS) and China Travel Service (CTS). These were later joined by the China Youth Travel Service (CYTS). These were known as the "three magnates" of travel service in China. In fact, they were not independent business operations, but part of the government bureaucracy. Hotel and transport services were also centralized at the national level, with little participation by regional and local entities. But with the deepening reform and booming tourism of the 1980s, government control has been gradually relaxed. The days when the "three magnates" dominated the travel business are now gone. There were over 2000 travel service offices in China by the end of 1992, among which 160 were entitled to do business directly with overseas tour operators (known as Category A travel services.)

These changes are due to a national policy made in 1985 to bring the initiatives of all sectors (namely, the central and local governments, government departments, collectives, and individuals) into the much needed improvement of China's tourism infrastructure. Travel conditions have improved greatly ever since. Hotels of various kinds have been built everywhere through joint efforts of the national government, local industries, collectives, and individuals, as well as foreign investors. International hotel chains and hotel management corporations, such as Sheraton, Holiday Inn Worldwide, Hilton, and Shangri-La have become involved in China.

In order to improve air services, the administration of civil aviation has been separated from the former CAAC airline. CAAC (Civil Aviation Administration of China) formerly operated the sole airline in the country. Beginning in 1985, it has now been divided into eight airlines. Air China (CA) is the national flag carrier. New regional airlines include: China Eastern Airlines (MU), China Southwest Airlines (SZ), China Southern Airlines (CZ), China Northwest Airlines (WH), China Northern Airlines (CJ), China General Aviation Corporation (GP), and Xinjiang Airlines (XO). In addition, some 20 local and allied airlines have been founded in recent years. In the high seasons there are also regular charter flights between Hong Kong and several popular tourist cities and scenic spots in China.

From a Product-oriented to a Market-oriented Mode

Due to nearly three decades of being closed to the outside world, combined with a limited receiving capacity, China's tourism in late 1970s and early 1980s enjoyed being in a seller's market. When China first opened its doors to the western world, tourists, particularly from USA and Japan, flooded in regardless of facilities, programs, or prices offered. Taking advantage of this demand, China exercised a product-oriented policy. The practice of rationing and quotas, which served as the traditional means of market control in the centrally-planned Chinese economy, was also implemented in the international tourism business. This made overseas tour operators both vexed and puzzled. Intoxicated with a temporary and abnormal situation of excessive demand, China showed little interest in marketing or market research and was hardly troubled with the problem of who their tourists were, except that of there were more than the infrastructure could handle.

However, with the increase in China's receiving capacity and the easing of the rush to visit China (especially after the Tiananmen Square incident), the seller's market has been replaced by a buyer's market. China has gradually realized the importance of the tourism market, which can be influenced or guided but not controlled at will. Only in the late 1980s did China begin to take the international tourist market seriously. Among actions recently taken, China has:

- simplified visa and frontier formalities for overseas tourists,
- introduced a star-rating classification for its hotels based on international standards,
- set up tourism offices in major markets abroad to provide necessary and up-to-date information on the country, and
- participated regularly in major world tourism exhibitions.

Year-long national tourism promotion campaigns were introduced in 1988 (Tourism Year of Dragon) and 1992 (Visit China Year). These further demonstrate the concern and determination in market development and enhancement felt by both the central and local governments alike. More recently, China joined members of the Pacific Asia Travel Association (PATA) to promote the "East Asia Year of Travel" in 1994. These actions, together with other marketing moves, show that China has now embarked on the right track for tourism development.

As an important economic sector, tourism has been closely tied to China's general market-oriented policy of economic development and its foreign policy of increased openness and cooperation. The national government is paying much more attention to the industry for both economic and political purposes, and is increasing facilities and services for the general touring public both at home and abroad. Similar in some respects to the past, the political goals of today are to allow the world to see for itself the changes and openness now found in China.

Experiences and Lessons

China is a late comer on the stage of world tourism. China has, in reality, only been an active player in world tourism since 1979. During this period, it has experienced the embarrassment of an unprepared takeoff, the joy of a surprising boom, and the panic of an unexpected slide. Nevertheless, through practice and experience, China has taken important steps in its tourism development. Outstanding progress has been made in understanding tourism, in searching for basic standards and principles for tourism development, and in seeking a way of developing tourism that is in accordance with the socialist politics and economics of China. The Chinese have gained experience in their successes and have learned many lessons from their failures. Some of these lessons may offer insight and guidance for tourism development in other developing countries. Some of the basic principles that guide tourism development in China today are:

To Base Tourism Development on the Country's Comparative Advantages

As a developing country, China is backward economically and technologically when compared to most industrialized countries. Owing to various reasons, its competitiveness is not strong in world trade and its total market share is relatively small. Yet its vast area, diverse landscapes, ancient history, rich culture, and distinctive political and economic system are among the attractions that constitute China's tourism. These abundant resources, many of which are unique to China, serve the country well in developing tourism. As a matter of fact, China had missed several opportunities for tourism development before the reforms of 1978, when the country favored heavy industries over the service sector, and preferred international trading in goods over trading in services. Although China cannot build its economy entirely on tourism, a much more important role for the tourism industry has now been recognized by the country's leaders. China can best triumph over competing destinations in international tourism by giving full play to its comparative advantage of cultural and historical resources, instead of by competing with them in beach resorts, amusement parks, or other costly projects.

Develop Tourism in Line with National Economic Development Policies

China's tourism development has followed the principles of "being active, acting according to one's abilities, and maintaining a steady advance." Tourism is a highly comprehensive business, and only policies that encourage the development of all of its related components will produce a successful industry. Tourism development may stimulate and promote other industries, yet it is also heavily dependent on the concurrent growth of other sectors. In fact, the tourist industry in China has long been ignored, and its size is actually smaller than most other major economic sectors. Therefore, a strategy of "appropriately faster growth" for tourism than for other industries in the national economy should be adopted for a certain number of years to come. Specific supporting policies favorable to the tourist industry should be issued to realize the goal. At the same time, it will do no good to develop tourism in a big way without regard to the ability of related economic sectors to support it. Also, it is not wise to blindly place the emphasis of development on increasing total tourist arrivals when economic gains, in real terms, should be the goal. China's experience has shown that the large scale construction of tourist attractions, accommodations, and recreational facilities, before the necessary infrastructure (e.g., transportation and education/training) is available will not achieve a sound development of tourism, but will probably waste resources and damage the destination's image.

Boldly Introduce Overseas Capital and Modern Management

Access to overseas capital and the use of management techniques and technologies from abroad can provide a shortcut to developing tourism in underdeveloped countries. Due to political unrest and past government policies, China has lagged behind the world's advanced countries in many ways. It is not easy (and probably impossible) for China to catch up in the short term. Tourism, especially international tourism, is a business full of intense competition. Facilities and services for more seasoned and sophisticated tourists must be attractive and distinctive. Above all, they must be up to the world standards. Since 1978, China has gradually introduced policies to encourage overseas capital investment and the adoption of modern technology and management techniques to build its hotel industry. The practice of overseas involvement in China has helped to greatly speed up hotel construction, improve the image of China's tourism industry, strengthen links with the rest of the world, and enhance the world's awareness of China. More importantly, joint ventures with international hotel developers have widened the horizons of the Chinese hoteliers and other businessmen in the country. In fact, the first joint-venture hotels have served as models for the country's hotel industry. An example of this is the Jianguo Hotel, which was the first Sino-US joint-venture hotel in Beijing, and was originally managed by Peninsular Hotel Corporation of Hong Kong. Without the introduction of modern overseas management and technology, China's hotel business could not be what it is today. To some extent, the hotel industry in China serves as a pioneer and vanguard in carrying out the policies of reform and openness to the outside world. The success in this field has become an outstanding example of China's current socialist market-oriented economic reform.

Be Aware of the Negative Impacts of Tourism

Tourism has brought foreign exchange and other economic benefits to many tourist destinations in China. Quite a few poverty-stricken areas have become prosperous and famous because of tourism. Many historical sites and natural features, which had long been left idle, have now become surprising money makers. However, this is not the whole story. With increasing tourist arrivals and business growth, some negative impacts have become visible and have drawn popular attention. Experience has shown that in terms of the economy, tourism is not always an industry which will generate quick economic results from limited investment, as has been described by some early writers.[5] With China's rather poor infrastructure, considerable capital must often be invested before profits from the industry can be realized. Adequate facilities for tourism development (including airplanes, airports, roads, deluxe tourist coaches, cruise ships, and accommodations) are rather costly, and the capital returns of some of them are very marginal, requiring a long development period. In addition, the tourist industry is subject to influences from a variety of factors, including natural disasters, economic fluctuations, and political unrest, most of which are beyond the control of tourist destinations and business operators. Tourism, therefore, can be a risky business.

The social and environmental impacts of tourism, which may often be insignificant when the business is very small, cannot be ignored with the expansion of the industry. For example, to describe tourism as a "smokeless" industry in terms of pollution is not a complete picture. In a developing country like China, which lacks of both experience and funds, pollution as a result of rapid tourism growth may be hard to avoid without careful planning. The environmental impacts of tourism in China result primarily from too many people producing an excessive wear on facilities and causing considerable waste problems. Poorly located and built hotels and other structures can also be a problem.

Because of some of its negative social impacts, the tourist industry is often used as a scapegoat in China for larger social problems. Prostitution, drug trafficking, airport con-artists, illegal street money-changers, and even the commercialization of traditional folkways would probably be less of a problem in China without the flood of overseas tourists. It is true, as stated in the *Manila Declaration on World Tourism* in 1980, that "the economic returns of tourism, however real and significant they may be, do not and returns of tourism, however real and significant they may be, do not and cannot constitute the only criterion for the decision by States to encourage this activity".[6] It is, therefore, necessary to keep an eye on the negative impacts of tourism.

Conclusion

The consistent growth in world tourism serves as an indication of world peace and economic development in general. China's political stability and the sustained growth of its economy will continue to boost the country's tourist industry. Thanks to its abundant and unique resources and its favorable government policies for tourism development, China's tourism (both foreign and domestic) has a promising future. Arduous efforts must be made to meet the serious challenges of other major tourist destinations, and to guard against the negative impacts which tourism can bring to the country and people. Given that the favorable situation will continue, China is striving to be the top tourist destination in Asia and one of the largest tourist countries in the world in the coming 21st century.

Notes

1. In 1971, Mao Zedong wrote that the "number of (international tourists) can be a bit bigger, and a few rightists can be allowed to come." The term "rightists" referred to people who opposed the Chinese political system, especially from countries like the United States.

2. Figures cited here are calculated from those published in various documents by the World Tourism Organization.

3. All statistics on tourism in China cited here are collected from various sources and published by the National Tourism Administration of the People's Republic of China (NTA) in its annual *Yearbook of China Tourism Statistics* and *China Tourism Bulletins*.

4. This statement was translated from the "Decision of the Central Committee of the CCP and the State Council on Speeding Up the Development of Tertiary Industries" issued on June 16, 1993.

5. Chinese authors who early on lauded the virtues of tourism development include He Lisun in his 1980 book, *Luyouye Mantan* (A Discussion of the Tourist Industry), and Wang Ligang and Liu Shijie's 1982 book, *Zhongguo Luyoujinjixue* (China's Tourism Economics).

6. The influential *Manila Declaration on World Tourism* was adopted by the World Tourism Conference held in Manila, Philippines, from 27 September to 10 October 1980. This extract is from Item 8 of the *Declaration*.

References

Hibbort, Peter. 1990. Cook's Peking Home. *Time Traveller* (15): 8-9. (Thomas Cook Travel Archive and Library, United Kingdom.)

Sun, Shangqing, ed. 1992. *Mianlin 21 Shiji de Xuanze* (Choices in the 21 Century: China's Tourism Development Strategies). Beijing: People's Publishing House.

Xu, Jiangshan. 1992. Laizi Eluosi de Nahan (Cries from Russia). *China Service Industry News* (April 8).

Zhang, Yuji. ed. 1990. *Luyoujingji Gongzuoshouce* (Work Manual of Tourism Economics). Beijing: China Encyclopedia Publishing House.

2

The June 4, 1989, Tiananmen Square Incident and Chinese Tourism

Wesley S. Roehl

No consideration of tourism in China can ignore the June, 1989 Tiananmen Square incident and the broader reaction of the Chinese government against the student democracy movement. Key events in this chronology began with the death of Hu Yaobang, former chairman of the Chinese Communist Party (CCP) and widely seen as both a political and economic reformer. This event resulted in student demonstrations memorializing Hu, the occupation by protesters of Tiananmen Square, failed negotiations between the government and protesters, and the government's declaration of martial law and subsequent growth in the number of protesters. Then, on June 3, the People's Liberation Army was ordered into action with the subsequent deaths of hundreds, if not thousands, of protesters. Suppression of individuals associated with the protests continue years after the incident.

In reaction to these events, the total number of foreign visitors to China fell from 1.84 million in 1988 to 1.46 million in 1989, a decline of 21 percent (World Tourism Organization 1990, 1992).[1] Furthermore, visitation from Japan and the USA, China's two largest markets and sources of high expenditure visitors, showed even larger declines. American visitation was down 29 percent in 1989 compared to 1988 while the number of Japanese visitors declined by 39 percent over this same period.

These events are considered by many to have brought one era of Chinese tourism to a close while simultaneously opening a new, and as yet uncertain, period for tourism in China (EIU 1990). The purpose of this chapter is to investigate how the new political environment in China has affected tourism to China. Specifically, this chapter will: (1) evaluate the overall impact Tiananmen Square had on Chinese tourism, (2) briefly discuss the impact of Tiananmen Square on the international hospitality industry, (3) investigate in some detail the response to Tiananmen Square by travelers and the travel trade in the United States of America, and (4) discuss the implications of these events for the future of the Chinese tourism industry.

Tourism, Economic Growth, and Tiananmen Square

The number of foreign visitors to China grew rapidly following the opening of China for tourism in 1978. Arrivals by foreigners grew from 229,646 in 1978 to over 1.8 million in 1988. Throughout this period, Japan and the USA were the two largest sources of visitors, accounting for between 48 percent and 52 percent of all foreign arrivals during this period (Zhang 1989). Visitation by compatriots also grew rapidly during this period, with the annual number of visits by residents of Hong Kong, Macao, and Taiwan (compatriots) reaching 29.8 million in 1988. However, it is worth noting that while visits by compatriots are more numerous than visits by foreigners, foreign visitors average much more spending per capita while in China (Tisdell and Wen 1991).

This is an important point since foreign tourism was encouraged by the Chinese government as part of its economic development strategy. For China to modernize, access to capital was necessary. However, most sources of capital were outside the People's Republic. In order to further develop both agriculture and necessary infrastructure, the Chinese government recognized that foreign capital had to be earned through export activities (Earle 1991). One export industry that China turned to was tourism. Receipts from tourism now represent the largest component in China's invisible (non-commodity) trade (Tisdell and Wen 1991).

However, there are considerable risks in promoting tourism as an earner of foreign exchange. Since the traveler must physically visit the destination country to consume the product, any event that persuades the potential traveler to either stay at home or travel elsewhere directly impacts that destination's export earnings. In recognition of this precarious situation, it has been suggested that "political serenity, not scenic or cultural attractions, constitute the first and central requirements for tourism" (Richter and Waugh 1986, p. 231). Numerous examples around the world illustrate the dire results awaiting destinations that fail to provide this very basic requirement.

International travelers responded quickly to the lack of political serenity brought about by Tiananmen Square. Visitation by all categories of visitors showed an immediate decline. Six million fewer compatriots arrived in

China in 1989 compared to 1988 and over 300,000 fewer foreign arrivals occurred. While these numbers are substantial, the overall trends obscure two factors critical to understanding the impact of Tiananmen Square on Chinese tourism. First, since yearly arrivals in China from most major origins had been increasing prior to Tiananmen Square, comparing actual arrivals in 1989 to arrivals in 1988 may underestimate the impact of Tiananmen Square. Second, there is considerable variation in how travelers from the major origins responded to the events. The following sections address these two points in more detail.

Estimating the Size of Tiananmen Square's Impact

Table 2.1 presents data illustrating arrivals in China from selected origins for the period 1984 to 1990. Data are presented for the 14 foreign origins sending the most visitors to China in 1984, other foreign origins, and compatriots. Overall, China received 6.8 million fewer visits by compatriots and more than 380,000 fewer visits by foreign travelers in 1989 than in 1988. The decline in arrivals by Japanese and American travelers accounted for 84 percent of the decrease in visitation by foreigners.

TABLE 2.1 Arrivals in China from Selected Origins, 1984-1990

Origin	1984	1985	1986	1987	1988	1989	1990
	(1,000s)						
Japan	368.0	470.5	483.5	577.7	591.9	358.8	463.3
United States	212.3	239.6	291.8	315.3	300.9	215.0	233.2
Australia	72.6	78.1	73.2	58.6	61.0	48.7	50.2
UK	62.1	71.4	79.4	83.7	96.6	72.2	78.9
Philippines	43.2	57.9	53.4	57.6	71.4	73.4	78.9
Singapore	37.4	46.5	48.6	64.1	65.4	57.9	71.7
Germany	34.2	43.1	48.2	60.1	69.0	47.1	51.8
Canada	30.3	35.2	41.0	52.3	63.3	46.0	47.6
France	27.0	39.0	40.3	53.6	63.2	51.9	50.7
Thailand	26.3	24.6	39.8	58.5	65.8	54.9	67.9
Korea (North)	20.9	22.3	25.4	23.4	20.1	20.5	54.7
Switzerland	16.0	12.4	12.8	17.0	16.4	13.6	11.5
Italy	15.9	18.8	16.0	29.8	30.7	17.8	26.3
Russia	14.0	17.7	19.2	24.7	34.8	81.3	109.8
Other	201.5	193.6	209.7	251.3	291.4	301.9	350.9
	(1,000,000s)						
Total Foreign	1.182	1.371	1.482	1.728	1.842	1.461	1.747
Compatriots	11.7	16.5	21.3	25.2	29.9	23.0	25.7

Source: WTO Yearbook of Tourism Statistics, various years

Specifically, the decline in Japanese visitors accounted for 61 percent of the decrease while fewer American visitors accounted for 23 percent of the total decline.

However, a visual inspection of Table 2.1 suggests that comparing visitation in 1989 to visitation in 1988 may underestimate the effect of Tiananmen Square. A number of origins show yearly growth in arrivals to China over the period 1984 to 1988. If the political stability of China had not been brought into questions this growth may well have continued in 1989.

The data in Table 2.1 were used to estimate what might have occurred with arrivals in China in 1989 if visitor growth trends had remained unchanged. A two step approach was used to derive these estimates. In the first step, the data for each of the 14 selected origins, the other foreign origins, total foreign arrivals, and the number of compatriot arrivals for the period 1984 to 1988 were used to estimate expected arrivals in 1989. Specifically, regression analysis was used to develop equations to estimate the number of arrivals in 1989 that would have been expected if the existing trends had continued. The dependent variable, the yearly total number of visits from a particular source, was modelled as a function of time (where 1984 was coded as year 1, 1985 as year 2, 1986 as year 3, 1987 as year 4, and 1988 as year 5). If this linear trend was statistically significant at the 0.05 confidence level, the derived equation was used to estimate arrivals in 1989 (where time = 1989 = 6). If the linear trend did not explain the pattern of arrivals over this five year period, a second step was conducted. In this second step, exponential smoothing was used to estimate arrivals for 1989. Results of either the linear estimates or the exponential smoothing estimates are presented in Table 2.2.

Arrivals from 11 of the 14 origin countries were explained well by linear equations with time as the independent variable. These equations were used to estimate the number of arrivals in China that might have occurred if the trends of the mid and late 1980s had continued. These estimates suggest that the impact of Tiananmen Square on arrivals was greater than previously estimated. Regression results suggest, for example, that China received over 300,000 fewer Japanese visitors in 1989 than would have been otherwise expected. Furthermore, if the trends in foreign visitor growth evident between 1984 and 1988 had continued through 1989, the total number of visitors expected in China would have been over two million (as estimated by the regression of total foreign visitors against time, $R^2 = 0.98$). This suggests that over one-half million fewer arrivals occurred in 1989 than should have been expected.

Similarly, there is a strong linear trend in arrivals by compatriots during the period 1984 to 1988. This linear trend explains over 99 percent of the variation in yearly arrivals. If this trend had continued in 1989, over 34

TABLE 2.2 Estimates of the Impact of Tiananmen Square on Arrivals in China from Selected Origins, 1989

Origin	1989 Arrivals	Forecasted 1989 Arrivals	Forecast Method[a]	Naive Impact Model[b]	Forecasted Impact Model[c]
Japan	358828	664846	R^2 .91	-233101	-306018
United States	214956	347866	R^2 .77	-85944	-132910
Australia	48747	61049	ES	-12302	-12302
UK	72211	103041	R^2 .97	-24379	-30830
Philippines	73354	73547	R^2 .69	1933	-193
Singapore	57860	74485	R^2 .91	-7553	-16625
Germany	47091	76896	R^2 .98	-21916	-29805
Canada	45955	69386	R^2 .96	-17373	-23431
France	51905	70784	R^2 .95	-11341	-18879
Thailand	54915	76906	R^2 .89	-10931	-21991
Korea (North)	20531	21885	ES	393	-1354
Switzerland	13562	15769	ES	-2858	-2207
Italy	17822	34396	R^2 .67	-12835	-16574
Russia	81347	36693	R^2 .87	46521	44654
Other Foreign	301886	300765	R^2 .78	10450	1121
Total Foreign	1.46 mil	2.02 mil	R^2 .98	-381236	-563408
Compatriots	23.0 mil	34.4 mil	R^2 .99	-6812174	-11381881

[a]Forecasts were made in a two step process. If the linear trend with time as the independent variable was statistically significant at the 0.05 level, the model's adjusted R^2 is presented. If there was no statistically significant linear trend, exponential smoothing (ES) was used to estimate expected 1989 arrivals.
[b]Naive impact model measures the impact of Tiananmen Square as arrivals in 1989 minus arrivals in 1988.
[c]Forecasted impact model measures the impact of Tiananmen Square as actual arrivals in 1989 minus forecasted arrivals for 1989.
Source: WTO Yearbook of Tourism Statistics.

million arrivals by compatriots would have been expected. When compared to actual compatriot arrivals of 23 million in 1989, this estimate suggests that the impact of events related to Tiananmen Square was in the neighborhood of 11 million fewer compatriot arrivals than might otherwise have occurred.

Overall, in ten of the 14 origins, when estimated arrivals for 1989 are compared to actual arrivals in 1989 the decline in arrivals attributable to Tiananmen Square is greater than when arrivals in 1988 are used to estimate what should have happened in 1989. This relationship also holds true for arrivals by compatriots.

Variation in Response to Tiananmen Square, by Origin

The impact of Tiananmen Square on visitation to China was not the same for all origins. Additionally, by 1990, the pattern of recovery in number of arrivals also varied across origins. These differential effects may best be illustrated by comparing arrivals in the post Tiananmen Square years of 1989 and 1990 to 1988. Overall, visitation by foreign travelers in 1989 was only 79 percent of the 1988 total (Figure 2.1). Eleven of the top fourteen origins sent fewer visitors to China in 1989 than they did in 1988. Italy and Japan displayed the largest percentage decrease, with 1989 totals that are only 58 percent and 61 percent, respectively, of their 1988 totals. In contrast, more travelers visited China in 1989 than did so in 1988 from three of the top fourteen origins. Arrivals from North Korea, the Philippines, and residual other foreign arrivals category grew in 1989. Most interestingly the total number of Russian visitors to China in 1989 was 234 percent of the 1988 totals. Not only were arrivals from Russia higher in 1989 than in 1988, they also exceeded forecasted growth based upon the historic trend in arrivals (Table 2.2). In contrast, arrivals from North Korea, the Philippines, and the residual other foreign arrivals category were very similar to what would have been expected given the historic trends in arrivals.

Arrivals from all origins under study except Switzerland and France increased in 1990 over 1989 levels (Figure 2.1). In fact, by 1990 five origins were sending more visitors to China than they had in 1988. In 1990, visitation from Thailand was at 103 percent of that in 1988, Singapore was at 109 percent, the Philippines was at 110 percent, North Korea was at 275 percent, and visitation from Russia was at 315 percent that of 1988 (Figure 2.1).

In evaluating the rate of recovery of the various origins, four distinct patterns became apparent by 1990. Two countries, Switzerland and France, show continued decline in visitation. Six countries, Australia, Canada, Germany, Philippines, United Kingdom, and the United States, show slow recovery, with visitation growing between two and eight percent in 1990. Four countries, Italy, Japan, Singapore, and Thailand, show rapid recovery. Visitation grew between 17 and 22 percent in 1990. Visitation by compatriots and the residual other foreign arrivals category also grew by 17 percent and 18 percent, respectively, in 1990. Finally, two countries, Russia and North Korea, showed even more vigorous growth. Russian visitation was up 82 percent in 1990 while North Korea was up 170 percent in 1990.

Three key points are suggested by this analysis. First, since the number of visitors to China from several origins was increasing yearly, the impact of Tiananmen Square on visitor arrivals in 1989 is probably greater than

origin

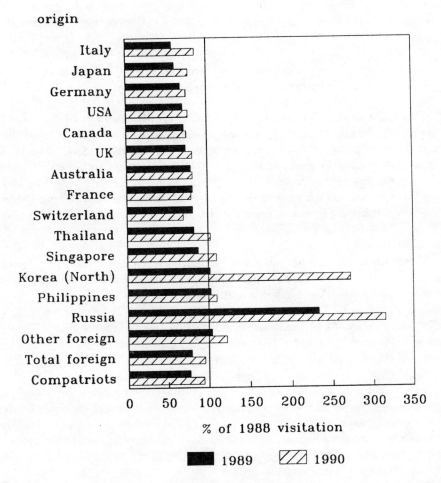

FIGURE 2.1 Response to Tiananmen Square, Visitation as a Percentage of 1988.
Source: WTO Yearbook of Tourism Statistics, various years.

generally recognized. Second, not all origins responded to Tiananmen Square similarly. Third, the events of Tiananmen Square seem to have resulted in diversification of markets for China as a destination. Foreign origins that historically dominated the volume of visitors to China became relatively less important, while new origins, often themselves reacting to changed political circumstances at home, grew relatively more important.

Tiananmen Square and the International Hospitality Industry

The Chinese tourism industry was not the only segment of the world economy to be affected by Tiananmen Square. Equity markets around the world were adversely affected by events in China. Asian markets experienced greater losses than did non-Asian markets and markets with closer economic and cultural ties with China sustained larger losses than did markets in nations with fewer ties to China (Mansur 1991). China's own economic standing in world markets also suffered. Following Tiananmen Square, Moody Investors Service lowered China's investment status from A3 to Baa1 (Earle 1991).

Tiananmen Square also affected foreign investment in China's hotel industry. Even before Tiananmen Square, evidence surfaced that many major tourist and business destinations in China were over built. For example, prior to Tiananmen Square, Deloitte Ross Tohmatsu projected that occupancy rates in Shanghai would decline from 68 percent in 1988 to only 41 percent in 1991. That estimate assumed a 10 percent *growth* in foreign visitors to China (Cheng 1990)!

Slumping occupancy rates in Chinese hotels after Tiananmen Square had dire consequences for both investors and lending institutions. After Tiananmen Square, it was estimated that 90 percent of foreign hotel loans either were rescheduled or were in need of restructuring (Cheng 1990). Tiananmen Square adversely affected banks and other financial guarantors in the major sources of investment in China, i.e., Hong Kong, the USA, and Japan (Cheng 1990; Earle 1991).

Finally, Tiananmen Square had economic consequences on hospitality businesses far from China's shores. For example, the events associated with Tiananmen Square and subsequent changes in both traveler preference and tour and cruise itineraries caused debilitating problems for some travel companies. Evidence from the USA suggests that cancelled trips and refunded deposits were a contributing factor in the bankruptcy of some large USA tour operators (Roehl 1990).

Tiananmen Square, the Travel Trade,
and Travelers in the USA

The behavior of American travelers is quite sensitive to risk and uncertainty, both real and perceived (Roehl 1990; Roehl and Fesenmaier 1992). Three characteristics of the American traveler must be considered in understanding their response to Tiananmen Square. First, surveys indicate that the average American has, at best, a fuzzy and imprecise mental map of the world (Gallup 1988). Because of widespread geographic illiteracy American travelers likely generalize specific events to areas far from that event. A prime example would be cancellation of travel to Western Europe during periods of tension in the Middle East (c.f. Hurly 1988). The second characteristic of American travelers is their reliance on what Gunn (1979) has called "nondirected information sources" when making travel decisions. For that part of the world in which the traveler has little or no first hand experience, meaning and understanding are derived from sources such as friends, family, and general media. These sources present information that is beyond the control of the destination. Finally, when Americans do consider long haul international travel, the interpersonal sales relationship with a travel agent is often highly influential (Dorsey 1989a; 1989b). Travel agents serve as a key source of specific destination and tourism product information.

Given these characteristics of the American traveler, the following sections (1) compare American arrivals in China with American arrivals in other competing Asian Pacific Rim destinations, (2) investigate how China and Tiananmen Square were covered in the American media, (3) review the effect of Tiananmen Square on a sample of travelers interested in China, and (4) evaluate the response of American travel agents and tour operators to Tiananmen Square.

Tiananmen Square and American Arrivals in the Pacific Rim

Figure 2.2 puts changes in American arrivals to China during the pre- and post-Tiananmen Square periods into context. Entries in this figure describe arrivals by Americans in China and in a number of other Pacific Rim destinations for the period 1987 to 1990. The pattern of arrivals gives further support to Tiananmen Square as one of the reasons for the decline in American visits to China. During the period in which American arrivals in China were declining, arrivals at other competing destinations were stable (Japan and South Korea) or were showing annual growth (Singapore and Thailand).

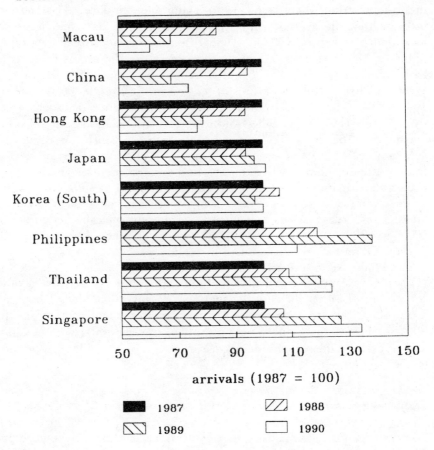

FIGURE 2.2 USA Travel to the Pacific Rim, Arrivals in Selected Destinations. *Source: WTO Yearbook of Tourism Statistics*, various years.

Two points about the data seem clear. First of all, the pattern of declining American arrivals to China cannot be completely attributed to the weakening American economy or the Gulf War since arrivals to other Pacific Rim destinations remained stable or experienced growth during this period. Second, although their official reincorporation into China does not occur until later this decade, American travelers seem to be treating Hong Kong and Macao as if they were currently part of China. Yearly arrivals to both these areas mirror the pattern of arrivals to China.

Tiananmen Square and the American Media

The mass media plays an important role in reporting disastrous events in tourism areas. Potential tourists look to these sources as opinion leaders who supply information that facilitates their assessment of risk (Milo and Yoda 1991). The visual aspect of Tiananmen Square, the mass demonstrations, and the advance of the People's Liberation Army, were well suited for television coverage. Fuller (1991) has argued that American television did a good job showing *what* happened but was less successful in explaining *why* the events happened. A sample of major daily newspapers was also criticized for stressing the more easily photographed "what" over the less visual (and also less easily identified) "why."

In order to get a better understanding of how China has been covered in travel-related articles in the American print media, a content analysis of article titles in the Reader's Guide to Periodic Literature was conducted. Understanding how China has been covered historically will help in identifying changes attributable to Tiananmen Square. All articles listed under the heading "China - Description and Travel" for the period 1977 to 1992 were identified. Two characteristics of these articles were evaluated, the number of articles per year (a measure of interest in China as a destination) and the theme or spin put on China as suggested by the article's title.

Figure 2.3 shows the number of articles appearing in American magazines that were general descriptions of China or specifically concentrated on travel to China during this period. Considerable year to year variation is present. To get a better visual picture of interest in travel to China in USA magazines, the actual number of articles per year was smoothed using a three year running average (Figure 2.3). The running average shows interest in China peaking after the opening of China in the late 1970s, achieving a steady plateau during the mid 1980s, then beginning to decline in the late 1980s. This decline in interest (as reflected in the number of articles on China) began before Tiananmen Square. The rate of decline appears to have been increased by events related to Tiananmen Square.

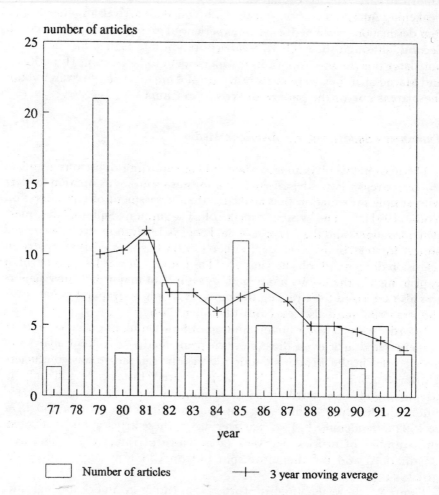

FIGURE 2.3 Magazine Articles on China Travel, General Interest Magazines, 1977-1992. *Source: Reader's Guide to Periodic Literature,* various years, compiled by author.

TABLE 2.3 Changing Themes in Articles on China Travel, 1977-1992

Examples of Article Titles	Year
Novelty:	
China alters course	78
China rolls out slightly ragged carpet	78
Cathay: the year's great adventure	79
Destination of the decade - the new China	79
Mainland China: destination of the year	80
How To:	
Playing your own China card	82
Two-wheeling tours	82
How to visit China from garden tours to commune stays	83
China independently	84
How to take the hitches out of a trip to China	84
Post Tiananmen Square:	
Free to fly inside the cage	89
China Syndrome	91
China's Faustian bargain	92
Traveling in the new China	92

Source: Reader's Guide to Periodic Literature, "China --Description and Travel," various years, compiled by author.

The themes of these magazine articles were also evaluated. Titles reflect a changing impression of China and travel to China. For example, titles in Table 2.3 illustrate what seems to be three periods in reporting China and China tourism. Articles in the late 1970s stress China as a new destination, the destination of the decade, and a place for great adventure. A second period followed where the novelty of travel to China was replaced by "how to" articles. Since Tiananmen Square fewer travel-related articles are being published about China. For example, in 1990 the only article published was in *Organic Gardening.* Finally, these few articles published since Tiananmen Square display a changed orientation. Key words stress a recognition that China's leaders see tourism (and economic reform in general) as a tool to achieve specific goals for the nation, not as a precursor to expanded political freedom.

Tiananmen Square and the American Traveler

The effects Tiananmen Square (and its coverage in the American media) have had on American travelers was addressed by Gartner and Shen (1992). They conducted a pair of surveys that allowed them to estimate the impact

Tiananmen Square had on the image of China held by a sample of potential travelers to China. Their sampling frame consisted of readers of *Modern Maturity* who requested information on China in response to an advertisement placed in the magazine. The first wave of the study was conducted immediately before Tiananmen Square (April 24, 1989 - June 1, 1989) and the second wave occurred approximately one year after Tiananmen Square (June 1, 1990 - August 10, 1990). Each sample's image of Chinese attractions and service-related attributes were compared.

Mean scale scores for a number of Chinese attractions and service attributes were significantly lower in the second sample. After Tiananmen Square, China was seen as a less attractive place. Service attributes seen as less attractive after Tiananmen Square addressed the attitudes of service personal and receptiveness of local people to tourists. Gartner and Shen's interpretation is that Tiananmen Square has raised questions among potential travelers to China on whether China can provide hospitable service after the events of 1989. Surprisingly, Gartner and Shen found that the image of natural resource attractions in China also declined in the wake of Tiananmen Square. This was an unexpected result.

Overall, Gartner and Shen's study indicates that one key market for China, older, up-scale Americans, now perceives China as a less attractive destination. Whether this is a permanent change, or whether these attitudes will return to pre-Tiananmen Square levels, is a key issue for the Chinese tourism industry.

Tiananmen Square and the American Travel Trade

A pair of studies address the reaction of the American travel trade to events in China. To better understand the response of the American travel trade to Tiananmen Square Roehl (1990) conducted a survey of California travel agents. These agents provided information on their personal reaction to selling China after Tiananmen Square. A majority favored USA government restrictions on the sale of high technology and military equipment to China but opposed banning travel or breaking diplomatic relations. Overall, agents opposed boycotting China and favored letting the consumer make an informed decision about travel to China.

Over one-half of the agents felt it would take one to two years, barring further negative events, for travel to return to pre-Tiananmen Square levels. Interestingly, agents who had sent more clients to China or who had clients cancel planned travel to China were relatively more hostile to China than were other agents. These agents expressed more support for sanctions and were more willing to question whether it was appropriate to sell travel to China. This suggests that the time it takes for travel to recover may, in fact, be longer than one or two years since agents who had been key players in selling travel to China were the most hesitant about resuming business as usual.

These agents also provided information on how their clients reacted to political events in China. Agents were asked to provide information on clients who had canceled planned travel to China and on clients who had been considering travel to China. Over one-half of the agents had clients cancel planned travel to China. A majority of the agents also reported dealing with clients who ceased considering China as a potential destination after Tiananmen Square. Travelers replaced China with a variety of alternative destinations (Table 2.4). These alternatives included other Asian destinations as well as Europe, Australia, and cruise vacations. Only five travel agents reported clients who did not substitute a new destination for canceled travel to China. Similar results were reported for individuals who were considering travel to China but had not yet finalized their travel plans (Table 2.4).

The ease with which substitute destinations were available to travelers who had previously considered travel to China but had changed their minds following Tiananmen Square is illustrated in Table 2.5. This table shows the probability that a travel agent in Roehl's 1990 study also sold competing Pacific Rim destinations. Almost all agents in the study who sold travel to China also offered travel to Japan and Hong Kong. Furthermore, a large majority also offered travel to Taiwan and the Southeast Asian countries of Singapore, Thailand, and Malaysia.

A second study into how the USA travel trade has responded to Tiananmen Square was conducted by Xiao (1993). Surveying a sample of USA tour operators, Xiao identified two key aspects of these operators' perception of China. First of all, operators had very consistent images of China. There were no significant differences between, for example, operators who did and who did not sell tours to China, or between operators who had and who had not been to China. Second, the five attributes of the Chinese travel experience seen as most important by this sample of tour operators were, in order of importance, safety and security, pleasant attitudes of service personnel, reliability of the reservation systems, cleanliness of buildings and the environment, and receptiveness of local people to tourism.

When discussing tourism to China after Tiananmen Square, USA tour operators cited concerns about the basic ability of China to satisfy the expectations of American travelers. This has been an issue since the novelty of travel to China wore off in the early 1980s (Choy, Dong, and Wen 1986; Zheng and Martin 1987; Cullen 1988). Additionally, Tiananmen Square appears to have created a new set of concerns about sending American travelers to China. Now, tour operators not only worry about dirty flatware,

TABLE 2.4 Destinations that Replaced China During Tiananmen Square
(as Reported by a Sample of California Travel Agents)

Destinations Visited by Travelers Who Canceled Planned Travel to China	Number of Agents Who Mentioned This Destination	Percent of Total
Asia	13	30.2
other Asia (not specified)	5	11.6
Hong Kong	5	11.6
Singapore	2	4.7
Thailand	1	2.3
Europe	9	20.9
Australia	4	9.3
Cruise	4	9.3
South Pacific	2	4.7
Other (no destination mentioned over once)	6	14.0
No destination visited in place of China	5	11.6
Total	**43**	**100**

Destinations Considered in Place of China by Travelers Without Finalized Plans	Number of Agents Who Mentioned This Destination	Percent of Total
Asia	21	41.2
other Asia (not specified)	10	19.6
Hong Kong	5	9.8
Singapore	3	5.9
Thailand	3	5.9
Europe	12	23.5
South Pacific	5	9.8
Australia	3	5.9
Other (no destination mentioned over once)	10	19.6
Total	**51**	**100**

Source: Roehl (1990), unpublished data.

TABLE 2.5 Probability of a California Travel Agents Selling Tour Packages to Other Pacific Rim Destinations in Addition to China

Sold Tour Package to China and to . . .	Probability
Japan	95%
Hong Kong	94%
Singapore	88%
Thailand	84%
Taiwan	75%
Malaysia	73%
Indonesia	72%
South Korea	67%
Philippines	58%

Source: Roehl (1990), unpublished data.

dirty linens and lost reservations, but also about the safety of sending clients to China. Since Tiananmen Square, tour operators have a new concern-- how their clients will be received by the Chinese population.

Implications of Tiananmen Square for the Chinese Tourism Industry

Tiananmen Square has ushered in a new era for the Chinese tourism industry. Tiananmen Square's impact on the volume of arrivals to China in 1989 was likely larger than generally reported since it interrupted growth from several key markets. However, a decline in visitor volume is not the most important consequence of Tiananmen Square. A one or two year drop in the number of foreign arrivals, while significant in the short term, can in the long term be reversed. Tiananmen Square's most important impact on the Chinese tourism industry is that a fundamental change in the type of visitor has occurred. While the number of visitors to China recovered soon after Tiananmen Square, in a basic way they were a different kind of visitor. Most critically, visitors from Japan, the USA, and other Western democracies have been replaced by visitors from Russia, North Korea, the Philippines, etc. While the volume of visitation has been maintained there are substantial consequences to replacing, for example, an American tourist with a Russian visitor.

Per capita expenditures of tourists from the Western democracies are likely much higher than similar expenditures by visitors from these emerging markets. In fact, many visitors from the emerging markets are not traditional pleasure travelers. For example, much Russian visitation appears to be "trade tourism" (Sneider 1992; Yu 1992). Entrepreneurs cross into China from border cities in the Russian Far East to buy inexpensive consumer goods for distribution throughout the former USSR. In fact, of the total Russian border trade of US$2 billion in 1991, it has been estimated that 59 percent occurred on the Russia-China border (Sneider 1992). Similarly, growth in visitation among compatriots has a lower per capita economic impact than visitation by high spending Westerners or Japanese. For example, Chinese from Taiwan are offered various incentives including discounted prices that are less than the official price for foreigners, together with additional discounts by provincial and local travel services within China that are eager for their business (Yu 1992). Furthermore, given the reasons compatriots visit China, they are more likely to either stay with friends or relatives, or utilize less expensive hotels (Bian 1990). Overall, this evidence suggests that on a per capita basis foreign visitors from the West make a much larger contribution than visitors from some of the emerging markets or compatriots.

These changes also have a geographical implication. Historically, there has been strong regional variation in the visitor mix to Chinese cities (Gormsen 1990). Cities in south China such as Guangzhou, Shenzhen, Zhuhai, and Zhengshan received a large number of tourists, with a high percentage of these visitors being compatriots and Overseas Chinese citizens (76 percent or higher of all visitors). In contrast, other important destinations such as Beijing, Shanghai, Xian, and Suzhou also received a large number of tourists, but a much higher percentage of their visitor mix was non-Chinese. Typically, 25 percent or less of the visitor mix to these cities consisted of compatriots or Overseas Chinese.

Change in the visitor mix, stressing the emerging markets, will have distinct regional implications. So even if the aggregate difference in per capita spending between Western visitors and compatriots can be compensated through increasing the volume of compatriot visits, there is still likely to be a considerable regional redistribution of economic impact, with destinations in South China benefiting.

Turning attention to the historically largest sources of foreign visitors, Japan and the USA, their responses in the long term are likely to be quite different. Japan will likely remain an important market for China. Two factors in favor of continued importance of Japan to the Chinese tourism industry are Japan's location and the important role China and Chinese culture have played in the development of Japanese culture (Yu 1992).

In contrast, China is not nearly as accessible from the USA, nor are there similar cultural bonds between the USA and China as there are between Japan and China. In the USA, China's appeal was originally one of novelty, mystery, and adventure (both physical and cultural). However, as indicated in the content analysis of popular magazine articles on China travel, the novelty of China appears to have worn off by the late 1980s, with interest in China wavering even before the Tiananmen Square incident. Furthermore, by the mid 1980s, individuals in the tourism industry noted that once it was no longer novel, China was handicapped by the poor service quality of the Chinese tourism product.

Today, post Tiananmen Square China has an additional handicap in the USA market. Both travelers and members of the travel trade no longer assume visitors to China will be well received. Concerns abound in both groups about the safety of travel to China. And even if visitors are objectively safe, both individual travelers and key segments of the travel trade are concerned about the type of welcome Americans will receive in China.

These concerns highlight the fact that a destination such as China faces fierce competition in attracting the American traveler. Whenever a destination area becomes less attractive due to cost, poor service, political strife, or Act of God, competitive destinations are poised to exploit these events. Results cited in this study reinforce the idea that destination areas are highly substitutable. Some American travelers replaced travel to China with travel to other, objectively similar destinations such as Thailand or Singapore. Other travelers, however, replaced travel to China with destinations such as Europe and Australia. These substitutes appear in many ways to be different from China. However, from the point of view of the traveler, the benefits provided by a trip to Europe were apparently acceptable substitutes for the benefits provided by a trip to China.

The Future of International Tourism to China

Tiananmen Square was a landmark event for the Chinese tourism industry. The industry's prospects in the post Tiananmen Square world may, at first glance, seem quite different than they did in 1988. However, it is important to recognize that even if the events associated with Tiananmen Square had never occurred, Chinese tourism would have faced difficulties in the 1990s. In fact, it has been argued that too much focus on the demonstrations and the government's reaction has obscured problems in the Chinese business environment that existed prior to Tiananmen Square (Earle 1991).

Before Tiananmen Square, the Chinese hotel industry was over built and lacked sufficient accommodations for mid-market travelers (Zhang 1989; Zhao 1989). Before Tiananmen Square, concerns abounded about China's ability to provide hospitality services that met international standards (Choy, Dong, and Wen 1986). Before Tiananmen Square, interest in China as a destination (measured by either arrivals or magazine articles) in one of its major markets, the USA, was clearly in decline. Tiananmen Square has added an additional layer of problems on top of this already shaky foundation.

Thus the Chinese tourism industry faces difficult prospects in the 1990s. Overcoming the negative effects of Tiananmen Square on the image of China is only a first step. Even if time and reform heal some of the wounds of Tiananmen Square, the Chinese tourism industry will still be faced with a number of severe problems that may handicap it well into the next century.

Notes

1. The Chinese government uses ethnic, national, and residential labels to describe visitors to China. In addition to foreign visitors, a second important category of visitors are labeled compatriots. Compatriots are residents of Hong Kong, Macao, and Taiwan and travel into China on a special home visit permit issued by the Chinese government. A third category are Overseas Chinese. These are Chinese nationals who reside abroad but hold Chinese passports.

References

Bian, J. 1990. Tourism in China. *World Leisure & Recreation* 32(1): 27-31.

Cheng, E. 1990. Ill-starred Ventures. *Far Eastern Economic Review* April 26: 54.

Choy, D.J.L., G.L. Dong, and Z. Wen. 1986. Tourism in PR China: Marketing Trends and Changing Policies. *Tourism Management* 7(4): 197-201.

Cullen, T.P. 1988. Filling China's Staffing Gap. *Cornell Hotel and Restaurant Administration Quarterly* 29(2): 76-8.

Dorsey, M. 1989a. The Influential Agent. *Travel Agent Magazine* (September 11): 10.
_____. 1989b. The Destination Decision. *Travel Agent Magazine* (September 18): 77-81.

Earle, B.H. 1991. China After Tiananmen Square: An Assessment of its Business Environment. *Case Western Reserve Journal of International Law* 23: 421-45.

EIU (Economist Intelligence Unit). 1990. China. *International Tourism Reports* No. 3: 22-48.

Fuller, L.K. 1991. Tiananmen as Treated by the Christian Science Monitor. *Political Communication and Persuasion* 8: 79-91.

Gallup Organization. 1988. Geographic Knowledge Deemed Vital, But Many Lack Basic Skills, *Gallup Report* 277: 35.

Gartner, W.C. and J. Shen. 1992. The Impact of Tiananmen Square on China's Tourism Image. *Journal of Travel Research* 30(4): 47-52.

Gormsen, E. 1990. The Impact of Tourism on Regional Change in China. *GeoJournal* 21(1/2): 127-35.

Gunn, C.A. 1979. *Tourism Planning*. New York: Crane Russak.

Hurly, J.A. 1988. The Hotels of Rome: Meeting the Marketing Challenge of Terrorism. *Cornell Hotel and Restaurant Administration Quarterly*, 29(1): 71-9.

Mansur, I. 1991. Tests of Market Efficiency on Major Equity Markets Following an Unanticipated Event: The Case of the Tiananmen Square uprising. *Journal of Economics and International Relations* 4(2): 89-97.

Milo, K.J. and S.L. Yoda. 1991. Recovery from Natural Disaster: Travel Writers and Tourist Destinations. *Journal of Travel Research* 30(1): 36-9.

Richter, L.K. and W.L. Waugh. 1986. Terrorism and Tourism as Logical Companions. *Tourism Management* 7(4): 230-38.

Roehl, W.S. 1990. Travel Agent Attitudes Toward China After Tiananmen Square. *Journal of Travel Research* 29(2): 16-22.

Roehl, W.S. and D.R. Fesenmaier. 1992. Risk Perception and Pleasure Travel: An Exploratory Analysis. *Journal of Travel Research* 30(4): 17-26.

Sneider, D. 1992. Tourists Replace Troops Along Russo-Chinese Border. *Christian Science Monitor* (August 4): 1,4.

Tisdell, C. and J. Wen. 1991. Foreign Tourism as an Element in PR China's Economic Development Strategy. *Tourism Management* 12(1): 55-67.

World Tourism Organization. (various years). *Yearbook of Tourism Statistics*. (Madrid: WTO).

Xiao, Z. 1993. China's Image as a Tourist Destination as Perceived by US Tour Operators. Unpublished Master's Thesis, University of Nevada, Las Vegas.

Yu, Lawrence. 1992. Emerging Markets for China's Tourism Industry. *Journal of Travel Research* 31(1): 10-3.

Zhang, Guangrui. 1989. Ten Years of Chinese Tourism. *Tourism Management* 10(1): 51-62.

Zhao, Jian. 1989. Overprovision in Chinese Hotels. *Tourism Management* 10(1): 63-6.

Zheng, G. and T. Martin. 1987. The Economic Significance of International Tourism for the People's Republic of China. *Hospitality Education and Research Journal* 11: 145-50.

3

An Assessment of China's Tourism Resources

Yongwei Zhang

The role of resources is essential to tourism development. McIntosh and Goeldner (1986: 200) have pointed out that the entire tourism industry rests on a base of natural resources. Researchers have found that spatial variations of tourism are closely linked to the availability, accessibility and the nature of tourism resources. "Clearly, tourism does not occur evenly or randomly in space. Various types of tourism will have differing requirements for favorable growth, and certain sites, regions, or nations will be more favorable for development than others" (Boniface and Cooper 1988: 17). China is endowed with a variety of tourism resources. The astonishing growth of tourism in China over the past 15 years, except a brief decline following the Tiananmen Square Incident, has adequately illustrated that resources are a fundamental component in the development of tourism. Mr. Liu Yi, the highest ranking official in China's National Tourism Administration (NTA), indicated that the future prospects for China's tourism will continue to lay on its "rich and world-famous" tourism resources (*Beijing Review* 1991: 20). In addition to the enormous economic and social changes that have taken place, Liu attributed China's attractiveness as a favored international tourist destination to its "5,000-year-old cultural civilization, wealth of national customs and varied geography and natural scenery." The following aims to examine the characteristics and regional patterns of distribution of China's tourism resources, natural and cultural, and to assess their development in recent years.

Geography and Heritage: Natural and Human Tourism Resources

China is truly one of the few countries in the world with such a vast territory, huge population, long-standing history, brilliant ancient civilization, stunning natural beauty, and multiethnic culture. This uniquely combined natural and cultural resource base has become a major asset for China in its effort to develop tourism. Located in the southeastern part of the Eurasian Continent on the western shores of the Pacific Ocean, China is the third largest country in the world with a total land area of 9.6 million square kilometers. Its geographic environment and physical landscape are enormously diverse due to the north-south differences in latitudes and the east-west variations in landform and moisture. China is a mountainous country. Hills, mountains, and plateaus cover two-thirds of the total area. The general topography descends from the high plateaus in the west to the lower-lying plains in the east. Most regions in China are influenced by the distinct Monsoon climate with large daily and annual ranges of temperature and four clearly defined seasons. From north to south, China covers cold-temperate, intermediate-temperate, warm-temperate, and subtropical climatic zones.

The vast size of the territory and the varied geography provide China with beautiful landscapes and a dazzling array of natural and scenic wonders. China's *shanshui* (mountains and rivers) has overwhelmed visitors from all over the world. In addition to its fabled Five Mountains (Taishan, Shanxi's Hengshan, Hunan's Hengshan, Huashan, and Songshan), China has many other famous peaks with equally enchanting and picturesque scenery. Huangshan, Lushan, and Emeishan are also among the most visited mountains in the country. A widely known saying among the Chinese people - "None of the Five Mountains need to be seen after coming back from Huangshan" - vividly describes the beauty of this mountain. There are also many great rivers in China. The mighty Changjiang (Yangtze River), with its breathtaking Three Gorges cliffs, is known the world over. Other spectacular views include:

- The Huangguoshu (Yellow Fruit Tree) Waterfalls on the Baihe River in Guizhou Province,
- The Hukou (Kettle Mouth) Waterfalls of the Yellow River in Shanxi Province,
- The famous karst (limestone) landscape along the Lijiang River between Guilin and Yangshuo, and

- The fantastic natural rock formations of Lunan Stone Forest in Yunnan Province.

Caves have always been the highlights of China's natural tourism resources. There are thousands of caverns in Zhejiang, Guangxi, Guizhou, and some other southern provinces. Many of these caves are huge and filled with magnificent stalactites and stalagmites produced by the hydrolysis of carbonate rocks. Recently, scientists have discovered in Guizhou Province a 35.2 kilometer long cave, the Double River Cave, which is 3 kilometers longer than the Flying Dragon Cave in Hubei Province, previously the longest cave in China (Yang, *People's Daily*, Dec. 2, 1993). Zhijin (Gold Embroidery) Cave was found recently in Guizhou. Because of its grand view and unparalleled beauty, it is now known as the "nation's number one underground art museum" (Yang and Liu, *People's Daily*, July 23, 1993).

Many of the most scenic localities are not only a gift of nature, but also the product of thousands of years of wisdom and hard work by the Chinese people. Among these places are Hangzhou's West Lake, Wuxi's Taihu Lake, Beijing's Summer Palace, and Suzhou's many picturesque gardens. Natural beauty and the human landscape are wonderfully intermingled in these places.

China's recorded history goes back over 4,000 years. This immensely long history of continuous economic and cultural development has left a rich legacy in many fields such as agriculture, handicrafts, science and technology, medicine, literature, architecture, art, and philosophy. The 6,700 kilometer-long Great Wall, built over two thousands years ago, is one of the most magnificent ancient structures in the world. Foreign trade and cultural exchanges created the well known Silk Road which linked China with central and western Asia, and with the Greek and Roman civilizations. Thousands of life-size, terra cotta warriors and horses with wooden chariots, arranged in battle formation, were unearthed in the tomb of Qin Shi Huang, the first emperor of Qin Dynasty (221-206 BC) in Xian, Shaanxi province. The Forbidden City, which was the Imperial Palace of the Ming (1368-1644) and Qing Dynasties (1644-1912), has a total floor space of 720,000 square meters and is the largest ancient architectural complex still standing in China. The Grand Canal, a man-made waterway first built in the 6th century BC between Tianjin and Hangzhou, is the longest of its kind throughout the world. Among China's many ancient cities, Beijing, Changan (today's Xian), Luoyang, Nanjing, Kaifeng, and Hangzhou have all served as the political and economic centers of past dynasties. They are now known as the "Six Great Ancient Capitals" (Zhang 1991: 176). In addition, China has numerous temples, pagodas, statues, and cave carvings, many of which are associated with Buddhism, Daoism, and Confucius.

Social heritage and ethnic diversity are also part of China's rich and varied tourism resources. A tradition of strong family ties based on the philosophy of Confucius, combined with the ideology enforced by the current government in its almost half-century rule, have created a unique social and cultural milieu for modern China which influences the behavior and interaction of most Chinese people. Many foreign visitors are fascinated with Chinese society and want to discover and learn more about it. On the other hand, Chinese society is also diverse. There are over fifty ethnic minority groups, and each one of them has its own distinct customs and traditions. Researchers have found that ethnic neighborhoods are increasingly becoming popular tourist attractions in China. The motivations of travelers who visit these places include the desire to "observe colorful folk life, native costumes, and house types, and to partake of regional food" (Rafferty 1993: 14). Yunnan Province, for example, has 24 minorities which account for about one-third of its 39 million people. An Ethnic Village Complex has been built in this province and is a major tourist attraction. Each section of the complex has an architectural style representative of a distinct minority group, and is tended to by real minority people. This miniature complex of different cultural landscapes and ethnic groups attracted over 1.6 million visitors in a period of nine months after it was opened in late 1992 (Zhao and Long, *People's Daily*, Sept. 7, 1993).

Festivals and public celebrations, together with a variety of other special events "are increasingly seen as unique tourist attractions and as destination image makers" (Getz 1992: xi). For most Chinese, the spectacular, week-long celebrations of the traditional Chinese New Year has always been the most important event of the year. Chinese who live in Hong Kong, Taiwan, and Macao flood into the mainland during this time. Many overseas Chinese take this opportunity to have family reunions and hold various kinds of celebrations. There are also other major traditional festivals such as the Zhongqiu Festival (known as the Mooncake Festival in the West), and the Qingming Festival when the dead are mourned. In 1993, China identified 40 state festivals and celebrations that could serve to promote tourism (*People's Daily*, Aug. 10, 1993). Most of these festivals feature one or more major cultural, social, or religious activities, such as

- The 1993 China Tourism and Shopping Festival,
- The Taishan International Mountain-climbing Festival,
- The Linxi International Calligraphy Festival, and
- The 1994 Leshan International Tourism and the Great Buddha Festival.

China is also known for its culinary arts, with over 5,000 traditional dishes of different flavors. Many westerners find Chinese cuisine delicate, exotic, and delicious. Each region has its own favored and distinct food. It is almost impossible to find appropriate words to describe the taste of the Chinese cuisine in general. Folklore characterizes the taste preference of people in different parts of China as "Sweet South, Salty North, Spicy East, and Sour West." This, however, does not come even near to a rough description of the diverse regional variations.

The distinct political landscapes of China may also be viewed as tourism resources. During the first 30 years of the People's Republic of China, few Westerners were allowed to visit the country. China completely isolated itself from the outside world. It was a mysterious nation in the eyes of foreigners. Curiosity has been one of the primary driving forces behind the travel motivations of many Westerners to China today. The huge portrait of Chairman Mao on the Tiananmen Gate, right across from the Square where his mausoleum stands, reminds travelers that they are in a Communist country. Numerous billboards of political propaganda, various statues of Chairman Mao and other "proletarian revolutionaries," locales and museums associated with the history of the Chinese Communist Party and with the legacy of Mao, and imprints of the Cultural Revolution, are political landscapes that are still visible throughout the country. Many revolutionary landmarks, such as Mao Zedong's birthplace in Hunan, Jiangxi's Jinggangshan Revolutionary Base, Yanan's cave dwellings, Guangzhou's Huang Hua Gang Cemetery of the Revolutionary Martyrs, and Nanjing's Zhongshan Tomb, are among China's major tourist attractions. During recent years, along with the ongoing economic reform, political billboards and banners proclaiming the virtues of the Party and socialism are interlaced with the neon signs of Coca Cola, Sony, Hitachi, and countless other capitalist commercial advertisements in many major industrial and population centers. Westerners find this unique landscape interesting and even amusingly appealing in its own way.

Regional Differences in Tourism Resource Distribution and Development

The strong influence of China's regional economic structure, which is characterized by a developed and industrial eastern coast region, a less developed and less industrial central inland region, and a least developed and least industrialized western interior region, is clearly seen in the spatial patterns of tourism (see Figure 3.1). Most tourist attractions are located in the eastern part of China where economies are highly developed and societies are predominantly urban. During the seventh Five-Year-Plan (1986-1990) period, China designated seven key tourism provinces (including autonomous regions and special municipalities). Five of these places, Beijing, Shanghai, Jiangsu, Zhejiang, and Guangdong, are located in the east coast (Shen 1993: 82). The remaining two, Shaanxi and Guangxi, are situated respectively in the northern and southern parts of the middle portion of the country. Since 1990, some other eastern provinces have also experienced dramatic growth in tourism, among which Liaoning, Fujian, and Hainan are most prominent. Geographically, Liaoning and Fujian are located on the coast and Hainan is an island in the South China Sea. Figure 3.1 illustrates the overwhelmingly coastal concentration of the major tourist destinations in comparison to the three economic regions identified by the State Council, the highest government administrative organ in China. Fujian has recently become the fourth largest tourism province (in terms of tourist receipts), following only Beijing, Guangdong, and Shanghai (Table 3.1). In 1992, tourist receipts and tourist arrivals in these 10 places accounted for 88.8 percent and 89.4 percent of the nation's totals in each category.

TABLE 3.1 Tourist Receipts of 10 Major Places in 1992

Place	Receipts (in million US$)	Place	Receipts (in million US$)
Beijing	657.0	Jiangsu	70.9
Guangdong	640.0	Liaoning	68.7
Shanghai	229.0	Zhejiang	50.2
Fujian	101.0	Hainan	43.6
Guangxi	88.7	Shaanxi	41.7

Source: Compiled from Wei and Feng 1993: 372.

The vast areas in the western part of the country, by contrast, have a much smaller role in the overall development of China's tourism. Well established and well-known tourist attractions are scarce in these areas, particularly in Ningxia, Qinghai, Xizang, Xinjiang, and Inner Mongolia. The Ningxia Autonomous Region is the only major region in China where even a medium-sized airport is not available. Ningxia's only high level accommodation facility, a three-star hotel, was not scheduled to be completed until 1994 (Lin, *People's Daily*, Aug. 6, 1993). Qinghai Province did not have an international travel service until 1983 and the average annual visitor arrivals has only been about 10,000 for the past 10 years. Xizang (Tibet) has received a total of 170,000 international tourists in a period of 11 years since 1981 (Hua Weilie and Hu Xisheng, *People's Daily*, Feb. 3, 1993). The State Council has twice officially designated places with favorable tourism resources as "State Level Scenic Wonders and Historical Sites." Of the 84 attractions (forty-four designated in 1982 and forty approved in 1988), only a few are located in western China (Table 3.2).

FIGURE 3.1   Coastal Concentration of China's Largest Tourist Provinces

TABLE 3.2 Eighty-four Scenic Wonders and Historical Sites Approved by China's State Council

Province, Autonomous Region, and Municipality (Number of sites)	List of Sites
SICHUAN (10)	Mt. Jinfuo (Golden Buddha), Mt. Gongga, Jianmenshudao (Sword Gate Path), Yalong River, Chongqing's Mt. Jinyun, Southern Sichuan's Sea of Bamboo, Mt. Emei, Mt. Qingchengshan and Dujiang Yan, Yellow Dragon Temple & Jiuzhaigou, Three Gorges of Changjiang (Sichuan and Hubei)
ZHEJIANG (7)	Mt. Tiantai, Hangzhou West Lake, Shengsi Liedao (Islands), Mt. Yandang, Mt. Putuo, Fuchun River and Xinan River, Nansi River
YUNNAN (6)	Jade Dragon Snow Mountain, Three Parallel Rivers, Mt. Dali Cangshan, Lunan Stone Forest, Lake Dianchi of Kunming, Xishuangbanna
GUIZHOU (5)	Red Maple Lake, Dragon Palace, Huangguoshu (Yellow Fruit Tree) Falls, Zhijin (Gold Embroidery) Cave, Wuyang River
LIAONING (5)	Gold Stone Shoal, Xingcheng Beach, Yalu River, Dalian Beach-Lushun, Mt. Qianshan
ANHUI (4)	Mt. Huangshan, Mt. Tianzhushan (Heavenly Pillar), Mt. Jiuhuashan, Mt. Langyashan
FUJIAN (4)	Mt. Qingyuanshan, Mt. Tailuaoshan, Gulangyu-Wanshishan (Ten Thousand Rocks Mountain), Mt. Wuyishan
HEBEI (4)	Waibamiao (Imperial Summer Villa), Mt. Cangyan, Wild Three Hills, Qinhuangdao-Beidaihe
JIANGSU (4)	Nanjing's Mt. Zhongshan, Mt. Yuntai, Lake Taihu, Shugang-Lake Souxi
JIANGXI (4)	Mt. Lushan, Mt. Longhushan (Dragon and Tiger), Mt. Jingganshan, Mt. Sanqingshan
GUANGDONG (3)	Mt. Xiqiao, Mt. Danxia (Rosy Cloud), Star Lake of Zaoqing
GUANGXI ZHUANG (3)	Mt. Guiping Xishan, Guilin Li River, Huashanfeng
HENAN (3)	Longmen (Dragon Gate) in Luoyang, Mt. Songshan, Mt. Jigong
HUBEI (3)	Mt. Dahongshan, Mt. Wudang, East Lake
HUNAN (3)	Wulingyuan, Lake Dongting-Yueyang Tower, Mt. Hengshan
SHANDONG (3)	Jiaodong Beach, Qingdao Laoshan Beach, Mt. Taishan
SHANXI (3)	Mt. Wutaishan, Mt.Hengshan, Yellow R. Hukou Waterfalls
HEILONGJIANG (2)	Lake Jingbo, Wudalianchi (Five Lakes)
JILIN (2)	Lake Songhua, Jingyuetan Lake
SHAANXI (2)	Mt. Lishan in Lintong, Mt. Huashan
BEIJING (1)	Badaling-Shisanling (Ming Tombs)
GANSU (1)	Mt. Maijishan
NINGXIA HUI (1)	Xixiasanling (West Xia Three Tombs)
XINJIANG UYGUR (1)	Heavenly Pond of Mt. Tianshan

Source: Compiled from Zhang, B. 1992.

In addition, the western part of China has long been perceived as a resource poor region by both international and domestic travelers because of its obvious lack of a large number of tourists and well established tourist attractions. According to Rafferty, "The landscape of China, at least in the eyes of most Westerners, is actually the landscape of Guilin" (1993: 475). A poll of overseas and domestic tourists was conducted by the Travel Services of China in 1991 on the most preferred tourist sites in the country. The results yielded the 40 most favored attractions (Table 3.3). Inner Mongolia had only one place on the list, while Xizang, Xinjiang, and Ningxia had none.

Contrary to its general image, the western part of China is by no means lacking in tourism resources. In fact, tremendous developmental potential exists in this region. For example, according to a recent survey Xinjiang tops all provinces, autonomous regions, and special municipalities in China in its total number and variety of tourism resources (The World Journal Report, Nov. 24, 1993). This survey found that Xinjiang possesses 56 different types of tourism resources, many of which are unique to this province. The survey used criteria specified by the official Survey Standard of Tourism Resources in China, in which a total of 68 kinds of tourism resources are identified. Compared with other provinces and autonomous regions, Xinjiang has the largest land area (one-sixth of the total land area of China) and the most contrasting landforms and climates. The world's most extensive middle-to-low latitude alpine glaciers are found there. The Altun Mountains comprise China's largest natural preservation zone with a wide variety of wild plant and animal species. The Taklimakan Mobile Desert ranks second in size for its kind in the world, and the Heavenly Pond of Tianshan has breathtaking views. Although Xinjiang has an abundant natural tourism resource base, nature attractions account for only 37.1 percent of the total inventory. The majority of the tourism resources identified are in the human category, including several routes of the Silk Road that pass through Xinjiang. Numerous historical relics along the Silk Road have become invaluable resources for tourism. In addition, the unique way of life of the Uygur people, including their famous music and dance, Islamic styles of architecture, and various types of local cuisine are all parts of Xinjiang's strong tourism assets. According to McColl, "The Western Regions are not remote, lonely, wind- and sand-swept 'nowheres.' Not a hinterland, this vast area instead has long been a center of creativity in the arts, sciences, technology and agriculture" (1991).

Other western provinces and autonomous regions are also rich in tourism resources. Ningxia has the largest concentration of the Hui nationality. Mosques are ubiquitous in Ningxia, and most Huis are devout Muslims. The extensive Tenggeli Desert, the roaring Yellow River, the Mt. Liupang (Six Spirals) Nature Preserve, and the newly developed Shahu (Sand Lake)

TABLE 3.3 Forty Most Favored Tourist Spots

Attraction (rank ordered)	Location
The Three Gorges of Changjiang (the Yangtze River)	Sichuan, Hubei
Guilin Lijiang River	Guangxi
Huangshan Mountain	Anhui
Lushan Mountain	Jiangxi
Hangzhou West Lake (Xihu)	Zhejiang
Emeishan Mountain	Sichuan
Huang Guo Shu Waterfalls	Guizhou
Taishan Mountain	Shangdong
Beidaihe Beach in Qinghuangdao	Hebei
Huashan Mountain	Shanxi
Jiuzhaigou Yellow Dragon Temple	Sichuan
Tonglu Yaolin Wonderland	Zhejiang
Gold Embroidery Cavern	Guizhou
Mt. Wushan Little Three Gorges	Sichuan
Jinggangshan Mountain	Jiangxi
Southern Sichuan Bamboo Sea	Sichuan
The Great East Sea - Ya Long Bay	Hainan
Wulingyuan	Hunan
Five Great Lakes	Heilongjiang
Hukou Falls of the Yellow River	Shanxi
The Badaling Great Wall	Beijing
Leshan Mountain Great Buddha	Sichuan
Suzhou Gardens	Jiangsu
Forbidden City	Beijing
Dunhuang Mogao Cave Paintings	Gansu
Qufu Three Confucius Sites	Shangdong
Summer Palace	Beijing
Ming Tombs	Beijing
Nanjing Sun Yatsen Tomb	Jiangsu
The Summer Villa - Waibamiao	Hebei
Qinshi Huangdi Tomb and the Terra Cotta Museum	Shaanxi
Zigong Dinosaur Museum	Sichuan
The Yellow Crane Place	Hubei
Beijing Daguan Garden	Beijing
Shanhai Gate and the Old Dragon Head Great Wall	Hebei
Genghis Khan Tomb	Nei Mongol
Zhuhai Tourist City	Guangdong
Shenzhen's "Magnificent China"	Guangdong
Confucius Temple and the Qin-Huai River	Jiangsu
The Gezhouba Dam	Hubei

Source: *Special Zones Herald*, Haikou, Jan. 28, 1992.

Scenic Zone provide much potential for sightseeing and nature enjoyment in Ningxia. The Xunishan Cave Complex consists of over 100 caves filled with records of the Silk Road. A group of 108 pagodas on the banks of the Yellow River stretch out along the surrounding hills in a unique triangular shape. The most splendid historical sites in Ningxia are probably the three tombs of nine emperors of the West Xia, a kingdom that existed here about 1,000 years ago. Foreigners visiting this place are overwhelmed by the magnificent architecture of the tombs and, giving high regard to their tourism value, have called them the "Pyramids of the Orient" (Lin, *People's Daily*, Aug. 6, 1993).

Xizang's (Tibet) tourism resources are characterized by its highland location and its Lama religion. The Qinghai-Tibetan Plateau, on which Xizang is located, is known as the "Roof of the World" and has a tremendous amount of highland scenery, including Mt. Qomolangma (Everest), the highest peak on earth. Numerous lakes and hot springs are scattered over the plateau. Yangbajing's Hot Water Lake has a huge geyser, that erupts up to 100 meters above the lake surface. Both the Medôg and Zayü Nature Preserves Zones have abundant climatic and biological resources. In Medôg, from the river valley of the Yarlung Zangbo to the top of Namjagbarwa Feng Peak, the elevation rises 6,000 meters within a horizontal range of 40 kilometers. A whole spectrum of physical landscapes is seen here, including tropical, subtropical, temperate, and polar. Nowhere else in China is such a great climatic and biological diversity found in such a small area.

The cultural landscape created by the Lama (Tibetan Buddhism) religion is unique to Tibet. The widespread temples are striking landscape features. Lhasa (holy land), the capital of Tibet, is the religious center of Tibetan Buddhism. The city is dominated by the Potala, a spectacular ancient palace complex and former residence of the Dalai Lama. Other landmarks in Lhasa include Jokhang (Great Cathedral), the Sera, Ganden, and the Drepung monasteries, and the Norbulingka (the former summer palace of the Dalai Lama).

Most of the religious establishments in Tibet were damaged to varying degrees during Mao Zedong's Cultural Revolution. The government is now trying to rebuild these places into valuable tourism resources. The Potala, for example, is being refurbished in stages. Hussey (1992) found that the continuing efforts of the government at restoration on the principle sites in Lhasa are evident, and that "the repairs are part of the development of [Xizang's] tourism infrastructure."

In summary, the eastern part of China possesses the most advanced tourism facilities, receives the most travelers, and produces most of the nation's tourism income. The western part of the country, on the other hand, remains largely untapped for tourism. With its tremendous tourism resources, however, this area is most likely to become a popular destination in the future when adequate funds for development become available.

Tourism Regions and Resource Patterns

Tourism researchers maintain that a scientific scheme of regional tourism divisions is a fundamental means for understanding the spatial patterns of a country's resources and for planning regional development (Zhang 1992: 1). Geographers have long been interested in developing theories and methods related to tourism regions. Factors such as the integrity and proximity of administrative units, and the similarity and interrelationship among the physical environment, history, culture, and tradition are always important considerations in the identification of tourism regions. Chen Chuankang of Beijing University argues that a tourism region should be the spatial integration of the physical environment, traditional cultural, and modern development (1993: 2). Scholars in China have different views regarding the manners in which China's tourism regions should be divided. A review of the literature has revealed, however, that most of them seem to agree that a tourism region should have the following characteristics:

1. A relative concentration of tourism resources,
2. A sufficient broadness of regional extent,
3. A distinctive and complementary combination of diverse resources, and
4. One or more well established tourist centers supported by adequate infrastructure, superstructure, and stable markets.

From this standpoint, various divisions of China have been proposed. Geographers at Hebei Normal University raised a nine-region scheme based on the geographic contiguousness of regions and the relative completeness of a historical or cultural resource (Shen 1993: 89). These nine regions include:

- Beijing Tourism Region
- Silk Road Tourism Region
- Northeast Tourism Region
- South China Tourism Region
- Southwest Tourism Region
- Taiwan Tourism Region
- Qingzang (Qinghai-Tibetan Plateaus) Tourism Region
- Yangtze River Valley Tourism Region
- Yellow River Valley Tourism Region

The perspectives of Zhou Jinbu of Hangzhou University have reflected his emphasis on climatic differentiations and destination characteristics (Shen 1993: 89). In an attempt to identify China's tourism regions, he proposed the following divisions:

- Zhongyuan (Central China) Ancient Civilization Tourism Region
- Eastern Coast Tourism Region
- Chuan Han (Sichuan) Tourism Region
- South China Tropical Landscape Tourism Region
- Southwest Karst Landform Tourism Region
- Northwest Silk Road Tourism Region
- North China Tourism Region
- Northern Border Frontier Fortress Tourism Region, and
- Qing-Zang Highland Tourism Region.

Guo Laixi of the Institute of Geography in the Chinese Academy of Sciences has characterized China's tourism regions as a three-level spatial system in which a series of primary, secondary, and tertiary structures can be further identified (Guo 1990). In order to make a distinction between these geographic units, he refers to the primary regions as *Luyou Dai* (Tourism Areas), the secondary regions as *Luyou Sheng* (Tourism Provinces), and the tertiary regions as *Luyou Qu* (Tourism Zones). Guo's system includes nine primary "areas," 29 secondary "provinces," and 149 tertiary "zones." Chen Chuankang (1993) has developed a similar system in which seven primary regions were specified. These include North, South, Northeast, Northwest, and Southwest China, the Qinghai-Xizang Plateau, and the Middle and Lower Reaches of the Changjiang River. Another classification was made by Zhang Baogao (1992). He presented a ten-region division (including Taiwan) as shown in Table 3.4.

The remarkable development of tourism in recent years has had a profound impact on regional tourism structures. Changes in the spatial pattern of tourism development and tourist behavior have not been accurately reflected in these classification schemes. Modifications need to be made to incorporate these changing patterns.

The area surrounding Bohai Bay, for example, has emerged as a distinct tourist region. This region has the nation's most intensive concentration of natural and human landscapes and developed tourist facilities (Liu 1993). This region, now widely referred to as the "Bohai Rim Tourism Circle," also coincides with one of the fastest growing economic areas in China, the "Bohai Rim Economic Region" (Zhang 1993: 3). The major administrative units included in this region (Beijing, Tianjin, Hebei, Shangdong, and Liaoning) possess over 40 percent of China's Five-Star and Four-Star level hotels and produced 35.95 percent of the country's total tourist receipts in

TABLE 3.4 China's Tourism Regions

Region	Extent	Landscape
Huadong (East China)	Shanghai, Jiangsu, Zhejiang, Anhui, and Jiangxi	Gardens, mountains, rivers and lakes
Huabei (North China)	Beijing, Tianjin, Hebei Shanxi, and Shaanxi	Ancient capitals, culture and civilization
Huanan (South China)	Guangdong, Fujian, and Hainan	Tropical products, markets, over-seas Chinese villages, islands
Huazhong (Middle China)	Hubei, Hunan, Sichuan	Golden Waterways, stone carvings
Southwest	Guangxi, Yunnan, Guizhou	Karst, wild life, ethnic cultures
Northeast	Liaoning, Jilin, Heilongjiang	Volcanoes, hot springs, snow plains, forests
Northwest	Gansu, Xinjiang	Silk Road, carvings, murals
Northern Territories	Inner Mongolia, Ningxia	Nomadic cultures
Highland	Xizang (Tibet), Qinghai	Religion, mountain environment

Source: Adapted from Zhang, B. 1992.

1991 (Liu 1993). Four of the six UNESCO designated World Relics in China are found in this region: the Forbidden City, the Great Wall, Mt. Taishan, and the Confucius' Shrine (*The World Journal Report,* Oct. 21, 1993). Beach resources and ocean landscapes are especially characteristic in this region. Numerous beach sites exist along the 5,800 kilometer long coast. In addition to the well established Beidaihe Resort and the newly developed Nandaihe Resort, the famous Cangli County is becoming one of the newest beach resort areas to offer a "sun, sand, and sea" experience with its "Golden Beach" on Bohai Bay (Li and Song, *People's Daily,* Aug. 6, 1993).

Recently, five southwestern provinces and autonomous regions (Xizang, Guangxi, Guizhou, Sichuan, and Yunnan) have decided to collectively plan and market their destinations. A "Five Province Tourism Network and Coordinate Committee" has been formed. Brochures, video tapes, and tour maps have also been produced emphasizing the tourist attractions and programs of the five provinces as a whole (Li, *People's Daily,* Aug. 13, 1993). These actions aim at coordinating the efforts and resources of the five areas in order to develop their tourism more effectively. From the standpoint that all these provinces are located contiguously along China's southwestern border with complementary resource advantages and disadvantages, it may be meaningful to group these five places as one tourist region.

Researchers still need to work hard toward a better understanding of China's regional tourism structures. After all, tourism per se is a relatively new phenomenon in China and most of the current regional divisions are preliminary and subject to further revisions and modifications.

Recent Developments in China's Tourism Resources

Since the beginning of the 1990s, the tourism industry in China has encountered many new challenges. First, the international tourist market has expanded significantly. During the entire 1980s, Japan and the U.S. were the only countries that produced total numbers of arrivals over 100,000 each year. The number of markets of this size increased to five in 1991 and to 12 in 1992. It is anticipated that this number will increase to 14 by the end of 1993 (Cui, *People's Daily*, Aug. 17, 1993). The total number of international tourist arrivals is expected to reach 40 million in 1993 (Xiao, *People's Daily*, Dec. 6, 1993). In order to meet this increasing demand, it becomes imperative for China to further explore new resources, develop new facilities, and create more opportunities.

Secondly, a phenomenal growth in domestic tourism has occurred because of the increasing incomes of the Chinese people. China experienced 350 million domestic person-trips in 1993 (Xiao, *People's Daily*, Overseas Edition, Dec. 6, 1993). This number is projected to reach 700 million by the year 2000 (Wei and Feng 1993: 345). Even more than for international visitors, tremendous pressure exists for the rapid and extensive development of tourism resources to meet the needs of increasing numbers of domestic tourists.

A significant event, symbolizing recent development efforts, is the establishment of national level "Tourism and Vacation Zones." The national government expects to "elevate China's tourism industry, currently primarily rendering service to the short-term sightseers, to attract long-term tourists combining sightseeing and holiday" (Kou 1992: 36). From proposals submitted by 26 places, the State Council has approved twelve for the establishment of long-stay tourist destinations. Funds for development are expected to come primarily from enterprises and individuals in Taiwan, Hong Kong, Macao, and the foreign countries. A series of incentives and preferential policies have also been provided by the government to encourage such investments. The twelve Tourism and Vacation Zones, and the provinces in which these facilities are to be located, are shown in Table 3.5. Most of these Tourism and Vacation Zones are currently under construction.

TABLE 3.5 The Twelve State Level Tourism and Vacation Zones

Tourism and Vacation Zone	Province
South Lake	Guangdong
Jinshi Beach in Dalian	Liaoning
Lake Taihu in Wuxi	Jiangsu
Lake Taihu in Suzhou	Jiangsu
Old Stone Man in Qingdao	Shandong
Zhijiang River in Hangzhou	Zhejiang
Yintan Beach in Beihai	Guangxi
Hengsha Island	Shanghai
Dianchi Lake in Kunming	Yunnan
Meizhou Island and Wuyishan Mountains	Fujian
Yalong Bay in Sanya	Hainan

Source: China Tourism News, July 17, 1993.

Another important new development is to further utilize China's forest resources as tourist attractions. Up to February of 1993, China has opened 350 new forest parks with a total area of some five million acres. Almost two-thirds of these parks were developed in the 1990s. In addition, there are also 420 nature preserves nationwide, providing a strong resource base for future tourism development. Hunan Province, for example, has the most developed forest park systems. The 31 forest parks located in this province received over one million visitors and a total income of US$5 million in 1992 (Fang L.G., *People's Daily*, Mar. 5, 1993).

Today, the development of tourism resources is seen almost everywhere in China. Many tourist resorts and summer villas are under construction. Numerous cultural attractions and scenic spots are being reinstated, repaired, or remodeled. Some of the major new tourism projects reported in the Tourism Section by the *People's Daily* in 1993 include:

- Seven tourism zones in Sanya City, Hainan Province
- A tourist amusement park in Jinan, Shandong Province
- Xinghe Amusement Park in Dalian, Liaoning Province
- Taihu Villa in Jiangsu Province
- Wan Lian Villa in Tianjin
- Xing Long Overseas Chinese Tourism Vacation City in Hainan
- The Shenzhen Tourism Zone, Guangdong Province
- Nandaihe Tourism City, Hebei Province
- Dragon Spring Holiday Villa and the Qingposhan Tourism Villa in Sichuan Province
- The Ninghai Holiday Center in Beihai, Guangxi Autonomous Region
- The Milky Way Tourism Zone in Weifang, Shandong Province

- White Dragon International Tourism City in Guangxi Autonomous Region
- The Rice Fragrant Lake Tourism Zone in Beijing
- The Golden Triangle Tourism Zone in eastern Sichuan, and
- A miniature Silk Road park in Xian, Shaanxi Province.

New and existing cultural, historical, and religious attractions are also being developed or refurbished. Some of these projects include:

- The Three Kingdoms Shu Han City in Chengdu, Sichuan Province
- The Guan Du Ancient Battlefield Tourist Zone in Zhangmu, Henan Province
- Kai Feng's North Song Cultural Tourism City, Henan Province
- Hunan Zhonghua Homeland Park in Changsha Mawangdui, Hunan Province
- Confucius' home town in Shandong Province
- The Xuan Zang Home Town Tourism Region in Henan Province, and
- China Great Buddha City in Xincang, Zhejiang Province.

Conclusion

The spatial organization of tourism has been an important subject of study for researchers. A scientific division of tourist regions can provide a useful reference for the government officials and tourism planners in making polices and allocating resources.

China has a variety of tourism resources because of its vast territory and its long-standing history. The general spatial configuration of China's tourism resources in relation to the levels of tourism development has demonstrated a strong regional disparity. The eastern part of the country has a highly developed tourist industry and is supported by a fast growing economy. The western part has an exceptional potential for future development because of its abundant resources. However, current development is hindered by western China's geographic remoteness and a shortage of development funds. One of the priorities for the eastern areas is to seek more foreign investment.

An enormous amount of construction on tourism projects is going on at the present time in many parts of China. Concerns have been raised regarding the economic feasibility and effectiveness of some projects. Blind construction, for example, has been a widespread problem in economic development in China, and tourism resource exploitation is no exception. More hotels than needed have been built in some places, causing substantial economic losses at both the local and national scale (Wei and Feng 1993:

52). Among the numerous problems that China has experienced in the area of tourism resource development are:

1. A lack of scientific studies on the locational advantages of resources, particularly in relation to the benefits and costs of different sites, and their short and long term planning goals.
2. A shortage of personnel with adequate understandings of tourist markets.
3. The poor and chaotic management of funds and resources associated with the transitional nature of Chinese society, as it moves from a centralized socialist economy to a socialist market economy.

Administrators and tourism planners will have to place these important tourism resource issues on their agendas, before the negative environmental, cultural, and social impacts of tourism are beyond their control.

References

Beijing Review. 1991. Vol.34, no.3 (January 21-7). San Francisco: China Books and Periodicals.

Boniface, Brian G. and Christopher P. Cooper.1988. *The Geography of Travel and Tourism.* Oxford, U.K.: Heinemann Professional Publishing.

Chen, Chuankang. 1993. An Overview of China's Tourism Resources and Strategies for Development. (Unpublished paper, Beijing University.)

Getz, Donald. 1991. *Festivals, Special Events, and Tourism.* New York: Van Nostrand Reinhold.

Guo, Laixi. 1990. Zhongguo Luyou Ziyuan de Jiben Tezheng yu Luyou Quhua Yanjiu (Basic Characteristics of China's Tourism Resources and the Study of Tourism Regions). In Shun Z., Qian Z., and Ding Z., eds., *Luyou Kaifa Yanjiu Lunji* (Collection of Papers on Tourism Development), Beijing: Luyou Jiaoyu Chubanshe (Tourism Education Press), pp. 1-17.

Hussey, Antonia. 1992. The Landscape of Lhasa, Tibet. *Focus* 42(1)(Spring): 8-12.

Kou, Zhengling. 1992. *Beijing Review.* Vol.35, no.38 (September 21-7). San Francisco: China Books and Periodicals.

Liu, Weiqiang. 1993. Huan Bohai Diqu Luyouye Chixu Fazhan de Sikuao (Considerations of the Continuing Development of International Tourism in the "Surrounding Bohai Rim Region"). *People's Daily,* Overseas Edition, November 23.

McColl, R.W. 1991. China's Silk Road: A Modern Journey to China's Western Regions. *Focus* 41(2)(Summer): 1-6.

McIntosh, Robert W., and Charles R. Goeldner. 1986. *Tourism: Principles, Practices, Philosophies,* fifth edition. New York: John Wiley and Sons, Inc.

Rafferty, Milton. 1993. *A Geography of World Tourism.* New Jersey: Prentice Hall.

Shen, Yanrong. 1993. Luyouye de Diqu Chanye Zhengce (Regional Policies of Tourist Industry). In Wei Xiaojing and Feng Zongsu, eds., *Zhongguo Luyouye: Chanye Zhengce ji Xiezuo Fazhan* (China's Tourism: Industry Policies and Coordinate Development), Beijing: Luyou Jiaoyu Chubanshe (Tourism Education Press), pp. 74-104.

Wei, Xiaoan and Feng Zongsu, eds. 1992. *Zhongguo Luyouye: Chanye Zhengce ji Xiezuo Fazhan* (China's Tourism: Industry Policies and Coordinate Development). Beijing: Luyou Jiaoyu Chubanshe (Tourism Education Press).

Zhang Baogao, ed. 1992. *Zhongguo Daoyou Zhishi Dachuan* (China's Tour Guide Almanac). Shanghai: Shanghai Wenhua Chubanshe (Shanghai Culture Press).

Zhang Wenkui. 1991. *Zhengzhi Dilixue* (Political Geography). Xuzhou, China: Jiangsu Jiaoyu Chubanshe (Jiangsu Education Press).

Zhang, Yongwei. 1993. Economic and Technological Development Zones in China. Paper presented at the Association of American Geographers, Southwest Division Annual Meeting, October 20-3, Fayetteville, Arkansas.

Organization

Tourism does not follow a single model for development. Its organization and administration depend on particular national and local needs and circumstances. China has developed its own special tourism organizations and is constantly modifying its organizational structures in order to meet the demands of both domestic and international travelers. The essays in Part Two describe how tourism is structured in China.

In the first essay, Erdmann Gormsen discusses the organization of international tourism to China. He identifies China's major international tourist markets, the patterns of international tourist flows to Chinese destinations, and the economic impact of international tourism on China's society. He substantiates his discussion and arguments with the most up-to-date statistical data available from the Chinese tourism authorities.

The second essay in Part Two examines the organization and operations of a major component of China's tourism industry: tourist hotels. Lawrence Yu outlines the organizational and functional aspects of tourists hotels, and analyzes their management effectiveness. He also discusses the impact of the introduction of western-style hotels on Chinese society and culture and their role in the transformation of China's cultural landscape. Recommendations for improving the management of tourist hotels are suggested, as well.

The availability of adequately trained workers in an area can have considerable influence on tourism development. Since 1979, China's tourism authorities have made great efforts to establish tourism and hospitality educational institutes to train competent people for work in the tourism industry. Xiao Qianhui and Liu Zhijiang's essay on China's tourism education explores the development of tourism and hospitality education programs and curricula at various levels of education in China. They also point out ways to improve China's tourism education, particularly in training competent managers who are able to provide services that meet high international standards.

4

International Tourism in China:
Its Organization and
Socio-economic Impact

Erdmann Gormsen

The People's Republic of China (PRC) owes much of its status as an major international tourist destination to its historical importance and a diversity of natural resources extending over its vast territory.[1] It stretches from tropical southern coastlines to inner-Asian deserts and the summits of the Himalayas. It encompasses superb landscapes, such as the Changjiang (Yangtze River) gorges, the Li River karst mountains in Guilin, the Stone Forest near Kunming, and the granite mountains of Emei Shan, Huang Shan, and Tai Shan.

Especially attractive for tourists are the cultural sights, which can be divided into two main areas: the Eastern heartland and the ethnic minority peripheral regions. The Eastern heartland is the "Land of the Middle Kingdom." Here, singular sights of Chinese history and art are to be found, including Beijing, the Ming Emperors' Tombs, the Great Wall, the ceramic army near Xian, Chinese gardens in Suzhou, as well as the impressive remnants of Chinese religious temples and pagodas. The peripheral regions, on the other hand, have been molded by the independent cultures of fifty-five ethnic minorities, including the Mongolians in the north, the Inner-Asian peoples scattered along the old silk road, the Tibetans, and the many groups in the southwest, of which 24 can be found in the Yunnan province alone.

Yet China's natural landscapes and cultural wealth became valuable for tourism development only after its economic opening began in earnest in

1979 (Kou 1992). In 1984, earnings from international holiday traffic had already surpassed one billion U.S. dollars and more than one million foreigners visited the country (Table 4.1). By 1991 this figure had increased to 2.7 million visitors, which was approximately twelve times as many foreigners as had visited China annually before the economic policy changes introduced by Deng Xiaoping in 1978. It should be kept in mind, however, that 2.7 million visitors comprise only about 8 percent of the 33.3 million travelers crossing China's borders in 1991. Besides foreigners, official PRC statistics contain two groups of Chinese visitors living outside the People's Republic:

- *Compatriots* - Chinese from Hong Kong, Macao, and Taiwan, which are considered to be separate provinces of the PRC (30.5 million visitors to China in 1991), and
- *Overseas Chinese* - PRC passport holders who are residing outside China (133,427 visitors to China in 1991).

Statistics concerning international tourism in China are published in *The Yearbook of China Tourism Statistics*, which is issued annually by the National Tourism Administration (NTA) of the PRC. In this chapter, it is cited as YEARBOOK and serves, unless otherwise stated, as the source for all data on visitors entering the country, including selected nationalities and social indicators, as well as data on international hotels, travel agencies, tourism employment, and foreign-exchange earnings. These statistics have some problems. For one, many researchers consider them inflated. Another problem is that the visitation numbers include both overnight and day visitors. The World Tourism Organization (WTO) defines international tourists as those who stay in a foreign country for at least twenty-four hours, and this definition is used by most of the world's countries. A third problem is the increasing decentralization of China's tourism industry, making data collection more difficult and estimations more the norm.

With regard to foreign-exchange earnings, it should be noted that until 1994 international travelers in China could legally make purchases only with a special currency, the Foreign Exchange Certificate (FEC¥), the value of which is set by the state bank. In recent years, the FEC¥ has been repeatedly adjusted for inflation as China has moved toward a more free market economy. (For example, in 1985 the official exchange rate was US$1 to FEC¥3.20; by 1993 the rate was FEC¥5.70). While exchanging foreign currency for China's regular Renminbi (RMB¥) currency is not officially permitted for tourists, a thriving black market has developed. Many Chinese themselves, however, strive for the possession of the FEC¥ because certain goods and services, and foreign travel could be financed only with this currency. (In the Special Economic Zones, discussed in the Geographic

TABLE 4.1 International Tourist Arrivals in China, 1978-1991

Year	Total (1,000)	Iª	Foreigners (1,000)	I	%	Overseas Chinese (1,000)	I	Compatriots (1,000)	I	Taiwan (1,000)	%	Foreign Revenue (mnᵇ)US$	I
1978	1,809	23	230	34	12.7	18	47	1,562	22	-	-	263	33
1979	4,204	54	362	54	8.6	21	54	3,821	54	-	-	449	57
1980	5,703	73	529	78	9.3	34	89	5,139	73	-	-	617	79
1981	7,767	100	675	100	8.7	39	100	7,053	100	-	-	785	100
1982	7,924	102	764	113	9.6	43	110	7,117	101	-	-	843	107
1983	9,477	122	873	129	9.2	40	104	8,564	121	-	-	941	120
1984	12,852	165	1,134	168	8.8	47	122	11,670	165	-	-	1,137	145
1985	17,833	230	1,370	203	7.7	85	218	16,378	232	-	-	1,250	159
1986	22,819	294	1,482	220	6.5	68	175	21,269	302	-	-	1,531	195
1987	26,902	346	1,728	256	6.4	87	224	25,087	356	-	-	1,862	237
1988	31,695	408	1,842	273	5.8	79	204	29,773	422	438	1.4	2,247	286
1989	24,501	315	1,461	216	6.0	69	176	22,972	326	541	2.2	1,860	237
1990	27,462	354	1,747	259	6.4	91	234	25,623	363	948	3.5	2,218	283
1991	33,350	429	2,710	401	8.1	133	343	30,506	433	947	2.8	2,845	362

ªI = Index (1981 = 100)
ᵇmn = million (1,000,000)
Source: The Yearbook of China Tourism Statistics, various years.

Distribution section below, the FEC¥ is practically unknown. Instead, railway tickets and other official prices are usually quoted in Hong Kong Dollars.)

Travel Motivations and the Organization
of International Tourists

While actual travel motivations are not included in the statistics provided by the NTA, it is possible to estimate motivations based on the type of travel agency that handles the travel arrangements of visitors. This information has been provided since 1985 (Table 4.2).

1. *Package tours* are those that cater to holiday and culture tourists whose round-trips must be carried out under the responsibility of the large state tourist bureaus. Most foreign tourists come under this category as this is practically the only way for them to receive a visa. Many compatriots also fall under this category. (This is the "Travel Agencies" category in Table 4.2.)

2. *Official trips* are those that fall under the auspices of government authorities and institutions, scientific and other organizations, or economic enterprises. Most of the foreign visitors to the PRC in recent years actually fall under this category. However, they are primarily business travelers instead of vacationing tourists. (This is the "Other Organizations" category in Table 4.2.) (Diplomats, students, foreign experts, and others who spend at least a year in the PRC are not included in any of the numbers shown in Table 4.2.)

TABLE 4.2 Tourists Received by Major Travel Agencies and Other Organizations, 1985-1991 (thousands)

	Total	Foreigners	Overseas Chinese	Compatriots	Foreigners % of Total
1985 Total of which:	17,833	1,370	85	16,378	7.7
Travel Agencies	2,360	933	25	1,403	39.5
Other Organizations	301	243	60	-	80.9
Crews	348	194	-	154	55.8
Private Visits	14,824	-	-	14,824	-

67

TABLE 4.2 *(continued)*

	Total	Foreigners	Overseas Chinese	Compatriots	Foreigners % of Total
1986 Total	22,819	1,482	68	21,269	6.5
of which:					
Travel Agencies	2,571	965	29	1,578	37.5
Other Organizations	385	345	40	-	89.7
Crews	312	173	-	140	55.3
Private Visits	19,551	-	-	19,551	-
1987 Total	26,902	1,728	87	25,087	6.4
of which:					
Travel Agencies	3,002	1,169	35	1,799	38.9
Other Organizations	441	388	52	-	88.1
Crews	341	171	-	171	50.0
Private Visits	23,118	-	-	23,118	-
1988 Total	31,695	1,842	79	29,773	5.8
of which:					
Travel Agencies	3,083	871	41	2,171	28.3
Other Organizations	816	777	38	-	95.3
Crews	451	194	>1	257	43.0
Private Visits	27,346	-	-	27,346	-
1989 Total	24,501	1,461	69	22,972	6.0
of which:					
Travel Agencies	1,905	499	26	1,381	26.2
Other Organizations	815	773	43	-	94.8
Crews	508	190	-	318	37.4
Private Visits	21,273	-	-	21,273	-
1990 Total	27,462	1,747	91	25,623	6.4
of which:					
Travel Agencies	2,792	667	48	2,077	23.9
Other Organizations	916	873	43	-	95.3
Crews	545	207	>1	337	38.1
Private Visits	23,210	-	-	23,210	-
1991 Total	33,350	2,710	133	30,506	8.1
of which:					
Travel Agencies	2,789	1,029	58	1,702	36.9
Other Organizations	1,392	1,317	75	-	94.6
Crews	782	364	-	418	46.5
Private Visits	28,387	-	-	28,387	-

Source: The Yearbook of China Tourism Statistics, various years.

3. *Airline and shipping crews* who visit the PRC are recorded under "Crews" category in Table 4.2.
4. *Private visits* to families or friends are typically conducted without the involvement of any of the forenamed offices. This category applies to compatriots only. Compatriots comprise by far the largest part of all travelers to China. Many compatriot business trips are also part of this number, especially to individual companies, as well as day visits without an overnight stay.

This typology, as seen in Table 4.2, provides a subdivision of travel motivations. It shows that the relative significance of holiday vacation trips by foreigners (category 1) has decreased steadily from 1985 to 1991. Between 1985 and 1987, two-thirds of the foreign visits to China took place in the form of package tours. However, these numbers decreased to only one-third in 1989 and have not significantly increased since then. In absolute figures, a peak of 1,168,705 vacationing foreign tourists was reached in 1987. Although the total number of foreign visitors has increased beyond that in recent years, the number of vacationing tourists to China was only about one million in 1991. The strong sensitivity of vacationing foreign tourists to political and other tribulations in a destination area can be readily seen in their 1989 drop to 499,000 following the Tiananmen Incident. The recent increase in foreign visitation to China can, therefore, be attributed mainly to business travelers, who comprise approximately 50 percent of foreign trips to the PRC. Unexpectedly high rates of visitation are seen for the airline and shipping crews, who comprise 10 percent to 14 percent of all foreign visitors in different years.

For 1986 the YEARBOOK provided data on travel agency use by the three main groups of international tourists to selected cities. For the well-known travel destinations of Guilin and Xian, the majority of all trips were booked through travel agencies, which points to the fact that even the compatriots went there first for sightseeing. In Beijing and Shanghai (and a few other cities) only among foreign visitors did a large percentage (80 percent for both cities) use travel agencies. The number of compatriots who organized their trips to these cities with the help of a travel agency was much more modest. The most popular travel destination for compatriots was the old southern trading city of Guangzhou (Canton). Here only 14 percent of the two million compatriot visitors in 1986 used travel agency services to plan their trip.

Since 1986, data on the hotel arrivals of foreigners, compatriots, and overseas Chinese in some fifty selected traffic areas, has been published in the YEARBOOK (Table 4.3). Over the following years, a few places have been added, while others were struck from the list. (The reasons for some of these additions or omissions were often not clear.) Therefore, while a

TABLE 4.3   Number of Visitors Received by Hotels in Selected Cities and Areas

		1986	1988	I	1989	I	1991	I	% share 1991 Foreign	Com- patriot
	I=Index (1986=100)									
1	Beijing	990,377	1,203,945	122	645,160	65	1,321,464	133	69.2	30.8
2	Tianjin	55,193	125,115	227	43,133	78	62,715	113	61.2	38.8
3	Shijiazhuang	7,690	8,435	110	6,312	82	8,828	114	53.5	46.5
4	Chengde	14,292	15,729	110	8,454	59	22,508	157	64.6	35.4
5	Qinhuangdao	15,920	16,372	103	5,987	38	13,282	83	64.2	35.8
6	Taiyuan	10,047	13,666	136	8,007	80	16,063	160	62.4	37.6
7	Datong	14,355	14,607	102	7,149	50	15,191	105	70.9	29.1
8	Hohhot	7,582	12,263	162	3,294	43	16,158	213	51.6	48.4
9	Shenyang	31,591	33,301	105	25,947	82	50,080	158	59.2	40.8
10	Dalian	43,085	53,696	125	38,780	90	72,967	169	71.4	28.6
11	Changchun	18,297	20,086	110	12,284	67	30,031	164	58.8	41.2
12	Jilin	13,073	19,512	149	10,837	83	16,113	123	21.1	78.9
13	Yanji	-	-	-	-	-	11,596	-	97.3	2.7
14	Harbin	43,554	43,102	99	25,814	59	67,891	156	57.4	42.6
15	Shanghai	659,340	916,392	139	655,779	99	981,804	149	62.4	37.6
16	Nanjing	153,532	269,045	175	172,378	112	221,300	144	43.7	56.3
17	Suzhou	160,997	254,783	158	159,546	99	227,677	141	51.1	48.9
18	Wuxi	101,133	164,591	163	99,748	99	116,380	115	49.0	51.0
19	Lianyungang	1,606	2,306	144	2,160	134	2,593	161	58.9	41.1
20	Nantong	4,330	8,732	202	9,412	217	11,035	255	56.2	43.8
21	Hangzhou	266,394	349,246	131	248,502	93	390,197	146	35.1	64.9
22	Ningbo	12,768	16,519	129	16,136	126	31,151	244	41.2	58.8
23	Wenzhou	3,365	4,716	140	2,622	78	11,125	331	20.8	79.2
24	Huangshan	15,144	-	-	-	-	121,364	801	21.5	78.5

(continues)

TABLE 4.3 *(continued)*

	1986	1988	I	1989	I	1991	I	% share 1991 Foreign	Com-patriot
	I=Index (1986=100)								
25	*Fuzhou* 69,111	105,195	152	96,027	139	148,135	214	23.4	76.6
26	*Xiamen* 90,035	152,169	169	138,508	154	205,102	228	32.6	67.4
27	*Quanzhou* 116,678	201,356	173	203,370	174	236,610	203	3.1	96.9
28	*Zhangzhou* 6,177	7,976	129	8,134	132	10,338	167	15.6	84.4
29	*Jiujiang* 13,132	8,468	64	5,695	43	8,481	65	23.4	76.6
30	*Jinan* 14,413	24,151	168	13,894	96	25,629	178	57.5	42.5
31	*Qingdao* 24,851	42,700	172	39,130	157	60,876	245	43.7	56.3
32	*Yantai* 4,829	11,950	247	8,192	170	19,958	413	54.4	45.6
33	*Zhengzhou* 28,476	24,443	86	21,913	77	44,461	156	24.2	75.8
34	*Luoyang* 35,792	55,169	154	21,180	59	33,725	94	73.5	27.9
35	*Wuhan* 66,531	72,827	109	49,138	74	89,598	135	31.5	68.5
36	*Changsha* 20,102	26,010	129	19,207	96	32,972	164	25.9	74.1
37	*Guangzhou* 2,512,385	2,044,368	81	1,229,777	49	2,034,369	81	21.9	78.1
38	*Shenzhen* 735,344	1,039,365	141	854,475	116	1,829,750	249	5.9	94.1
39	*Zhuhai* 766,363	345,381	45	244,579	32	460,251	60	5.2	94.8
40	*Shantou* 102,272	173,922	170	140,051	137	198,321	194	38.7	61.3
41	*Zhanjiang* 14,177	17,148	121	13,556	96	26,793	189	12.0	88.0
42	*Nanning* 17,070	11,899	70	5,639	33	17,521	103	32.8	67.2
43	*Guilin* 356,853	459,431	129	282,127	79	429,113	120	46.4	53.6
44	*Beihai* 2,274	2,589	114	2,539	112	2,614	115	21.6	78.4
45	*Haikou* -	90,436	-	51,349	-	118,107	-	16.1	83.9
46	*Sanya* -	38,359	-	21,632	-	56,436	-	13.3	86.7
47	*Chengdu* 101,372	111,000	109	62,763	62	139,502	138	38.2	61.8
48	*Chongqing* 52,092	59,753	115	38,487	74	73,108	140	36.7	63.3
49	*Guiyang* 7,540	17,943	238	10,002	133	26,820	356	26.0	74.0

TABLE 4.3 *(continued)*

	1986	1988	I	1989	I	1991	I	% share 1991 Foreign	Compatriot
	I=Index (1986=100)								
50	*Kunming* 95,327	121,312	127	74,431	78	160,165	168	35.9	64.1
51	*Xian* 257,832	365,785	142	212,036	82	310,073	120	76.7	23.3
52	*Lanzhou* 29,297	36,609	125	16,553	57	40,657	139	74.1	25.9
53	*Urumqi* 25,805	40,081	155	25,697	100	54,380	211	78.7	21.3
54	*Lhasa* 7,791	-	-	-	-	15,200	195	93.0	7.0

Source: The Yearbook of China Tourism Statistics, various years.

Additional Place Names in Figures 4.1 and 4.2:

55 Wutaishan	63 Emeishan	71 Dunhuang	79 Sakya
56 Baotan	64 Dazu	72 Turfan	80 Tsedang
57 Taishan	65 Yangtze	73 Kuqa	81 Hefei
58 Qufu	66 Jinghong	74 Aksu	82 Nanchang
59 Kaifeng	67 Dali	75 Kashgar	83 Yinchuan
60 Xinglong	68 Lijiang	76 Hotan	84 Zhongshan
61 Tongzha	69 Xining	77 Gyantze	
62 Leshan	70 Jiayuguan	78 Shigatze	

total of 54 places have been included in Table 4.3, only 43 are comparable from 1986 to 1991. The total number of the tourist destinations is, of course, much larger. In 1991 there were 733 places or areas officially authorized for foreigners to visit, in contrast to only 122 in 1979.

International tourist arrivals at all hotels in each of China's provinces were published for the first time in the YEARBOOK for 1991 (Table 4.4). This number totaled 13.4 million for the entire country. Since 10.7 million were reported in the selected major cities, the share of these cities in international tourism is amounting to 80 percent of all hotel arrivals, while among foreign arrivals alone it is 90 percent (3.8 million of 4.3 million total arrivals). An apparent discrepancy exists in that 33.3 million visitors entered the country is 1991, yet only 13.4 million hotel arrivals were recorded (with many visitors recording multiple arrivals for multiple cities.) This discrepancy is apparently due to the 30.6 million compatriot Chinese coming across the border, for whom only 9.2 million hotel arrivals were recorded for the entire country. This figure includes business travelers, especially in the southern provinces, who may visit China without staying overnight. It is unclear, however, how many of the remaining 28.4 million

TABLE 4.4 International Visitor Arrivals at Hotels, 1991

	Total	Foreigners	%	Compatriots & Overseas Chin.	%
Total Frontier Arrivals	33,349,761	2,710,103	8.1	30,639,658	91.9
Hotel Arrivals in					
Selected Major Cities	10,733,378	3,811,776	35.5	6,921,602	64.5
Total Hotel Arrivals	13,439,800	4,258,100	31.7	9,181,700	68.3
Total Tourist Nights	28,299,600	11,245,400	39.7	17,054,200	60.3

Source: The Yearbook of China Tourism Statistics 1991.

(85 percent of all visitors) enter the country on one-day trips or how many stay with relatives during their visits. The latter have gained in importance, especially among citizens of Taiwan, who, after decades of separation, were only allowed to enter mainland China after a bilateral accord became effective in November 1987.

For foreign visitors who do not live in Hong Kong or in the neighboring border areas, day trips to China are much less common. Therefore, the situation is very different from that of compatriots. In 1991 there were 2.7 million border crossings by foreigners, which resulted in 4.3 million hotel arrivals (of which 3.8 million were in the major selected cities.) An unknown number of foreign visitors take one-day trips into China (without staying the night) from Hong Kong, Macao, and other border areas.

A new source of visitors to China is the citizens of the former USSR. In 1991, eight times as many visited China as in 1988 (Table 4.5). After the abolition of visa requirement and the opening of more border stations, they reached a share of more than 10.5 percent of all foreigners, and as a group were surpassed in numbers only by Japanese and Americans. Further growth has occurred with the completion of the railway line from Urumqi over the Alataw Pass to Alma Ata in 1992 (the building of which was interrupted in 1962 for political reasons and only resumed in 1985) (Kampen 1993; *China aktuell* 1991, October: 626).

This is an interesting example of a form of border tourism that has becoming increasingly important between neighboring countries of the developing world, serving trade objectives in addition to sightseeing purposes (Yu 1992; Gormsen 1988: 72). Apparently considerable quantities of Chinese consumer goods are exported by travelers directly into the CIS countries, whereby the local border traffic, without overnight stays, plays an important role (Kremb 1993; *Beijing Rundschau* 1992, 24: 33). This is confirmed by the fact that 284,885 CIS citizens entered the PRC in 1991, whereas only 86,297 arrived in hotels in the major selected cities. Harbin, with 22 percent of CIS arrivals, takes second place,

TABLE 4.5 Foreign Visitor Arrivals by Nationality and Region, 1981-1991

Nationality	1981	1985	1988	I	1989	I	1991	I	1991%
I = Index (1981° = 100)									
Japan	223.5	470.5	591.9	265	358.8	161	640.9	287	23.6
Philippines	27.7	57.9	71.4	258	73.4	265	104.8	378	3.9
Thailand	14.4	24.6	65.8	459	54.9	382	88.6	617	3.3
Singapore	16.2	46.5	65.4	403	57.9	357	98.1	605	3.6
India	4.6	7.0	10.8	235	10.8	236	22.2	484	0.8
other	49.9	109.6	140.0	281	137.5	276	433.2	869	16.0
Total Asia									
	336.2	716.0	945.3	281	693.3	206	1,387.8	413	51.2
U.K.	41.8	71.4	96.6	231	72.2	173	114.6	274	4.2
France	21.4	39.0	63.2	296	51.9	243	86.0	402	3.2
Germany	18.4	44.8	72.8	395	52.8	286	92.4	501	3.4
Italy	9.4	18.8	30.7	328	17.8	191	45.4	485	1.7
Switzerland	5.8	12.4	16.4	283	13.6	234	18.7	323	0.7
Sweden	3.8	8.3	13.2	347	9.8	258	16.2	426	0.6
Netherlands	4.3	9.5	16.5	388	13.8	325	20.5	481	0.8
USSR/CIS	3.7	17.7	34.8	934	81.3	2,181	284.9	7,640	10.5
other	24.6	52.5	77.7	316	81.2	330	110.9	451	4.1
Total Europe									
	133.1	272.5	421.9	317	394.5	296	789.5	593	29.1
U.S.	130.4	239.6	300.9	231	215.0	165	314.1	241	11.6
Canada	14.2	35.2	63.3	445	46.0	323	69.2	487	2.6
Latin Am.	12.0	14.1	21.3	178	28.0	233	35.1	292	1.3
Total Americas									
	156.6	288.9	385.6	246	289.0	184	418.5	267	15.4
Australia	40.3	78.1	61.0	152	48.7	121	65.1	162	2.4
N.Z.	4.9	7.5	12.4	256	11.6	239	12.1	248	0.4
Africa and other	4.0	7.4	16.0	395	23.9	593	37.2	921	1.4
TOTAL	**675.2**	**1,370.5**	**1,842.2**	**273**	**1,461.0**	**216**	**2,710.1**	**401**	**100.0**

Source: The Yearbook of China Tourism Statistics, various years.

behind Beijing, which received 41 percent. Shanghai, at 11 percent, is the third most popular CIS overnight visitor destination, followed by Urumqi at 9 percent. Famous tourist centers, such as Xian and Guilin, are insignificant. Even the southern metropolis of Guangzhou received a mere 1.6 percent of CIS hotel arrivals (YEARBOOK 1991: 64-7). Similar cross border visitation patterns for other nationals are also seen elsewhere in China, as well (Yu 1992).

The Geographic Distribution of Tourism
Supply and Demand

It has already been mentioned that China possesses a wealth of tourism resources. An overview of the provinces, however, reveals a considerable decline in visitation from the coastal areas toward the interior. This is not only due to the larger interest in traditional Han Chinese culture, but also to the economic importance that is concentrated in industrial and commercial centers of eastern China.

Shenzhen is one of the newer commercial centers of eastern China. It lies across from Hong Kong and, with 1.8 million hotel arrivals (1991), takes second place among all international travel destinations behind Guangzhou's 2.0 million hotel arrivals (Figure 4.1). Beijing, with 1.3 million hotel arrivals, and Shanghai with almost one million are significantly behind. Shenzhen is one of several Special Economic Zones (SEZs) in China. Similar to the Zhuhai SEZ (adjacent to Macao) and others in coastal cities of the southeast, the Shenzhen SEZ was set up by the PRC government in the early 1980s with special laws and investment incentives. It serves as a kind of "experiment in capitalism." Many SEZs have grown into booming big cities and have also developed a high volume of foreign travel. Table 4.6 shows the enormous rise in hotel arrivals in Shenzhen in the early 1980s. By 1985, overnight hotel visitors were nearly double the number of day visitors to Shenzhen. This increase is comprised almost entirely of compatriots on business trips (Gormsen 1990a: 146; 1990b: 128). This is also true for most of the other SEZs, which are known more for economic activities than sightseeing opportunities.

In order to encourage Chinese workers to migrate to Shenzhen for employment, the SEZ government has built numerous Chinese gardens, all of which closely follow traditional models. They are, especially on weekends, the preferred destination for urban dwellers and their children, who have few opportunities to recreate outside during the week. Shenzhen

TABLE 4.6 Tourism in Shenzhen SEZ, 1979-1985

	1979	1981	%	1983	%	1985	%
Total Arrivals	522,156	651,323	100	1,251,309	100	1,259,375	100
Day Visitors	522,003	646,489	99.3	824,612	65.9	480,839	38.2
Hotel Arrivals:							
Total	153	4,834	0.7	426,697	34.1	778,536	61.8
Compatriots	35	3,828	0.6	420,541	33.6	742,077	58.9
Foreigners	118	971	0.1	3,831	0.3	34,930	2.8

Source: Shenzhen Statistical Office.

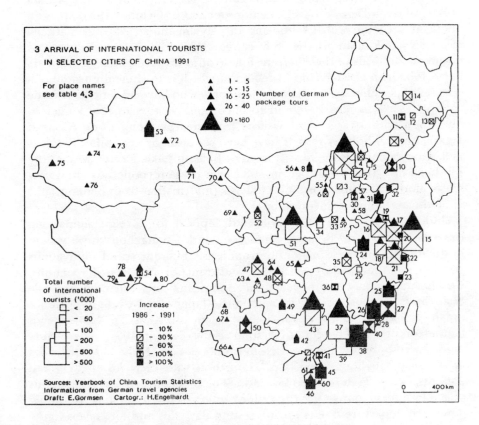

FIGURE 4.1 Arrival of International Tourists in Selected Cities
of China, 1991

offers two special attractions. The first is "Splendid China," which claims which claims to be the world's largest miniature scenic spot, and contains an impressive miniaturized display of almost 100 of the best known Chinese buildings and landscapes over a 30-hectare area. The second is the "China Folk Culture Village." This attraction opened in October 1991. It is an open air museum with 24 housing displays in the styles of 21 national minorities built in an area of 18 hectares. Here folk dances, theater, and traditional festivals of the different folk groups are presented. It appears like a folklorish "Disneyland," the aim of which is to show the traditional customs of peripheral regions to local people who have no time to visit the real places. It is also designed to encourage visitors to stay longer in Shenzhen and attracts many visitors from nearby Hong Kong (Conrad 1993). Several holiday resorts have been set up in or near other SEZs, as well. One example is the tourist town of Baiteng Lake, located west of the Zhuhai SEZ. It was founded in 1984 by a peasant cooperative and now offers modern facilities for 3,600 tourists (information from Baiteng Lake United Development Corporation).

Understandably, the SEZs hold little appeal for foreign sightseeing tourists, for whom Beijing, Shanghai, and Guangzhou are the top destinations. In these major metropolises, different travel motivations overlap, including culture, business, and transportation transfer stations. Guangzhou is more important for Americans and Australians, while Shanghai is the most visited city among the Japanese. Next in importance are the well-known tourist destinations of Guilin and Xian. In Xian, foreign visitors comprised 75 percent of its total visitor count in 1991. These cities are followed by others that are rich in tradition, namely the old canal cities of Nanjing, Suzhou, Wuxi, and Hangzhou with their historical urban patterns, located in the eastern lowlands. The remaining major destinations visited by foreign tourists are the traffic centers of Chengdu and Kunming. They are departure points for interesting day trips and for travels to the peripheral minority areas, which are especially attractive to westerners.

At this point, a comparison of the regional distribution of supply and demand in Chinese tourism proves very informative. An analysis of travel programs from thirteen German tour operators revealed a total of 58 places where their China tour groups stayed overnight (Figure 4.2). Of these, 34 are located in the eastern and southern core areas of the country, including the Red Basin of Sichuan. The rest were in the periphery. The three municipalities, plus Xian and Guilin, were visited over 80 times, whereas 21 places appear only in one to five of the trips. Although this survey only dealt with travel from one country, it can be assumed from observations and investigations that package tours from other countries are very similar.

The coincidence between the places most visited by German tourists and those most visited overall in China is low (Table 4.3). Only 33 places appear

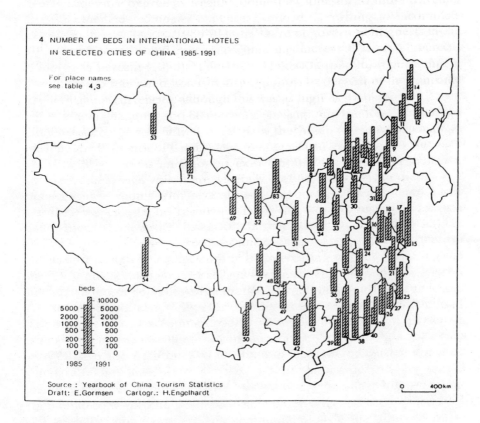

FIGURE 4.2 Number of Beds in International Hotels in Selected Cities of China, 1985 and 1991

on both lists (indicated by a combined square with a triangle in Figure 4.1). Of the 25 places that can be found in German holiday programs, and also rate high in Table 4.3, the majority lie in the periphery.

Tibet is an example of how the official selection of places to list in the YEARBOOK does not depend entirely on the number of foreign visitor arrivals. In 1986, there were 7,791 tourists counted in Lhasa (of which 7,633 were foreigners). Lhasa, however, has not been listed in the YEARBOOK since 1986. Both the low number of arrivals in Lhasa and its subsequently being dropped from the YEARBOOK lists relates to the political turmoil in Tibet. In addition, travel to Tibet is limited to those on package tours organized by one of the major state travel agencies. This regulation, which includes the flight and at least three nights in a contract hotel, is frequently circumvented by individual travelers, who upon arrival switch to more inexpensive hotels and move around freely in the autonomous region.

In 1991, there were 15,200 hotel arrivals (14,200 foreigners) reported for all of Tibet. Since almost all arrivals in Tibet pass through Lhasa, this is an accurate estimate of the number of international hotel arrivals for the capital city, as well (and has, therefore, been added to Tables 4.3 and 4.7). Furthermore, Lhasa is where most of the major contract hotels are located. Tibet receives a higher percentage (93 percent) of foreign visitors at its hotels than any other place in China (Table 4.3). At 7.8 days, the average stay there is also the longest of any destination in China. Lhasa has, therefore, a more important position than many of the other places listed in the YEARBOOK, some of which receive fewer than 3,000 total hotel arrivals. The city's importance becomes obvious when one notes the increase in accommodations, growing from three hotels with 1,271 beds in 1985 to 10 hotels with 2,234 beds in 1990 (Table 4.7, Fig. 4.2).

The large percentage of foreigners among visitors to Inner Mongolia, Ningxia, Gansu, and Qinghai also corresponds to greater foreign interest in seeing more *exotic* cultures and landscapes. This is also true for Xishuangbanna in the southwest of Yunnan Province, a tropical mountain land whose original tribes are related to ethnic groups in Burma and northern Thailand. Apart from these minority areas, many Europeans feel it is exotic, if not adventurous, to ride a common Chinese train with a steam engine. A few tour operators even offered a tour of the last factory for such engines in Datong, until it was closed in 1988.

Very different travel motivations exist for citizens of the former Soviet Union, Pakistan (who frequently visit Xinjiang), and travelers from Southeast Asia. For example, 48 percent of all the foreigners registered in 1991 in Shantou came from Thailand, which means that 30 percent of all tourists from Thailand were received in this relatively small harbor town in Guangdong Province. The reason for this is that a large part of the ethnic Chinese population of Thailand came from the Shantou area in the

TABLE 4.7 Hotels, Rooms, and Occupancy Rates in Selected Cities in China

City	Hotels 1985	Hotels 1991	Rooms 1985	Rooms 1991	Occupancy Rate (%) 1987	Occupancy Rate (%) 1991
1 Beijing	64	203	33,191	90,946	83	54
5 Qinhuangdao	3	33	704	12,017	55	52
14 Harbin	8	15	3,812	7,183	69	84
15 Shanghai	24	85	11,438	41,464	77	60
17 Suzhou	5	14	1,051	4,614	59	51
26 Xiamen	12	24	3,446	6,508	77	56
31 Qingdao	2	29	465	10,263	70	59
37 Guangzhou	53	112	28,433	56,118	76	72
38 Shenzhen	21	143	6,725	38,901	73	72
43 Guilin	6	29	3,151	12,122	53	38
47 Chengdu	1	16	1,1021	10,207	71	67
50 Kunming	3	18	1,294	5,688	75	74
51 Xian	6	22	3,458	11,753	65	42
53 Urumqi	3	9	1,196	3,635	71	72
54 Lhasa	3	10	569	2,234	41	27

[a] Numbers refer to locations in Figures 4.1 and 4.2.
Source: The Yearbook of China Tourism Statistics, various years.

previous century (Somers-Heidhues 1974). Approximately 13 percent of the population of Thailand is ethnic Chinese (Jones 1981: 254). Understandably, visitors from Thailand also comprise the largest share of foreign hotel arrivals in Kunming (Yunnan Province). This number may even increase with the extension of the Burma Road from Kunming to Southeast Asia. In a similar manner, Fujian Province with its old harbor of Xiamen, is the third most visited place among travelers from the Philippines (18 percent) and from Singapore (10 percent).

Forms of Tourist Accommodations

In the 1970s and early 1980s the first international tourists traveling through modern China saw themselves, in many ways, as adventurers because the infrastructure was so poor in almost every regard. Most major cities had only one or two hotels of an international standard, and these were built either before World War II or under the Soviet influence in the 1950s as "Friendship Hotels" for foreign experts and delegations from the socialist countries. The latter show several peculiar combinations of the monumental "Stalin style" and traditional Chinese architecture. Many, modern, international hotels have been built since 1978. Up to 1991, their number quintupled from 431 to 2,130. Among the latter, 421 (20 percent) were joint ventures or cooperatives with foreign participation

TABLE 4.8 Accommodation Types in China

	1987	1991
International Tourist Accommodations	1,283	2,130
- Foreign Joint Ventures &		
Cooperative Agreements	162	421
- Domestically Owned	1,121	1,709
Domestic Tourist Accommodations	62,282	95,556
Total Domestically Owned Accommodations	63,403	97,265
Total Accommodations	64,565	98,686

Source: The Yearbook of China Tourism Statistics, various years.

(Table 4.8). The number of beds quadrupled in the same period from 165,000 to 680,000. Apart from special events (for example, the Guangzhou Trade Fair) the capacity is more than adequate in most cities. The drop in the average occupancy from 66 percent (1987) to 61 percent (1991) shows that a serious surplus had developed. This is especially true in the cities that developed early, such as Xian (42 percent in 1991) and Guilin (38 percent), Beijing (54 percent), and Shanghai (60 percent) (Table 4.7).

Only half (339,386) of the hotel beds are in the 853 hotels that are star-rated by the NTA. These hotels average 400 beds each. Most packaged tours for foreign visitors and compatriots are limited to three, four, and five star hotels. Compatriots and domestic tourists use the one and two star hotels. In contrast, the other half (340,072 beds) are in the 1,277 non-star-rated hotels. Many of these are smaller, although there are also some large international hotels who choose to remain outside of the NTA's star-rating system. (The star-rating system requires maintaining certain standards. By not being star-rated the hotel has greater management flexibility.) The non-star-rated hotels average 266 beds per facility. These hotels are used almost exclusively by domestic tourists and have lower prices and more modest furnishings, as well as certain shortcomings of the personnel in the area of foreign language proficiency. In addition, they are not always listed in the local hotel registry and, because of this, are less accessible for foreign tourists traveling alone.

The differences between the various cities, for which statistical hotel data has been available since 1985 (Table 4.7), are considerable and do not agree with the corresponding hotel arrivals of foreign tourists (Figure 4.2). An especially glaring discrepancy appears, for example, in Qinhuangdao. Including Beidaihe, the number of hotels there increased between 1985 and 1991 from three to 33, and the number of beds rose from 704 to 12,107. However, the number of international visitors registered at these hotels peaked in 1988 with only 16,372 (Table 4.3). The 1991 occupancy rate in Qinhuangdao, while low, was still 52 percent. One apparent explanation is that even hotels of a higher star rating category were visited to a considerable degree by wealthy domestic Chinese and those traveling at government or company expense. Indeed, according to incomplete statistics in the YEARBOOK (1986-91), the share of government guests in the 102 largest state owned hotels in China has increased from 41 percent (1986) to 64 percent (1990). The 1992 YEARBOOK (p. 106) reports that in 1991, the 853 star-rated hotels registered only 40 percent of their income in international currencies, although this was as high as 87 percent in Tibet, 65 percent in Shanghai, and 60 percent in Beijing. On the low end, foreign currencies comprised only 6 percent of the hotel revenues in Guangxi (despite the presence of Guilin) and remote Gansu Provinces.

Inexpensive hotels and hostels exist throughout China for domestic travelers, and foreign visitors are generally not allowed to stay in them. The majority have rooms with several beds and modest furnishings. Their number, which can be calculated from the "total number of tourism enterprises" listing in the YEARBOOK, has increased from 62,282 (1987) to 95,556 (1991) (Table 4.8). However, the capacity of the state and collective hotels and hostels is insufficient for the increasing demand. During the busy summer months, local government and collective (e.g., a neighborhood or company organization) owned buildings, such as school classrooms, public bath houses, and underground shelters, are often used as domestic tourist accommodations. Hawkers at bus and train depots solicit travelers to use these accommodations. Recently, many private houses have also been opened in China to meet the increasing domestic demand. They have up to 30 beds in four to six rooms and very simple sanitary facilities. Some bed-and-breakfast/pensions have opened using traditional courtyard houses on which another story has been added.

A special example of these new accommodations is the "tourist village" south of the city of Xian. Here, 94 families, who have been resettled in an urban renewal program, received not only a new apartment but also a small, one-family house. This building can be set up as a privately owned guest house, using their own funds and state credit. In spite of the high building costs, the program has been very successful. One family reported that in 1986 their 20 beds were occupied every night for nine months and that, consequently, they vacationed in Southern China during the winter on their profits (Gormsen 1990a: 150). Aside from this, they could afford household appliances that were not yet generally available in China, including a color television, a telephone, and a motorcycle. The latter two are being used to buy tickets and to make other travel arrangements for their guests. As there are no official accommodation assistant services in Xian many "tourist village" owners offer their rooms to travelers directly at the railway station.

Transportation System Problems for Tourism

Contrary to the accommodations situation, considerable transportation problems exist in China. Serious capacity problems can be observed, not only for the airline companies, but also for railways, road traffic, and river navigation, despite the fact that since the establishment of the PRC all of these systems have been improved to a large extent (Table 4.9). From 1949 to 1987, the railway network, always the backbone of China's long-distance transportation network, has more than tripled from 30,000 to 99,000 km. Recently it was equipped with diesel engines and partly electrified (*China aktuell* 1991, February: 77; *Beijing Rundschau* 1991, 37: 4-5). However, asphalt roads, which predominantly serve the intermediate distances, expanded over the same period from 32,000 to 982,000 km. Road construction is still done, for the most part, by farmers who are only equipped with the ubiquitous two-wheel tractors. One-third of the road development has taken place since 1980, and further intensification can be observed throughout China today. Despite this, there are still extensive areas where secondary roads are without pavement.

In the same period, the number of transportation vehicles also increased substantially (Table 4.9). Between 1980 and 1987, passenger train carriages increased 44 percent and the number of passenger buses grew 218 percent. While the fleet of Chinese airlines only grew 2.3 percent in this period, there was a major shift whereby smaller aircraft were exchanged for larger planes. Actually, the growth rate for the number of passengers is highest for air traffic, a fact that every traveler who has ever been on one of China's frequently overbooked flights can confirm. Airlines have also experienced the greatest percentage increase in kilometers per person in China. By 1975, the number of bus passengers exceeded train passengers, and by 1987, buses transported approximately (80 percent) of a total 7.4 billion people recorded traveling by public transportation. However, because of its large average distance of 253 km/person, train travel still maintains the leading position in total passenger-kilometers in China. In addition, inland-navigation has always been important in China and, with 50 km/person, has doubled its transportation performance since 1978.

The total of 7.4 billion passenger trips in 1978 means that each Chinese citizens, on average, used public transportation seven times. Compared to those values, the 290 million holiday trips that were estimated by the NTA for 1987, comprise only a meager 4 percent of all public transportation trips. Instead, business trips, in the broadest sense of the word, make up the largest part. Apparently this includes many bus trips by farmers who sell their products at the open markets in the nearby cities and towns, and sojourners from rural areas who travel to larger cities seeking work. Depending upon the durability of the products, other methods of trans-

TABLE 4.9 China's Transportation System, 1949-1989

Year	1,000 km: Rail (#)	Road (#)	# of Public Conveyances: RailCars (1000)	Buses (1000)	Planes (#)	Number of Passengers: Total (mn³)	Rail (mn)	Road (mn)	Water (mn)	Air (mn)	Transport Turnover (Billion Persons x km): Rail	Road	Water	Air
1949	30	32	3	17	-	137	103	18	15	0.27	13.0	0.8	1.5	0.2
1952	35	55	5	19	45	245	163	45	36	0.02	20.1	2.2	2.4	0.1
1957	43	121	8	34	105	638	312	237	87	0.07	36.1	8.8	4.6	0.1
1962	55	263	10	47	245	1,221	741	307	163	0.17	85.9	14.1	8.3	0.1
1965	58	304	10	60	287	963	412	436	113	0.27	47.9	16.8	4.7	0.2
1970	70	411	11	75	293	1,300	524	618	157	0.22	71.8	24.0	7.1	0.1
1975	77	551	14	173	357	1,929	704	1,013	210	1.39	95.4	37.4	9.0	1.5
1978	83	651	15	259	382	2,539	815	1,492	230	2.31	109.3	52.1	10.0	2.7
1979	85	647	15	297	380	2,896	863	1,786	243	2.98	121.6	60.3	11.4	3.5
1980	86	662	16	351	393	3,417	921	2,227	264	3.43	138.3	72.9	12.9	3.9
1981	88	676	17	406	395	3,847	952	2,615	275	4.01	147.2	83.9	13.7	5.0
1982	89	692	18	442	380	4,289	999	3,006	279	4.45	157.4	96.3	14.4	5.9
1983	92	706	19	478	388	4,706	1,060	3,369	272	3.91	177.6	110.5	15.3	8.3
1984	94	725	20	563	391	5,302	1,133	3,903	259	5.54	204.6	133.6	15.3	8.4
1985	95	750	21	795	390	6,202	1,121	4,764	308	7.47	241.6	172.4	17.8	11.7
1986	97	780	22	966	414	6,882	1,085	5,442	343	9.96	258.6	198.1	18.2	14.6
1987	99	982	23	1,115	402	7,464	1,124	5,936	389	13.10	284.3	219.0	19.5	18.8
1988											326.0	252.8	20.3	21.4
1989											303.7	266.2	18.8	18.5
Index 1987 (1978 = 100):						294	138	398	169	570	261	421	196	674
Index 1989 (1978 = 100):											279	512	188	661
Average km per Person:											253	37	50	1,435

ᵃmn = million (1,000,000)

Sources: "The Development of Transportation and Communication in China," compiled by the National Statistics Bureau, China's Statistics Publishing House, 1989; "Historical Statistics by Provinces," China, 1949-1990, compiled by the National Statistics Bureau, China's Statistics Publishing House, 1990.

portation are also used over long stretches. In 1987, several egg traders in Nanjing reported to the author that every 10 days they would transport 1,000 eggs per person approximately 200 km by ship along the Changjiang (Yangtze River).

In the last few years, noticeable efforts to improve China's transportation situation have been undertaken, including the purchase and lease of larger airplanes (*China aktuell* 1991, August: 500-1) and new train coaches, as well as continuing construction and maintenance of roadways. In spite of these efforts, undercapacity at all levels of the transportation system remains a problem. Foreign tourists, who must pay higher prices than citizens of China (and even compatriots), receive preferential treatment on the public transportation lines. This creates a kind of two-class society, not only on the railway between soft-seats and hard-seats, but also at the entrance to museums and other leisure facilities. But international travelers also meet with organizational difficulties. With a few exceptions, one can buy neither a round-trip ticket nor a return-trip ticket for the train in China. Instead, one must buy a separate ticket at each stopover on the trip, which means long waiting periods at transfer stations for the individual traveler. Even with good contacts at every station, or being part of an organized tour group, one cannot be certain of avoiding unpleasant delays and mishaps.

In an effort to increase efficiency in air traffic, the domestic operations of China's state airline (the Civil Aviation Administration of China, also known as CAAC and Air China) have been divided into seven regional airlines since 1985 (Westlake 1993). Air China is still the national carrier, with CAAC more of a regulatory body. In addition, five other formerly CAAC-related airlines are now in operations, as well as 16 private airline companies. At the same time, airline ticket prices have been increasing for both international travelers and domestic Chinese. The price increases have provided a temporary relief to the airlines by depressing airline ticket demand. A computerized booking system was introduced, which now makes it possible to reserve a seat on some flights at very short notice. (Although, typical of China's service industry, a representative of the CAAC at the 1989 International Tourism Fair (ITB) in Berlin stated that such a system was not necessary because all flights were completely sold out.)

Socio-economic Consequences of Tourism

The PRC government's interest in tourism, as in most other countries, exists mainly in increasing foreign currency income. Foreign currency growth in China appears very pronounced at first glance. However, over the entire period since 1978, its growth rate has remained behind the growth rate of border arrivals (Table 4.1), which translates into a consistent

‗ecline in expenditures per visitor. The main reason for this lies in the large proportion of private visitors (Table 4.2) who do not stay overnight in hotels and, therefore, have only low additional costs. Only in recent years has the rate of foreign currency revenues begun to increase sharply because of higher prices. Indeed, the average expenses of international visitors (excluding private visits) have steadily increased to almost US$600 (Table 4.10). A decrease in 1990 was probably caused by discounts for international package arrangements, which were granted to revive tourism demand after the political events of 1989. There is no data available to estimate the loss of foreign currency through the importation of goods that are connected with tourism, such as hotel equipment, vehicles, and special foodstuffs.

Because of the recent increase in tourism to China, the number of employees in the international tourism trade grew from 64,736 (1982) to 708,263 (1991). Among these, some 547,532 are in the hotel trade, 55,176 are in travel agencies, and 40,085 are in the coach and cruise industry (the remainder are listed as administration and other). The demand for qualified personnel to fill these positions in China has been very high. By 1991 a total of 266 tourism-related training institutions had been created, in which 58,141 students were being taught. These institutions included 68 at universities (7,567 students), 20 at professional schools (3,701 students), and 178 at vocational trade schools (46,873 students) (YEARBOOK 1992:

TABLE 4.10 Domestic and International Arrivals and Revenues, 1985-1991

	1985	1986	1987	1988	1989	1990	1991
Domestic Tourists (Million)	240	270	290	300	240	280	300
Index (1985)	100	113	121	125	100	117	125
Arrivals at Frontiers	17.8	22.8	26.9	31.7	24.5	27.5	33.4
Index	100	128	151	178	137	154	187
Private Visits	14.8	19.6	23.1	27.3	21.3	23.2	28.4
Index	100	132	156	184	144	157	191
Organized Tourists	3.00	3.27	3.78	4.35	3.23	4.25	4.97
Index	100	109	126	145	107	141	165
Revenue							
Domestic Tourists							
(Billion RMB¥)	8	10.6	14	18.7	15	17	20
Index (1985)	100	133	175	234	188	213	250
International Tourists							
(Billion US$)	1.3	1.5	1.9	2.2	1.9	2.2	2.8
Index	100	122	149	180	149	177	228
Revenue per Organized Tourist							
(US$)	415.3	468.4	491.9	516.6	576.4	521.5	573.2

Source: National Tourism Administration.

100-1). Contracts exist with many foreign tourism schools, as well. In addition, there are training programs in cooperation with international hotel companies, most of which are English language courses (Han 1987).

In the entire tourism and accommodations industry, including domestic tourism, there were almost 1.8 million jobs recorded by the NTA in 1991. This compares with 1.4 million in 1987. These numbers are probably underestimated because employees in family-run businesses are almost impossible to estimate precisely. However, the employment effects of tourism in China can probably never be entirely comprehended because of the large and rapidly growing number of related private and informal occupations. There are, for example, hot food stands on street corners, mobile souvenir traders, photographers at view points, bicycle renters, and so on (Gormsen 1990a: 154; Gormsen et al. 1991; Wagner 1990: 165). Connected to this is the rapidly expanding souvenir industry. In addition to larger enterprises, (e.g., silk weaving-mills and fan factories), there are many private workshops producing a variety of arts and crafts, especially those representing ethnic minority cultures. Frequently, traditional commodities and clothing, which are still used in the producers' society, are adapted to the tastes of tourists. For example, in the batik clothing in Dali (Yunnan Province), the patterns sold no longer have any relationship to the local dress (Hemberger 1990: 175; Gormsen 1990c; Gormsen et al. 1991).

Examples of tourism's direct and indirect impact on cultural change are, on the one hand, evidence of the economic success of China's open door policy with its emphasis on strengthening private economic initiative. On the other hand, the ultimate effects of change on the social and cultural of behavior of local people are not easy to estimate. These changes are clearly in addition to the specific influence of tourism. However, their manifestations are often most apparent in the spatially defined areas most closely associated with tourism activities.

Conclusions

Tourism will continue to play an important role in the economic development of China. Its local and regional impacts should not be underestimated in relation to its economic impact on the nation as a whole. It is not easy to distinguish between the different influencing factors that impact an area. For tourism, these impacts may range from the individual backpacking tourists to international package tours, and include every level of domestic tourism. Varied interactions and intersections between different forms of supply and demand exist. It should, however, be emphasized that the remarkable results in tourism development have been only minimally related to foreign holiday and vacation travel, and that this part of the international travel market has actually been stagnant in absolute figures. The reasons behind this are certainly manifold. However, the problems of transportation, inefficient services, and inadequate maintenance are certainly among them. Therefore, if China, with all its outstanding natural and cultural sights, wants to attract more foreign tourists it should try to solve these problems as soon as possible. Regarding foreign currency earnings, the many business people and the enormous number of compatriots are more important than foreign visitors. It remains, therefore, to the government to decide which of the various tourism sectors should receive appropriate support for modernization.

Notes

1. Much of the information contained in this chapter comes from the author's personal observations and communications that he collected during six prolonged journeys to China between 1987 and 1993, as well as from a major research project on tourism in China that he is conducting with Martin Hübner, M.A. and Xu Gang, M.S., supported by the Volkswagen Foundation.

References

Beijing Rundschau (weekly review). Beijing.

China aktuell (monthly review). Hamburg, Germany: Institut für Asienkunde.

Das neue China (quarterly review). Dortmund, Germany: Montania Verlag.

Conrad, Dorte. 1993. Der Reiz des Exotischen, Tourismus und Minderheiten in China. *Das neue China* 20(1): 22-4.

Gormsen, Erdmann. 1988. Tourism in Latin America: Spatial Distribution and impact on regional change. *Applied Geography and Development* 32: 65-80. (Institute for Scientific Co-operation, Tübingen, Germany.)

_____. 1990a. Tourismus in China; Entwicklung, Probleme und Perspektiven. *Inst. für Tourismus, FU Berlin, Berichte und Materialen* 8: 143-56.

_____. 1990b. The Impact of Tourism on Regional Change in China. *GeoJournal*, 21(1/2): 127-35.

_____. 1990c. Kunsthandwerk in der Dritten Welt unter dem Einfluß des Tourismus. *Geographische Rundschau*, 42(1): 42-7.

Gormsen, E.; R. Hemberger; and S. Wagner. 1991. Leben von den Fremden; Strukturwandel als Folge des Tourismus. *Das neue China* 18(1): 31-5.

Han, Guojian. 1987. Ausbildung im Tourismusbereich. *Beijing Rundschau*, 24: 34.

Hemberger, Ralf. 1990. Tourismus in Dali. *Inst. für Tourismus, FU Berlin, Berichte und Materialen* 8: 169-77

Jones, H. R. 1981. *Population Geography*. London: Harper and Row.

Kampen, Thomas.1993. Politik, Freundschaft und Verkehr; die Eisenbahnverbindung von Xinjiang nach Kasachstan. *Das neue China* 20(1): 30-2.

Kou, Zhengling. 1992. Chinesischer Tourismus auf neuer Etappe. *Beijing Rundschau* 26: 20-6.

Kremb, Jürgen. 1993. Wir brauchen und hassen uns. Handel und Schmuggel in Rußlands Fernem Osten. *Der Spiegel* 47(5): 152-8.

Somers-Heidhues, Mary F. 1974. *Southeast Asia's Chinese Minorities*. Camberwell, Australia: Longman.

Wagner, Susanne. 1990. Fremdenverkehr in den Bergen von Huang Shan. *Inst. für Tourismus, FU Berlin, Berichte und Materialen* 8: 157-68

Westlake, Michael. 1993. Troubled Take-off. *Far Eastern Economic Review* 156(7): 52-3.

The Yearbook of China Tourism Statistics (annual). Beijing: China Travel and Tourism Press.

Yu, Lawrence. 1992. Emerging Markets for China's Tourism Industry. *Journal of Travel Research* 31(1): 10-3.

5

China's Hotel Landscape:
A Marker of Economic Development
and Social Change

Lawrence Yu

One of the most dramatic international tourism developments that figures prominently in the Chinese cultural landscape is the construction of tourist hotels. Modern, luxury and western-style hotels constitute the landscape of international tourism in China. The creation of a tourism landscape demonstrates the search by modern tourists for novelty, escape, nostalgia and variety (Eckbo 1969). The hotel landscape, as an element of the total tourism landscape, can be variously studied as an indicator of economic growth, morphological identity, and social change in values and fashion (Ayala 1991). The hotel landscape in China serves as a vivid marker illustrating rapid international tourism development and profound social change. The following examines the formation of a hotel landscape in China during the past decade and evaluates the hotel landscape as a revealing marker of economic growth and social change.

The Formation of a Hotel Landscape

Lodging facilities in China have generally been divided into two major categories for accommodating overseas and domestic tourists, based on the amount of amenities and level of services. The high-level lodging facilities, known as *binguan* or *fandian* (guest house or hotel), are the hotels for overseas tourists. This type of lodging facility is equipped with amenities and luxuries that meet international hotel standards. The lower level lodging facilities, called *ludian*, accommodate only domestic tourists and offer very simple amenities and services, including having more than three beds in a room, and a shared bathroom, television, and telephone. This paper focuses only on the higher level lodging accommodations that serve the overseas tourists for two reasons: (1) the tremendous impact of these hotels on China's economy and society, and (2) the statistical data on hotel development, compiled by National Tourism Administration of the People's Republic of China (CNTA), only include hotels for overseas tourists (the *shewai luyou fandian*). Therefore, the word "hotel" used here refers only to the higher level lodging facilities for overseas tourists.

When China first embarked on international tourism development in 1978, there was a great shortage of lodging accommodations which could meet the western hospitality standards, particularly in the most-visited destination areas, such as in Beijing, Shanghai, Xian, Guilin, and Hangzhou. Many tourists who had reservations at the Beijing Hotel were told upon arrival that it was overbooked and that they had to look for lodging facilities elsewhere in the city, or even in the small towns outside Beijing. Sometimes, these unlucky tourists had to be transported to Tianjin, a municipality 138 km from Beijing, for overnight accommodations. The lack of adequate lodging facilities drew constant complaints from international tourists and criticism from the international travel industry (Cook 1989; Schrock, et al. 1989). The development of lodging facilities with western standards thus became an urgent and critical issue concerning the future success of China's burgeoning international tourism industry.

Hotel development, therefore, was singled out by the Chinese government as a major area for infrastructure investment in the *Sixth Five-Year Plan (1981-1985) for China's Economic and Social Development* (1984). In order to accelerate hotel development and meet the demands of western tourists, the Chinese government initiated several strategies: (1) opening up the luxury state guest houses to accommodate international tourists; (2) domestic investment which included direct investment by the central government, local government tourism agencies, various other government agencies, and collective enterprises, and (3) foreign investment in the form of foreign direct investment, joint ventures and cooperative agreements with foreign hospitality management companies. All these development measures have contributed to the formation of a hotel landscape in China over the last decade.

State Guest House Hotels

The opening up of the state guest houses and exclusive resorts was one of the first measures taken by the Chinese government to ease the hotel shortage problem. Since the founding of the People's Republic in 1949, the Chinese Communist Party (CCP) and the central government have developed many large, world-class lodging facilities and resorts in the country for the purpose of accommodating foreign leaders and dignitaries. They were also used by the top party and government leaders as vacation homes and travel accommodations. These lodging facilities and resorts are commonly known as "state guest houses" (*goubinguan*), and often occupied the most desirable physical settings in the country. They were equipped with modern amenities and luxuries, and were guarded by uniformed soldiers who kept them off limits to the general public.

When the shortage of hotels became a serious problem in the late 1970s, the central government decided to open up parts of many state guest houses in the country to accommodate international tourists, in part because most state guest houses were underutilized. Consequently, state guest houses throughout the country adjusted their operations to service international tourists. The well-known state guest houses, such as Diaoyudai Guobinguan in Beijing, Xijiao Binguan in Shanghai, Liu Zhuang (presently, Xizi Binguan) and Wang Zhuang (presently, Xihu Binguan) in Hangzhou, all opened several buildings or villas to international tourists (Figure 5.1). Some state guest houses even built new facilities to cater to international tourists. Xijiao Binguan in Shanghai built a new building, Building No. 7, in its expansive and exclusive compound.

This strategy has had considerable impact on the development of China's hotel industry. Obviously, the opening up of China's most exclusive state guest houses alleviated international tourist demands for lodging facilities. These guest houses also generated foreign currencies, turning themselves from heavily subsidized government enterprises into profit making properties. The partial conversion from diplomatic to commercial use reduced the financial burden on the government.

In addition, these state guest houses became instant tourist attractions themselves. All of these properties were built in a garden setting and designed with traditional Chinese architectural motifs. Many of them included beautiful scenic and recreational amenities in the surrounding land, lakes, vegetation, and mountains. Some of the villa buildings and presidential suites formally used by world leaders are particularly appealing to overseas tourists. Some international travel companies that primarily organized luxury tours to China in the early 1980s would reserve blocks of rooms in state guest houses for their clients. The conversion of portions of state guest houses into tourist hotels had a profound impact on the

FIGURE 5.1 Villa No. 1 in the Xizi Guest House in Hangzhou. Photo by Lawrence Yu.

formation of the hotel landscape in China, particularly in the initial stages of the country's hotel development.

Domestic Investment in Hotels

The second strategy to alleviate the shortage of accommodations was to have new hotels funded and built by government at various administrative levels. The central government allocated development funds and loans for selected major tourist destination cities, such as Beijing, Guangzhou, Shanghai, Xian, and Guilin. This direct development incentive was channelled through the NTA, the country's tourism development authority, to provincial and municipal tourism bureaus. Beyond this, additional hotel projects were being initiated independently by the provincial and municipal governments. New, multistoried hotels were erected in downtown commercial areas and famous scenic spots. These new highrise structures contrasted sharply with the smaller buildings in the older Chinese cities.

As the central government encouraged provincial and local government tourism agencies' involvement in developing new hotels, other government agencies, quasi-governmental, collective, and even private investors seized the opportunity and invested in the lodging industry. Hotels built by the collective farmers and the People's Liberation Army are used as examples to illustrate such development.

With the profound and rapid rural economic reform that China was experiencing since the late 1970s, rural communities along the coastal regions and outside the major metropolitan areas massed a fortune by diversifying their economies. They were not only just engaged in farming operations, but also in developing light manufacturing industries and traditional artisan handicrafts. Any deviation from agricultural practice by the farmers was considered capitalist activities and banned in the people's communes before the rural economic reform initiated by Deng Xiaoping in 1978. The rural economic reform allowed the farmers in the coastal regions and near major metropolitan areas to diversify their economic base and, consequently, accumulate rapid wealth.

Collectively, the farmers could invest their surplus income in business ventures. Attracted by the demand-driven hotel market at the time, and the potential for a quick return on their investment, the rural farmers from wealthy communities moved into the major tourist cities and built lodging facilities for international and domestic tourists, as well as domestic conference delegates. The Huiqiao Hotel, in the Hepingli District of Beijing, is such a property. It was built and managed by farmers from the suburbs of the city.

The People's Liberation Army has also been involved in investing and building tourist hotels (The Economist 1991). At peace time, the Chinese army has been asked to to reduce its operating budget and to participate in economic development. To achieve these goals, the Chinese army took an active part in many commercial business ventures. Building and managing hotels for international and domestic tourists is one of these business ventures. The Lantian (Blue Sky) Hotel in Shanghai is owned and managed by the local air force unit. Because of its adequate accommodations and services, this hotel was awarded the 3-star rating by the NTA, and is often booked by international travel services in other parts of the country. For example, Hangzhou International Travel Service used to reserve a block of up to 200 rooms in this hotel for overseas tourists during the peak tourist season in Shanghai.

Hotel development by various government agencies at different levels, and by collective and private investors, has contributed the most to the formation of the contemporary hotel landscape in China (Table 5.1). Of the 2,130 hotels recorded in China by 1991, 71 percent were developed by various government agencies. This obviously indicates that China is still a largely socialized economy with central planning and public ownership.

Due to the market situation, building enough hotel rooms was a top priority in China's international tourism development during the early part of the 1980s. However, with the emergence of luxury and western-style hotels through foreign investment and joint-ventures in the late 1980s, many hotels built by non-tourism government agencies and collective investors, such as the hotels built by farmers and the army, were reduced to receiving only domestic tourists and conferences due to their inadequate management and services.

TABLE 5.1 Hotel Ownership in China, 1991

Ownership	No. of Hotels	No. of Rooms	No. of Beds	Occupancy Rate
Domestically-Owned				
State-Owned	1,528	213,525	470,718	63.47
Multi-Gov. Agency Owned	8	1,298	2,679	55.01
Collective Ownership	171	16,692	38,188	65.88
Private Ownership	2	35	86	60.00
Foreign-Invested and Operated				
Sole Foreign Investment	4	843	1,516	44.84
Joint-Venture	202	48,212	87,100	52.35
Management Contracts	215	40,511	79,081	59.58
Total	2,130	321,116	679,458	61.35

Source: The Yearbook of China's Tourism Statistics 1992, pp. 86-7.

Foreign Investment in Hotels

As a developing country, China encountered substantial financial difficulty in financing hotels with western amenities, services and management. In order to speed up the development to meet the needs of foreign visitors, the Chinese government initiated foreign investment and joint-venture incentives for overseas investors to develop lodging facilities in China (Liu 1980). This strategy served not only to attract badly-needed financing from overseas, but also service management know-how as technology transfer (Pine 1992). The concept of service was almost non-existent during the era that Mao Zedong ruled China. Since the communist ideology was to eradicate social class difference, leisure travel was considered a bourgeois lifestyle. Many hotel employees had service attitude problems which drew constant complaints from international tourists. The introduction of western hospitality management would help improve service standards and enable China's hotel industry to compete at the international level.

The first successful joint-venture hotel was the Jianguo Hotel in Beijing, built in 1982 with a total capital investment of US$22.3 million. This joint-construction and management effort was an instant success. In the first six months of operation the hotel generated a gross income of US$7.66 million (Zhou 1989). Its financial success and systematic management encouraged government agencies at various levels to aggressively seek overseas investors and management partners. A wave of joint-venture and cooperative agreement hotel development swept the country in the 1980s and, at present, most of the major international hotel corporations are present in the Chinese hotel market (Schneider 1985; Yu 1992a). It is this type of hotel development that accentuated the hotel landscape in terms of modern architecture, contemporary technology, vertical morphology, and luxury amenities (Figure 5.2).

The Hotel Landscape

Geographically, the hotel landscape is most commonly seen in the major tourist destination cities and in the economically-developed coastal provinces (Table 5.2). Guangdong Province leads all others in hotel development. By the end of 1991, there were 685 hotels with a total of 82,970 rooms in this province (Sun 1992). The capital city Guangzhou and the Special Economic Zone (SEZ) cities of Shenzhen and Zhuhai are the most popular places in the entire country for foreign investment, trade and travel (Fong 1985). In addition, many overseas ethnic Chinese have made substantial investments in their home villages or counties for economic development, an advantage other provinces in China do not have.

FIGURE 5.2 The Shanghai Hilton International, the first hotel in China that was solely invested in and managed by foreign companies. Photo by Lawrence Yu.

TABLE 5.2 Hotel Distributions by Municipality/Province, 1991

Municipality or Province	# of Hotels	Hotel Capacity (number of rooms)				
		500 +	300-499	200-299	100-199	< 100
Municipality						
Beijing	203	21	32	33	59	58
Shanghai	85	13	13	17	25	17
Tianjin	22	1	3	5	6	7
Province						
Guangdong	685	13	37	56	165	414
Sichuan	90	1	9	19	35	26
Fujian	87	0	5	14	28	40
Hubei	81	0	6	10	36	29
Shandong	76	0	4	17	26	29
Liaoning	73	0	5	10	25	33
Hebei	64	2	5	11	25	21
Zhejiang	64	1	4	5	23	31
Guangxi	57	1	11	14	13	18
Anhui	51	0	0	7	20	24
Jiangsu	49	1	5	9	18	16
Xingjiang	49	0	1	2	15	31
Jiangxi	48	0	2	7	21	18
Hainan	44	0	1	5	20	18
Yunnan	40	0	1	4	20	15
Hunan	38	0	4	8	15	11
Heilongjiang	36	0	4	4	13	15
Jilin	36	0	1	1	14	20
Gansu	26	1	3	1	9	12
Shaanxi	23	5	5	2	7	4
Shanxi	22	0	3	3	10	6
Henan	20	0	3	4	4	9
Inner Mongolia	16	0	1	4	4	7
Guizhou	13	0	1	2	7	3
Ningxia	13	0	1	0	4	8
Tibet	12	1	0	0	2	9
Qinghai	7	0	2	1	1	3
Total	**2130**	**61**	**172**	**275**	**670**	**952**

Source: The Yearbook of China's Tourism Statistics 1992, pp. 90-1.

The national capital city of Beijing witnessed a dramatic hotel boom in the 1980s, and its 203 hotels with 48,510 rooms clearly demonstrated the magnitude of the tourism development in the city. The hotel landscape in Beijing is dotted with hotels developed by all levels of government agencies, collective investors, as well as many international hotel corporations. Gone

are the days when international tourists had to be transported to a nearby
city or county for an overnight sleep because of overbooking in Beijing
hotels.

The spatial distribution of hotels clearly reflects the tourism demand and
supply factors in other municipalities and provinces. The popular tourist
destinations of the coastal regions and the Changjiang (Yangtze) River
region have more hotels than the interior, periphery provinces, and ethnic
autonomous regions. The coastal municipality of Shanghai, and the
Provinces of Hebei, Liaoning, Zhejiang, Fujian, and Shangdong all
registered more than 60 hotels in 1991. The two provinces situated on the
Changjiang Range, Hubei and Sichuan, recorded 81 and 90 hotels
respectively in 1991, a clear indication of the Three Guorges on the
Changjiang River as a popular destination for international tourists. The
interior, periphery provinces and autonomous regions of Inner Mongolia,
Guizhou, Tibet, Qinghai and Ningxia all reported no more than 20 hotels
respectively in 1991. It is interesting to note that Xinjiang, the Uygur
Autonomous Region in northwest China, recorded 49 hotels in 1991, more
than doubling the hotel capacity of its neighboring provinces and
autonomous regions. This development pattern may be explained by the
increasing border trade and travel between Xinjiang and the many
Commonwealth of Independent States (CIS) in the former Soviet Union.

A Marker of Economic Growth

The hotel landscape is a revealing marker of the economic impact that
tourism has had on China. An observant eye can detect clues as to the
financial returns and management effectiveness of each individual property.
Financially, the lodging industry in China has made a significant
contribution to China's international tourist revenues. Table 5.3 shows the
breakdown of international tourism revenues in 1991. Receipts from hotels
made up 22 percent of the total tourism revenues.

From the lodging industry's standpoint, the cash return of the hotels in
1991 reached RMB¥ 18.868 billion, a 35.6 percent increase over that of
1990. Of the total hotel revenues, RMB¥ 6.096 billion was in foreign
currency receipt of Chinese FEC¥, an increase of 32.3 percent over the
previous year. (Until 1994 China issued two types of currencies, RMB¥ for
its own citizens and Foreign Exchange Certificate (FEC¥) for foreigners.
The foreign currency receipt from tourism is measured in FEC¥.) Table
5.4 describes the breakdown of hotel operating revenues for China in 1991.

Further analysis of the hotel revenues by hotel ownership reveals that
over 70 percent of total receipts came from the state-owned hotels, which
comprise 71 percent of all hotels in China. In terms of profitability, 79.3

percent of the state-owned hotels made profits in 1991, while the remainder lost money that year. As for the 421 hotels with either direct foreign investment or contractual management agreement (four solely foreign owned hotels, 202 joint-venture hotels, and 215 foreign management company operated hotels), 172 (40.1 percent) properties were profitable in 1991 (Sun 1992: 19-20).

The financial performance of the solely foreign owned hotels, joint-venture hotels, and foreign management hotels can be partially explained by the relatively low room occupancy rate they experienced in 1991. In 1991, the average room occupancy rate for the 2130 hotels in China was 61.4 percent. The domestically-owned and operated hotels all had average room occupancy rates above 60 percent (63.47 percent for state-owned hotels, 65.88 percent for collectively owned hotels, and 60 percent for individually owned hotels), except for the category of joint-government agency ownership, which recorded 55.01 percent (Sun 1992: 86-7).

None of the hotels with foreign investment and management achieved a 61 percent room occupancy rate in 1991, a general indicator of profitable

TABLE 5.3 Breakdown of International Tourism Receipts 1991

Receipt Category	Revenue (Million US$)	%
Long Distance Transportation & Communication	818.08	28.7
Shopping	704.21	24.8
Lodging	627.35	22.1
Local Transportation & Entertainment	410.48	14.4
Food & Beverage	284.85	10.0
Total	2,844.97	100

Source: The Yearbook of China's Tourism Statistics 1992, p. 103.

TABLE 5.4 Breakdown of Hotel Revenues in China 1991

Sales Category	Revenues (Billion RMB¥)	%
Room Sales	7.272	38.4
Food & Beverage	6.907	35.1
Gift Shops	2.622	14.4
Others	2.067	12.1
Total	18.868	100

Source: The Yearbook of China's Tourism Statistics 1992, p. 19.

operations. Hotels operated under foreign management contract had the best performance with a 59.58 percent occupancy rate, the joint-venture hotels averaged only 52.35 percent nationwide, and the solely foreign owned hotels reported a national average of 44.84 percent room occupancy in 1990 (Sun 1992: 86-7).

This unsatisfactory financial performance, resulting from the relatively low room occupancy rates in the hotels with foreign investment and management, deserves further discussion. The difference of financial accounting and reporting systems between the domestically-owned hotels and foreign owned and operated hotels may make the comparison difficult (Sun 1992: 19). However, the low occupancy rates experienced by these hotels reveal some managerial and operational deficiencies, such as cultural clashes between foreign and local management personnel, ineffective marketing promotions, and high room rates. In international hospitality operations, it is of paramount importance to have smooth cooperation between the expatriate and local managers. However, management conflicts often occur due to the personal and cultural differences. This will naturally have an impact on the performance of the lower level management and employees, and directly influence the financial performance of the hotels (Shenker 1990; Stross 1991).

Marketing is another very important operational strategy to increase room sales, particularly in a very competitive market with an oversupply of hotels. However, marketing also needs to take into account the local cultural values and ways of conducting business. In the Chinese cultural and business environment, the hotel marketing or sales manager's personal rapport with the Chinese travel services is vital to room sales because the Chinese travel services provide them with a substantial number of overseas group tours. It requires time for foreign sales managers to make close friends within the local travel services, and a good friendship with your business partners is needed to guarantee a steady business for the hotel.

High room rates are also a major hinderance in increasing occupancy at foreign owned and operated hotels. Because of the high investment cost per room for modern and luxury amenities, these hotels have to charge a higher room rate. This excludes the moderate and budget travel market segments, leaving their appeal exclusively to business travelers, high-income individual tourists, and deluxe leisure travel groups. The financial performance of foreign owned and operated hotels is a very important topic for further study. Management differences, marketing strategies, and high room costs are some of the factors that have caused such performance. Only through further investigation will the importance of factors that affect hotel success in China be fully understood.

The Five-Star Rating System

A major development recently in the Chinese hotel industry is the implementation of a five-star rating system for the hotels in China. The rating of China's hotels under a five-star system was instituted to: (1) enhance hotel management and service standards, and (2) protect the interests of hoteliers, travel companies, and consumers (Yin 1987). To make China's hotels meet international standards while still reflecting China's national or regional cultural characteristics, the NTA developed the five-star rating system based on hotel architecture, decoration, facilities, maintenance, management level, service quality, sanitation and hygiene, and guest satisfaction (Yu 1992b). By 1991, 853 of the 2130 hotels in China were rated by CNTA as starred hotels: 21 hotels were rated as five-star hotels, 48 as four-star hotels, 235 as three-star hotels, 393 as two-star hotels, and 156 as one-star hotels (Sun 1992). At present, this hotel rating program is continuing. The five-star hotel rating system illustrates the adoption of a systematic hotel management scheme in China and has demonstrated China's efforts in meeting international standards of hotel operations. Further improvement of China's hotel management will definitely have a great impact on the international hotel industry.

A Marker of Social Change

Hotels can shape and change life in a community, and they are almost always at the center of such change in China. The hotel landscape of China reveals a dramatic change in the cultural values and the way of life in modern Chinese society (Lew 1987). Physically, hotels figure prominently in the traditional Chinese landscape, overshadowing the traditional low and small dwellings in the old city centers. In the newly-developed areas of major cities, architecturally distinctive hotels add radiance and vitality to nearby highrise residential and commercial buildings (Figure 5.3).

The hotels are often the first places where the general public experiences new technology and modern architectural styles (Cain 1981; Spritzer 1991). The glass building of the Golden Flower Hotel in Xian, the Jinjiang Tower with the revolving restaurant in Shanghai, and the Great Wall Sheraton in Beijing have clearly illustrated the cultural diffusion of western architectural styles into the traditionally austere Chinese landscape. Hotels, as a cultural landscape marker, vividly reveal the introduction of western lifestyle into a traditional society.

Hotels also play an important role as an information disseminator in Chinese society. The Chinese government used to have tight information control over all national and international political and economic developments. News from the outside world was carefully censored and broadcast through the government controlled propaganda apparatus. Such control over information from the western world served to check the infiltration of western ideology into Chinese society. Such infiltration was viewed by the central government as influential in the student uprising which lead to the Tienanmen Incident in 1989. However, such information control actually increased the public's thirst for news from the outside world, particularly from the west.

At the same time, hotels in China were attempting to create a comfortable lodging environment for international tourists and make them feel as though the hotels were their "home away from home." Thus, many hotels, especially those with foreign investment and management, were equipped with satellite communication systems. CNN World News from U.S. and Star TV from Hong Kong can now be conveniently received in each guest room. Most hotels also provide newsstands that offer western daily newspapers, journals, and paperback best sellers to visiting international tourists. The Wall Street Journal, Time Magazine, and novels by Stephen King and Danniel Steele illustrate the infiltration of western values through the hotel industry.

Consequently, the hotels come to serve as information disseminators in China. Local hotel employees acquire direct access to the most up-to-date western news and literature. Many tourists also leave their travel readings behind for hotel employees. Such information can then be disseminated by the hotel employees to their families, relatives, and friends. For an information-starved society, word of mouth spreads rapidly.

Besides the local hotel employees, Chinese people who are involved in any aspect of international business (including the travel industry) frequent hotels. These include government officials, trade representatives, and tour guides. Local people can also go to the hotels to visit their relatives from overseas. Their visits to hotels also give them direct exposure to news information and literary works from the west. Western information has proven to be a powerful ideological influence, which is challenging and changing the traditional Chinese value system.

Hotels are also centers of lavish entertainment. Night entertainment was almost non-existent in China before the advent of an international tourism industry. To enrich the nightlife of international tourists, many hotels opened discotheque and more recently *Karaoke* clubs, a new form of entertainment introduced from Japan. These fancy and expensive nightclubs have become popular entertainment centers for the local young people. The latest popular music, songs, and dance styles from the west are often first introduced in the hotels.

FIGURE 5.3 The Peninsula Group's Palace Hotel in Beijing. Photo courtesy of the Peninsula Group.

Additionally, hotels are the source of new fashions because the hotel employees have direct contact with international tourists. Young hotel employees tend to emulate the consumption patterns of foreign visitors, and clothing fashion is an explicit demonstration that they can use to show off their new cultured ways to the larger society. This cultural borrowing, the so-called "demonstration effect," has a great impact on expectations and values of younger Chinese. The tourist hotels are, without doubt, a powerful agent in catalyzing the social and cultural changes in the traditional Chinese value system and way of life.

Conclusions

The dramatic changes that the international tourism industry has brought to China are clearly imprinted in the country's landscape through the development of modern lodging facilities. The formation of a hotel landscape is a good indicator of the rapid growth in tourism stimulated by various development forces. Various Chinese government agencies, collective and individual Chinese investors, joint-ventures, sole foreign investment, and foreign management companies combined to transform the traditional Chinese cultural landscape into a more colorful and modern one, with a blend of Chinese and western-style hotels.

The hotel landscape also reflects the overall accelerating economic growth in China. The lodging industry generates substantial revenues and creates new jobs in the Chinese economy. Differences in profitability between domestically-owned hotels and hotels with foreign investment and management show some revealing and interesting developments and management patterns in the areas of cultural diversity, cross-cultural marketing practice and pricing development. Substantial research is needed to further compare and analyze the operational differences between hotels of these two different categories.

The hotel landscape has witnessed the introduction of western technology in hotel design and construction, the cultural diffusion of western ideology through news media and literature, and the demonstration of western cultural behavior in dress style and night entertainment. As a cornerstone of tourist cities, hotels have had a profound impact in changing and reshaping the cultural values and norms of China's younger generation. Furthermore, the hotel landscape in China has become an essential element of the dissemination of global popular culture, and has brought about the further development of cultural convergence in the world.

The cultural landscape reflects the continuous accumulation of cultural, economic, and technological changes in a society. Each element in the totality of the cultural landscape marks the cultural values of the people that have created it. These markers, in turn, illustrate the inspirations and cultural behaviors of a particular group of people. By examining the landscape markers of tourist hotels in China, one can understand the economic, social, and cultural changes occuring in the past decade. The tourist hotels in China have documented the country's great economic growth and social changes, and will continue to witness new development and changes in future.

References

Ayala, Hana 1991. Resort Hotel Landscape as an International Megatrend. *Annals of Tourism Research* 18: 568-87.

Cain, Ray 1981. Landscape Architecture in Asia: The Shangri-La Hotel. *Landscape Architectural Forum* (Winter): 15-9.

Cook, David. 1989. China's Hotels: Still Playing Catch-Up. *The Cornell Hotel and Restaurant Administration Quarterly* 30(3): 64-7.

The Economist. 1991. China: The Army that Makes Money. (October 5th): 38.

Eckbo, Garrett. 1969. The Landscape of Tourism. *Landscape* 18(2): 29-31.

Fong, Mo-Kwan Lee. 1985. Tourism: A Critical Review. In Kwan-yiu Wong and David K.Y. Chu, eds., *Modernization in China: The Case of the Shenzhen Special Economic Zone*, New York: Oxford University Press, pp. 79-88.

Lew, Alan A. 1987. History, Politics and Social Impact of International Tourism in the People's Republic of China. *Asian Profile* 15(2): 117-28.

Liu, Chu. 1980. China's Joint-Venture Policies. In N.T. Wang, ed., *Business with China: An international reassessment*, New York: Pergamon Press, pp. 73-7.

Pine, Ray. 1992. Technology Transfer in the Hotel Industry. In Peter Jones and Abraham Pizam, eds., *The International Hospitality Industry: Organizational and operational issues*, New York: John Wiley & Sons, pp. 226-40.

Schneider, M. 1985. China's Hotel Fever Peaks. *Hotels & Restaurants International* 9: 7.

Schrock, Jay R., Charlie R. Adams, and Jiayi Lung, 1989. China's Need for Tourism Development. *The Cornell Hotel and Restaurant Administration Quarterly* 30(3): 68-71.

Shenker, Oded. 1990. International Joint Ventures' Problems in China: Risks and remedies. *Long Range Planning* 23(3): 82-90.

Sixth Five-Year Plan of the People's Republic of China for Economic and Social Development 1981-1985. 1984. Beijing: Foreign Language Press.

Spritzer, Dinah A. 1991. The Hotel Is Oasis of Western Comfort. *Travel Weekly* (April 25): 72,74.

Stross, Randall E. 1991. *Bulls in the China Shop: And other Sino-American business encounters*. New York: Pantheon.

Sun, Gang. 1992. *The Yearbook of China's Tourism Statistics*. Beijing: China Travel and Tourism Press.

Yin, MinLian. 1987. Notes on the Criteria for Rating and Ranking Tourist Hotels. *Tourism Research and Tourist Hotels* (Special Edition): 1-9, internal publication of China Institute of Tourism.

Yu, Lawrence. 1992a. China's Hotel Development and Structures. *International Journal of Hospitality Management* 11(2): 99-110.

_____. 1992b. Seeing Stars: China's Hotel-Rating System. *The Cornell Hotel and Restaurant Administration Quarterly* 33(5): 24-7.

Zhou, Jian. 1989. Overprovision in Chinese Hotels. *Tourism Management* 10(1): 63-6.

6

Tourism and Hospitality Education in China

Xiao Qianhui and Liu Zhijiang

When China opened its doors to the outside world in 1978, it gave birth to a new industry in which travel, tourism, and hospitality became money-making business activities, as opposed to foreign policy functions. The new and rapidly developing tourism industry created a great demand for competent tourism and hospitality managers and service personnel. Tourism and hospitality education programs were quickly developed to try to meet this new demand (Jin and Yu 1990; Zhao 1992). In China, high schools, professional schools, technical schools, and vocational schools comprise the secondary school level. Post-secondary schools include Universities, Colleges, and Institutes. Continuing and adult education are offered in training centers.

The first tourism school in China, the Jiangsu Technical School of Tourism, was established in 1978. However, this school initially did not have tour guiding, guest service, and culinary courses in its curriculum. Several other schools were established in the period from 1979 to 1981, including the Shanghai Tourism Institute, the Beijing Tourism Institute, and the Sichuan Tourism School. The Beijing Second Foreign Language Institute also developed tourism economics courses on a trial basis.

Between 1983 and 1988 the travel and tourism industry in China experienced incredibly rapid growth and was in urgent need of personnel with tourism and hospitality management and operation knowledge and skills. The existing tourism schools, however, were far from able to meet the industry's needs. Under these circumstances, the National Tourism Administration of the People's Republic of China (NTA), along with some of the provincial and municipal tourism bureaus, established a large number of new tourism and hospitality schools and programs at both the secondary and post-secondary levels. Many other schools also began to offer travel and hospitality courses and degrees. This period was the *Golden Age* in the development of Chinese tourism and hospitality education. The following are examples of the many tourism schools and programs that were opened during this period:

- Tourism Department in Nankai University in Tianjin
- Hotel Management Department in Zhongshan University in Guangzhou
- Tourism Department in Northwest University in Xian
- Tourism Department in Hangzhou University
- Tourism Department in Xian Foreign Language Institute
- Guilin Tourism Institute
- Zhejiang Tourism School
- Hubei Tourism School
- Shanxi Tourism School
- Jinsong Vocational School in Beijing

Since 1988, there has been only a slight increase in the number of tourism and hospitality schools in China. The recent period has been characterized by the development of continuing education training centers targeted at improving the job skills of tourism and hospitality managers and employees. Nine new tourism training centers and two continuing education schools were founded between 1988 and 1991, including the China Tourism Management Institute in Tianjin, with the funding of US$3 million from United Nations Development Program, and the Jinling Hotel Management College in Nanjing. By the end of 1991, there were altogether 268 tourism and hospitality education programs at various levels in China, with a total enrollment of 58,141 students (Sun 1992).

At present, tourism education in China is in a stable period. The emphasis is not on expanding the number of schools, but on optimizing existing resources and improving educational quality.

Institutional Organization

The various tourism and hospitality education programs in China are institutionalized in many different ways. Tourism economics and hotel management programs are normally found in the economics and business management departments of four-year comprehensive universities. Tour guiding programs are often offered in the foreign language institutes since the primary requirement for a tour guide is the ability to speak a foreign language. There are also specialized tourism and hospitality education colleges, professional schools, and high schools that offer comprehensive training with academic degrees and professional certificates. Other schools simply offer tourism and hospitality courses (such as hotel operations, culinary skills, and guest services) in their curricula as a career focus. By 1991, 68 tourism education programs were offered by post-secondary institutions of higher learning. These programs were either 3 or 4 years in length and enrolled 7,567 students. An additional 198 programs were run by secondary schools, with 46,873 students enrolled (Sun 1992). The regional distribution of these schools is directly associated with the level of tourism development in China. Tourism education is well developed in places where international travel is strongest (Table 6.1). Beijing, the third most visited area in China, has the largest number of tourism schools for any one city. Shanghai and neighboring Jiangsu Province are the second most frequented area by international visitors and together have the largest number of schools for any region. Guangdong Province is the most visited by international tourists and also has a large number of schools. Liaoning Province is close to the Beijing area, while Guangxi Province borders Guangdong. The reason for the large number of schools in Heilongjiang Province is unclear.

The secondary high school and professional school tourism programs offer two or three years of studies. They recruit qualified students who have had three years of junior high school education. The three year programs are typically found in secondary schools which specialize in tourism and hospitality only. Most of the students who graduate from these

TABLE 6.1. Principal Locations of Tourism and Hospitality Schools in China in 1991

Province or Municipality[a]	*Post-secondary Schools*	*Secondary Schools*	*Total Students Enrolled*
Beijing	10	37	13,372
Shanghai	14	20	7,395
Liaoning	4	17	5,098
Jiangsu	4	21	4,463
Guangdong	15	15	4,226
Guangxi	2	8	3,516
Heilongjiang	0	21	3,351
Total for China	68	198	58,141

[a]Provinces and municipalities not listed above have fewer than 1,600 students enrolled in tourism and hospitality schools.
Source: The Yearbook of China Tourism Statistics 1992

schools are employed as service-personnel, although some of those in three-year programs are trained for more specialized work such as cooks and entry-level management.

The purpose of tourism education programs at post-secondary higher education institutions is to train senior tourism and hospitality management personnel. Tourism educational programs at post-secondary schools offer both three-year diplomas and four-year bachelor of art degrees. Students graduating with a bachelors degree are hired at the highest management levels. The university tourism programs enroll qualified students who have had six years of junior high and high school education. Two universities now offer a master degree in tourism economics. No doctoral programs are available in tourism or hospitality, although a tourism is a major focus in some selected disciplines, such as in the Geography Department of Beijing University.

Curriculum Development

Courses offered in Chinese tourism and hospitality institutions follow educational guidelines and policies established by the government to meet the needs of the industry. Most of the schools adopt, to varying degrees, international pedagogical methods and curriculum structure when setting up tourism and hospitality courses. Variations in curriculum structures reflect different levels of training. The majors offered in schools of higher education typically include tourism economics, hotel management, tourism finance, food and beverage management, culinary arts, and tour guiding and interpretation. Majors offered in secondary school tourism programs are usually limited to hotel service and management, and cooking skills. Table 6.2 shows the core courses offered to tourism and hotel management majors in most higher education schools, and to hotel service and management majors in most secondary schools.

Tourism and Hospitality Faculty

The quality of teachers in China's tourism and hospitality schools is considered a major factor in the success of tourism and hospitality education in the country. School administrators pay great attention to the composition and development of their teaching staff. Teachers for tourism and hospitality schools are educated and recruited in one or more of the following ways.

The majority of the Chinese faculty are trained domestically. Domestic training mainly includes school coursework, short-term training programs, and internship in the tourism and hospitality industry. Currently, all of the

TABLE 6.2 Major Tourism and Hospitality Courses Offered in China

Higher Learning Institutions (colleges, universities, etc.) with 3 to 4 Year programs	*Professional Schools and High Schools with 2 Year programs*
Political Economics	Hotel Housekeeping
Western Economics	Food and Beverage Management
Management Theory & Practice	Front Desk Operations
Accounting	Hospitality Accounting
Quantitative Methods	Introduction to Hospitality Mgmnt.
Computer Applications	Introduction to the Travel Industry
Travel Psychology	
Introduction to the Travel Industry	
Travel Laws and Regulations	
Introduction to Hotel Management	
Property Management	
Food and Beverage Management	
Guest Service Management	
Human Resource Management	
Hotel Engineering and Maintenance	
Hotel Safety and Security	
Hospitality Marketing	

Source: Department of Personnel, Labor and Education of National Tourism Administration of the People's Republic of China, 1991.

major secondary and post-secondary tourism schools in China have programs to train teachers. Among the more prominent are the graduate program in the Tourism Department at Nankai University and the tourism and hospitality education major in the Shanghai Tourism Institute. These programs were established for the purpose of training qualified tourism and hospitality educators. The Department of Personnel, Labor and Education (DPLE) of the NTA organizes short-term teacher training programs on a regular basis. An example of this was the 1990 Hospitality Educator Training Program on Food and Beverage, which was co-sponsored by the Hong Kong Education Fund, and included tourism and hospitality industry and education experts from Hong Kong. Another example was the Training Program for Professional Tourism Educators in 1992, which included United Nations volunteer experts. This program is scheduled to be offered every three years. Most of China's tourism schools have a rule that professional teachers must work as interns for six months to a year in a travel or hospitality enterprise before they can officially start teaching. This industry experience is designed to bring practical experience to the classroom.

Some Chinese faculty are also sent to foreign tourism and hospitality schools for further education and training. More than 200 faculty have been trained overseas in recent years. Courses they take include travel industry management, hotel management, and western culinary arts. Among the more prominent schools they attend are:

- Austria: the Salzberg Tourism Institute
- Britain: the University of Surrey, University of Strathclyde
- Germany: Bavaria Hotelfachschule Altötting, and Fachhochschule Rheinland-Pfalz
- Italy: the Turin Training Center, and the Tourism Science International School
- Japan: Linai University
- Switzerland: Ecole hôteliere de Lausanne
- United States: Cornell University, the New School of New York, Northern Arizona University, and the University of Hawaii

This overseas education and training greatly enhances the academic level of the Chinese tourism and hospitality faculty.

Tourism schools often invite foreign experts to conduct short teaching and training courses for the Chinese faculty in China. Over the years, more than 500 foreign teachers have been invited to teach in China's tourism and hospitality schools. In 1992, there were approximately 110 foreign teachers in the country. The Beijing Second Foreign Language Institute (also known as the China Tourism Institute), and the China Tourism Training Institute in Tianjin employ the most foreign teachers and experts. The foreign teachers and experts in these two institutions all have had at least one year of previous work experience in China. The number of foreign teachers and experts who have come to China to lecture on a short-term basis is much higher.

Finally, many tourism and hospitality institutions offer adjunct teaching positions to professionals in the industry in order to better integrate teaching with practice. These industry professionals include travel agency managers, hotel managers and highly skilled chefs. Their classes are well received by the students because of their rich experience in the industry.

Textbook Development

Teaching materials for tourism and hospitality courses were developed rapidly after China became serious about the industry in 1978, and many left much to be desired. Most of the textbooks in China are written by faculty members in various tourism and hospitality schools. Recent textbooks are incorporating more concepts from foreign tourism and hospitality sources, as well as new developments from Chinese authors. The DPLE is primarily responsible for compiling professional and academic teaching materials for nationwide use. The DPLE's Committee on Teaching Material Compilation and Evaluation organizes faculty from four-year tourism and hospitality institutes to write textbooks. Experts from the industry and professors from related disciplines are usually invited to participate in the development of textbook outlines and drafts. The goal is to assure that the textbooks are both academically acceptable and are well integrated with practice. In some cases, experts from the industry directly participate in the writing of teaching materials.

At present, there are five series of textbooks which were written and published under DPLE guidance. They include:

- the standard series of textbooks for colleges
- the series of reference materials for colleges
- the series of translated textbooks from overseas
- the series of textbooks for professional and high schools
- the series of textbooks for continuing adult education

All of these teaching materials are recommended by the DPLE to schools for adoption. Individual schools can compile their own teaching materials or choose textbooks other than the recommended ones. A survey conducted by the DPLE, however, found that these materials are very popular and well received in most of the country's tourism and hospitality schools.

Quality of Education

In October, 1991, the DPLE conducted an extensive study on the quality of tourism and hospitality education offered in China. In particular, the study examined the job performance of students who had graduated from tourism schools. Workplace supervisors were asked to evaluate some 1,000 tourism and hospitality graduates. These graduates were employed in travel services, hotels, tourism bureaus, and other tourism enterprises and organizations in six different cities and provinces in the country.

Table 6.3 summarizes the average work performance evaluation scores of the former students. The graduates were evaluated on three categories: political behavior (or attitude), professional development and skills, and physical fitness and stamina. The results show that the tourism and hospitality graduates are generally held in a positive light by their employers. The lowest scores, however, are in the areas of organizing ability and professional knowledge. This indicates that there are still some

TABLE 6.3. Job Performance of Tourism and Hospitality Graduates in Six Cities and Provinces[a]

	Beijing	Yunnan	Shanghai	Guangzhou	Xian	Gansu	Mean
Sample Size	390	108	180	172	198	66	
Physical Health	4.79	4.70	4.79	4.84	4.75	4.76	4.77
Political Behavior	4.22	4.35	4.22	4.21	4.09	3.95	4.17
Team Player	4.28	4.28	4.21	4.23	4.04	3.86	4.15
Foreign Language Ability	4.36	4.04	4.11	4.06	4.09	3.89	4.09
Communication Skills	4.32	4.06	4.13	4.02	4.00	3.83	4.06
Discipline	4.13	4.25	4.06	4.01	3.99	3.77	4.04
Professional Skills	4.14	4.00	4.07	4.01	3.90	3.79	3.99
Performance	4.16	4.09	4.03	4.00	3.84	3.68	3.97
Independence	4.16	4.04	3.99	3.95	3.85	3.82	3.97
Professional Knowledge	4.06	3.89	3.84	3.87	3.83	3.55	3.84
Organizational Ability	3.90	3.81	3.74	3.77	3.58	2.95	3.63
Three Major Categories							
Physical	95.79	94.07	95.89	96.86	95.05	76.36	92.34
Political	83.95	84.86	82.56	82.21	79.82	76.36	81.63
Professional	83.04	79.40	79.55	78.90	77.32	72.60	78.47
OVERALL SCORE	84.68	83.05	82.38	82.92	80.10	76.36	

[a]Each individual item is evaluated on a five-point scale with 5 being highly positive. The three category scores are evaluated on a 100-point scale with 100 being highly positive.
Source: Department of Personnel, Labor and Education, National Tourism Administration of the People's Republic of China, 1991.

educational areas in need of improvement. In addition, the evaluations of students in Gansu Province, which is the least visited region in the survey, were significantly lower.

Continuing Education Programs

The Yearbook of China Tourism Statistics recorded 1.7 million people employed in China's tourism industry at the end of 1991 (Sun 1992). The majority of these workers were transferred from other industries without adequate professional education and training. Therefore, one of the major tasks of Chinese tourism education is to enhance the professionalism of its work force through various forms of continuing education. At present, continuing education for tourism and hospitality employees in China continues to be given low priority because the nationwide demand for university education is so high that faculty at all levels have little time to teach students who are not enrolled full-time in their schools.

However, national and local governments have recently begun to develop continuing education training centers, including the Tianjin Tourism Training Center and the Jinling Hotel Training Center. These two continuing education schools are relatively large in size, and are intended mainly for training management personnel from hotels, travel agencies and tourism administrative bureaus. They also train teachers from tourism schools in newer techniques and technologies. These two training centers recruit students all over the country. Smaller continuing education training centers have been established in more than a dozen of other provinces for local training. In addition, post-secondary tourism and hospitality universities, colleges, and institutes have begun to offer continuing education classes for tourism and hospitality managers and employees.

Job Qualification Program

Most of the continuing education programs are centered around the Job Qualification Program, which serves as the main means of improving the in-service skill of managers and employees. This series of training programs is designed by the DPLE and provides two-month courses aimed at establishing basic skill and knowledge standards for workers in different aspects of tourism and hospitality. The programs are offered to all levels of management and employees, but are especially designed to provide professional skills and knowledge to workers with limited formal education. The training focuses on management and service procedures by using a uniform teaching plan, curriculum, and materials. A job qualification certificate is issued to those who pass the final examinations. By 1996, a job qualification certificate will be required for certain positions in the industry, under a policy recently introduced by the NTA. By 1992, hundreds of thousands of tourism and hospitality employees had taken the job qualification training. The quality of tourism and hospitality services in China has shown considerable improvement as a result. This has become the main measure for improving the professionalism of tourism and hospitality employees.

An example of one of the training programs offered under the DPLE's guidelines is the travel service management certification. The tour guide qualification examination is conducted to ensure that potential tour guides meet the qualification for this particular job position. The tour guide qualification program was initiated in 1989 and is now conducted on an annual basis at most training centers. Over 70,000 tour guides had taken the examination by the end of 1991. Of these, more than 30,000 passed the examinations and received tour guide certificates. Those who failed the examination are not permitted to work as tour guides. Additional job qualification programs are currently under development.

At a higher level of tourism administration, the National Seminar for Directors of Tourism Bureaus at provincial and municipal levels is conducted directly by DPLE staff. Started in 1987, this 20-day program is targeted at improving the professional quality of public tourism bureau directors at the provincial, municipal, and autonomous region levels. It provides a forum for exchanging experience and sharing information on international tourism development in order to improve the macro-management of the industry. Seminar speakers are both from China and abroad. By 1991, five such programs had been organized and 250 tourism directors were trained. This program has been well received by its participants.

Conclusions

Since 1978, Chinese tourism authorities have made great efforts in developing tourism and hospitality education programs. The demand for qualified managerial and service personnel, however, remains high. The DPLE has developed an integrated approach to tourism education, which includes both international advances in tourism and practical knowledge from China's tourism development experience. Academically, tourism and hospitality programs are found in a variety of different types of schools, from post-secondary tourism and hospitality departments in four-year higher education institutions, to two-year professional and high-school tourism programs, to continuing education training centers. These academic and professional education programs train both managers and service employees for the tourism and hospitality industry. Qualification certificate programs, such as the tour guide qualification program, enhance the service quality and skills. Starting from a base of no tourism and hospitality education of any kind prior to 1978, China has made remarkable advances. Today, China's well-trained and highly-skilled tourism and hospitality work force is able to increasingly compete at the globe level as they help to build China into the major tourist destination in Asia by the end of the century.

References

Jin, Hui, and Lawrence Yu 1990. Hospitality Education in China: Great Stride in the Land of the Great Wall. *Arizona Hospitality Trends* 4(3): 6-8.

Job Performance of Tourism and Hospitality Graduates in Six Cities and Provinces. 1991. Survey conducted by the Department of Personnel, Labor and Education of the National Tourism Administration of the People's Republic of China.

Sun, Gang, ed. 1992. *The Yearbook of China's Tourism Statistics.* Beijing: China Travel and Tourism Press.

Zhao, Jinlin. 1992. A Current Look at Hospitality and Tourism Education in China's Colleges and Universities. *International Journal of Hospitality Management* 10(4): 357-67.

PART THREE

Chinese Tourists

The essays in Part Three look at tourism in China from several perspectives, all of which have ethnic Chinese tourists as the central focus. These essays address topics on which very little has been written in the past, in part because domestic tourism is an even newer phenomenon in China than is international tourism. The first two essays review the recent development of the thriving domestic tourism industry in China today. Qiao Yuxia discusses the changing governmental policies on domestic tourism. She analyzes the inception and the characteristics of domestic tourism in China, and reveals the current political thought on domestic tourist flows and their socio-economic impact. Erdmann Gormsen examines the types of places that are popular for domestic tourists, and the environmental impacts that result from their popularity. With over one billion potential domestic tourists, China faces tourism management problems that are potentially overwhelming.

Ying Yang Peterson reveals some of the cultural background that drives Chinese domestic tourism in the third essay. She explains that due to the influence of historical and artistic images, Chinese view natural and historical attractions in a different light than do foreign tourists. She also argues that the Chinese perception colors the tourist product that is promoted to foreign tourists, and suggests that China needs to develop alternative forms of tourism to expand the potential market for tourism growth.

For statistical compilation, China's tourism authorities divide international travelers into three major categories: foreigners, overseas Chinese citizens of China, and compatriots. In the fourth essay, Alan Lew looks at the compatriot Chinese, as well as a fourth category that is not easily measured, but has a tremendous impact on tourism in China, the overseas ethnic Chinese. Few other developing countries have the resources that China has in its compatriots (residents of Hong Kong, Macao, and Taiwan) and overseas ethnic Chinese populations.

7

Domestic Tourism in China: Policies and Development

Qiao Yuxia[1]

Domestic tourism, as discussed in this essay, consists of leisure and business travel activities conducted by citizens within their own country. Domestic tourism inevitably grows in response to a country's economic development and rising living standards. Travel and tourism, as a socioeconomic behavior, is very closely related to advances in the economy and culture of a society. Like many other socio-cultural and economic activities, travel and tourism follows the law of self-development, moving from lower level development to higher level development and extending from domestic travel to international travel. Travel and tourism is a form of modern consumer behavior. The realization of one's desire to travel depends not only on discretionary money and leisure time, but also on many complex social and political factors, including the social stability of the destination.

In general, the world's developed nations, owing to the advanced development of their economies and scientific technology, have experienced high levels of tourism demand and supply. Tourist facilities and services have been expanded and developed around the world to meet the rising demand of travelers from developed countries. But, the unbalanced levels of economic growth among different countries have led to disparities in tourism development. In developing countries, the low level of economic livelihood restricts the development of a domestic tourism industry. This is true even in those countries with a strong international tourism sector.

Most of the people in the developing world are still struggling to make ends meet. Thus, leisure travel for them remains a distant dream.

To improve their national economy, the governments of many developing nations give priority in their strategic tourism planning to the development of international tourism, because it generates badly-needed hard currency. Only after the economy of a developing nation has been improved, as measured by increases in personal income and more leisure time, can the development of mass domestic tourism occur.

While inbound international tourism often precedes the expansion of domestic tourism in a developing country, the development of domestic tourism is a necessary foundation for the development of outbound international travel. For the domestic market, outbound international tourism is an extension of domestic tourism. The governments of the developing nations, therefore, should adopt policies and measures to coordinate and integrate the development of domestic tourism with inbound and outbound international travel. Only by coordinating and balancing the development of all aspects of domestic and international tourism can a country's travel and tourism industry experience the greatest success and prosperity. One example of this in China is the use of older international hotels to serve the newly developing domestic market, while newer and more expensive international hotels are designated for the international market.

Domestic Tourism Development in China

Modern tourism in China began in the 1920s. The first travel agencies were established in Shanghai in 1923 (Yang and Jiang 1983: 9). These early travel agencies handled both domestic travel and outbound travel for Chinese citizens to visit foreign countries. Travel services for transportation, lodging and meals were also provided for inbound foreign travelers. But this burgeoning tourism industry was short-lived due to political upheavals and continuous warfare in the country.

After the founding of the People's Republic of China (PRC) in 1949, the Overseas Travel Service (the predecessor of today's China Travel Service) and the China International Travel Service (CITS) were set up to service overseas ethnic Chinese who came back to visit their relatives, as well as foreign travelers, primarily coming from socialist countries. In 1978, China adopted an open-door policy for the country's economic reform. As a result, the travel industry changed from a political propaganda machine to a foreign currency generator. The travel and tourism industry also became a vehicle for overseas visitors to conduct commercial, scientific, technological, and cultural exchanges.

However, when China first opened its door to the outside world, the tourism industry could not meet the demands of overseas tourists, particularly the demands for lodging, transportation, and communication. To alleviate the problems of infrastructure and superstructure development, the Chinese government gave special priority to the development of international tourism in the 1980s. The government policy for domestic tourism development during this time period was to "take the local situations into consideration and develop a positive and steady domestic tourism" (Ma and Sun 1993, vol.3: 2025). In other words, while it was not a high priority, domestic tourism would not be discouraged, and would be addressed as needed on a case by case basis.

In the 1990s, a major increase in the development of China's service industry occurred, driven by a tremendous growth in the country's economy.[2] This was particularly pronounced after the Chinese Communist Party's (CCP) Congress in 1992 when it was declared that China would establish a market economy within the broad tenets of socialism (Liu 1993). As a result of this policy, China's economy grew an amazing 12.8 percent in 1992 and recorded a phenomenal 13.9 percent increase in the first half of 1993 alone. The International Monetary Fund now rates China's GNP third in the world after the United States and Japan. The booming economy has translated into increased personal income. The structure of consumer spending has changed considerably and travel has rapidly become an important leisure activity pursued by many Chinese. In addition, the government has now begun to discuss the issue of developing the domestic tourism industry in China because the travel infrastructure and superstructure were finally considered adequate after a decade of development.

The coastal regions and major metropolitan areas were first to experience mass domestic tourism. Table 7.1 illustrates the total number of domestic tourists and expenditures in China from 1984 to 1992. At present, domestic travel and tourism in China has the following characteristics:

1. Highly diversified market segments. The major market segments include: urban residents and wealthy farmers in and around the major metropolitan areas and coastal towns; incentive tours for employees offered by their companies; resort vacations arranged by various organizations and associations; public holidays and annual leave vacations for employees; summer and winter break vacation travel by college and high school students; and leisure travel by retired people.
2. The principal tourist generating markets are concentrated in the coastal regions and large metropolitan areas. There are very low levels of participation among residents in the less developed interior of the country.

3. Per capita domestic tourist expenditures are low. The average per person/trip expenditure for domestic tourist between 1985 and 1992 was only RMB¥58. This amount, however, is expected to grow dramatically in the coming years.
4. Operationally, all-inclusive package tours are not popular among domestic tourists, except when organized by their work unit. The majority of Chinese domestic tourists travel independently.

TABLE 7.1   China's Domestic Tourist Trips and Expenditures, 1984-1993

Year	Trips (million)	Change (%)	Expenditures (billion RMB¥)	Change (%)
1984	200	-	-	-
1985	240	20.0	8.0	-
1986	270	12.5	10.6	32.5
1987	290	7.4	14.0	32.1
1988	300	3.4	18.7	33.6
1989	240	-20.0	15.0	-19.8
1990	280	16.7	17.0	13.3
1991	300	7.1	20.0	17.6
1992	330	10.0	25.0	25.0
1993[a]	360	9.0	50.0	100.0

[a]1993 is an estimate
Source: National Tourism Administration for the People's Republic of China, 1993.

Due to the uneven distribution of economic growth and wealth in China, these characteristics will probably continue for some time. The expected economic growth and expansion of China's socialistic market economy in coming years has led the National Tourism Administration (NTA) to forecast 360 million domestic tourists and RMB¥50 billion in tourist receipts for 1993 (*China Tourism News* 1992).

Economic and Socio-cultural Impacts

The rapid development of China's domestic tourism industry has had a great impact on the nation's overall economic development and on the cultural life of the Chinese people. Summarizing the development experience of China's domestic tourism industry over the past few years, one can identify five important economic and socio-cultural impacts.

1. The development of the domestic tourism industry creates employment opportunities. Registered travel agencies which serve domestic tourists numbered 1,400 by the end of 1992 (*Travel and Tourism Investigation and Research* 1993). This was an increase of over 85 percent from the 750 registered travel agencies in the previous year. These domestic travel agencies generate many direct and indirect jobs, particularly in the most-visited tourist destination areas. The creation of these service-related jobs contributes to higher personal income and a more stable society.

2. The tourism industry is highly fragmented. The development of China's domestic tourism industry has impacts on a variety of services, including food services, lodging accommodations, transportation, telecommunication, and shopping facilities. Like the growth in the number of travel agencies, these companies create new jobs and contribute to a more stable society.

3. The Chinese government considers the development of the domestic tourism industry as a very important means of withdrawing currency from circulation. It was estimated that RMB¥130 billion non-commodity currency was withdrawn from circulation as result of domestic tourism development from 1985 to 1992 (*China Tourism News* 1992). It is forecast that RMB¥50 billion will be withdrawn from circulation because of domestic tourism spending in 1995 and RMB¥120 billion in the year 2000. This helps to alleviate China's excess money supply, which has been a major cause for high rates of inflation in the early 1990s.

4. China's domestic tourism industry promotes the development of local cottage industries that produce handicrafts and tourist souvenirs. Facing an increase in domestic tourist demand, many enterprises have begun to produce travel products and souvenirs with local materials and local cultural motifs. The production of travel merchandise and souvenirs can thus increase a company's profits and create more jobs.

5. With 56 ethnic nationalities, China has a great diversity of cultural traditions. Domestic travel has the potential to strengthen local cultural traditions and better cultural understanding among people in different parts of the country.

Domestic Tourism Development Measures

The importance of developing China's domestic tourism industry has recently drawn great attention from the government and various sectors of the service industry. Many regions and cities have formulated strategic plans for promoting domestic tourism as a leading sector of China's emerging service industry, such as Tonglu County of Zhejiang Province, and the cities of Dunhuang in Gansu Province, and Chengde in Hebei Province. To ensure the successful development of China's domestic tourism and better serve tourist needs, four development measures are proposed.

Proposal One. The NTA classifies travel agencies in China as First, Second, and Third Category Travel Agencies. Third Category Agencies cater only to domestic tourists and have been rapidly increasing in number, while the other two categories, which cater to international visitors, have been declining (Sun 1992: 93). It is, therefore, vital that Third Category Travel Agencies be systematically organized and managed. Despite their large number (1,400 in 1992), both their quantity and their service quality have still been unable to meet the needs of the rapidly growing domestic travel market. To meet this service challenge, domestic travel agencies must improve service quality and treat domestic tourists with greater consideration. Qualified tour guides need to be trained for the domestic market and more service products and tour itineraries should be introduced.

In management, domestic travel agencies should pursue the separation of political intervention from daily management operations. Each domestic travel agency should have an independent accounting system and be held liable for any business losses. They should also be given management autonomy from the local political system and be allowed to compete openly in domestic travel markets.

Proposal Two. More tourism facilities need to be developed for domestic travelers. At present, domestic tourism is restricted by transportation system limitations. Railway development has been singled out by the government as the principal means of improving China's transportation network, but it will take time to build a sufficient national railway system. In the mean time, domestic tourists are encouraged to take a variety of different modes of transportation for their travel.

Special attention should be paid to the fragmented nature of the tourism infrastructure and superstructure. Different levels of tourist facilities need to be developed, including tourist products for the luxury market, the midscale market, and the budget market. The domestic travel industry needs to constantly improve tourist products and coordinate the development of transportation, restaurants, lodging, sightseeing, entertainment, and shopping activities. Capital investment will be needed to build tourist facilities. The sources for such investment should come from a concerted effort by the national government, local governments, foreign investors, Chinese collective enterprises, and even private Chinese investors.

Proposal Three. There is an urgent need for the formulation of an "industry code of conduct" to protect the interests of both the tourism industry and consumers. The domestic travel industry involves many governmental agencies and economic sectors each of which has its special interest in developing tourism. Disagreements may occur over development issues due to conflicts of interest. In addition, during periods of rapid growth in demand, consumers may not always be treated fairly by unscrupulous business people. An industry code of conduct could help to alleviate these problems.

Proposal Four. The government should strengthen measures to guide the steady growth of domestic tourism. China has a huge population and is endowed with a rich diversity of tourism resources. In the rush to expand the country's service industry, many government agencies, government businesses, and private businesses have been enthusiastic in their efforts to develop domestic tourism. However, the country's overloaded transportation system and overcrowded destinations cannot continue to endure the current explosion of mass domestic tourism. Rapid development requires government regulations and coordination. Based on general planning principles, with flexibility for local situations, the national government's tourism authorities should suggest guidelines for the domestic tourism industry. In the near term, it may be necessary to intervene administratively to correct poorly planned and constructed development projects.

Future Prospects

It is of paramount importance that government tourism authorities and travel business operators fully research and understand the domestic tourism market. By doing this they will be able to formulate effective strategic plans and apply efficient management practices. China's domestic tourism market has exploded into its initial stage in the development cycle. Some management and operational practices are still fettered by the centrally planned economy and traditional ideas of China under earlier communist leaders. As the country shifts from a totally planned economy to a socialist market economy, the development of the domestic travel market deserves detailed analysis.

China's domestic tourism market has tremendous potential for future development. There were 330 million domestic tourists in China in 1992, and 360 million people are forecast to travel domestically in 1993. This volume of travel has significant impacts on China's economy and culture. The phenomenal expansion of the Chinese economy will spur the domestic travel market to continue to grow dramatically in the near future. At present, the development of domestic tourism services should be focused on the economically advanced coastal regions and major metropolitan areas. For instance, the Pearl River Delta in Guangdong Province is the largest generator of domestic tourists. This region is adjacent to Hong Kong and Macao and experienced greater exposure to the outside world than the rest of China. Residents of this region have higher personal incomes and have come to enjoy travel as a modern way of life. The residents of the three municipalities of Shanghai, Beijing, and Tianjin also have higher incomes and are more educated than much of China. They, too, have expressed a strong interest in travel to other parts of the country. In China's interior, some newly rich residents of smaller cities and wealthy farmers in rural areas will likely be the next major domestic tourism market.

As far as the demand for travel services is concerned, most luxury travel is still out of the reach of domestic tourists (although this too is gradually changing). Midscale and budget travel will continue to be the mainstay of China's domestic tourism industry. Consequently, there is a great need for midscale and budget level lodging accommodations in China.

The supply and demand equilibrium of China's domestic travel industry is at present unbalanced, with demand far exceeding supply. Domestic travel services in Shanghai, Guangzhou, Beijing, Hangzhou, Chengdu, and Xian have been improved the most in recent years. Travel agencies in these cities offer tours and other services that are sufficient to meet current tourist demand. In these cities, the travel supply and demand equilibrium tilts in favor of the tourist. But, the tourist is disadvantaged in the rest of the country, where service providers benefit from a lack of competition. This situation will change as the country shifts to a more market economy. Travel service operators will need to rid themselves of non-market practices used under the communist planned economy and design travel products centering around the needs and wants of tourists. This requires careful forecasting and analysis of the domestic tourist market and adjustments in management strategies and service orientations to satisfy different levels of domestic tourist demand.

To be successful in a competitive market economy, domestic travel services should design their travel products to suit tourist needs and market these products aggressively. In doing this, new travel products and promotions should consider the following.

1. Sightseeing tours will be the primary tour product for the domestic tourist market. China is renowned for its rich and diverse physical resources and cultural heritage. These are also the major attractions for domestic tourists. Of the 1.1 billion Chinese population, 900 million are rural farmers. Many of them have never taken a leisure trip outside of their home county. Once they have the financial means

to travel, they will go to see the ancient capital cities of China and other sites of its 5000-year-old civilization. On the other hand, urban dwellers want to go back to nature and visit areas with fascinating physical landscapes and bucolic rural scenes. Sightseeing tours to meet these varied interests should provide tourists with both an educational and cultural learning experience.

2. Domestic travel agencies should design short distance tour products. Based on local conditions, short regional tours appeal to many tourists who cannot travel long distance because of time or money. These short distance tours can satisfy many domestic travel needs and also reduce the heavy burden on the transportation system for long-haul domestic travel.

3. Special interest and special events travel should be developed by domestic travel services. More than 100 special travel festivals and activities were held in various places in the country in 1992 (*China Tourism News* 1992). Those large-scale festivals and events were well received by domestic tourists because of their appealing content and participatory nature. Many of these one-time events could be developed into annual tourist activities.

4. Regional cooperation in tourism development needs to be strengthened. Regional cooperation can help to avoid redundancy in the creation of tourist attractions and the copying another region's cultural characteristics. Travel service operators should avoid a self-centered development approach in which they try to build everything within their own territory. They should apply the law of the market economy to guide the development of their tourism industry and allow each region to capitalize on its intrinsic strengths.

5. As the domestic tourism industry matures, competition will become increasingly intense. Marketing and promotion will be key operating factors in managing a successful domestic travel service. Marketing should promote the nature, content, service, and value of travel products to potential consumers. Effective marketing strategies can enhance a travel product's popularity and persuade potential consumers into becoming traveling tourists. If a tourist's pre-tour expectations match the actual travel experience, they will feel satisfied and tell their families and friends about their experience, thereby providing word of mouth publicity.

In conclusion, China has great potential for the development of its domestic tourism industry. As the tourism development experience of other countries has shown, there is a close, positive correlation between increased personal income and increased travel activities. As one of the most rapidly growing economies in the world in the 1990s, China is now experiencing the initial stage of the domestic tourism development cycle. The demand for travel related products and services will increase dramatically in the near future.

As China's economy shifts to a more market system, the domestic travel industry will face increasing challenges in a more highly competitive environment. This will require domestic travel services to constantly study their market conditions, design travel products according to the needs and wants of tourists, and sell their travel products effectively to potential markets. A successful domestic tourism industry in China relies on two levels of coordination and operation. National and provincial governments need to monitor regional trends in domestic travel patterns and develop measures for guiding domestic travel growth. At the individual business level, domestic travel services need to implement systematic management practices and operations. China can only develop a successful domestic tourism industry if there is a well-coordinated effort between the government and the private travel industry.

Notes

1. Translated from the Chinese version by Lawrence Yu and Alan A. Lew.

2. In 1990, China's gross national product reached RMB¥1,769 billion, 3.9 times more than that of 1978 (RMB¥359 billion). After inflation, the actual growth was 1.74 times, showing an average annual growth of 8.8 percent. Nationwide, personal income increased at an average annual rate of 6.7 percent from 1952 to 1990 (Ma and Sun 1993, vol.1: 9).

References

China Tourism News (Zhongguo Luyoubao). 1992. December 1, p. 1.

Liu, Phillip. 1993. Mixed Diagnosis for Mainland Fever. *Free China Review* 43(9): 42-7.

Sun, Gang, ed. 1992. *The Yearbook of China Tourism Statistics 1992*. Beijing: Travel and Tourism Press.

Ma, Hong, and Sun Shangqing, eds. 1993. *Modern Chinese Economic Dictionary* (Xiandai Zhongguo Jingji Dacidian). Beijing: China Finance and Economics Press.

Travel and Tourism Investigation and Research (Luyou Diaoyan). 1993. Vol. 2: 27.

Yang Shijin, and Jiang Xinmao. 1983. *Introduction to Travel and Tourism* (Luyou Gailun). Beijing: China Travel and Tourism Press.

8

Travel Behavior and the Impacts of Domestic Tourism in China

Erdmann Gormsen

The number of international tourists to the People's Republic of China (PRC), while impressive in comparison to other Asian destinations, is modest in comparison with the approximately 300 million domestic tourists estimated by the National Tourism Administration (NTA) to have toured the country in 1991. This figure is in line with the author's observations, because not only are all means of transportation overcrowded, but the masses of tourists also squeeze themselves into museums, parks, historical sights, and scenic points throughout the country.[1] In addition, all forms of public transport have experienced rapid growth rates, due in part to the fact that private, long distance automobile trips are still rare in China.

Unfortunately, numbers for domestic tourism are not available for subregions within the country. Since 1985, domestic tourism has grown at approximately the same rate as international tourism, including a substantial decrease in the politically disruptive year of 1989 (See Table 7.1 in chapter 7). In financial terms, the increase in domestic tourism appears even more significant. Per capita domestic expenditures have consistently grown faster than international tourist expenditures (although exchange rate fluctuations, and the difference in buying power between Foreign Exchange Certificates (FEC¥) and local Renminbi Yuan (RMB¥) currency, should be taken into account.)

These figures reflect an enormous increase in the desire and ability of China's citizens to travel, and is a direct consequence of the PRC government's economic policies, including the development of international tourism. Country-wide investigations into domestic travel behavior have not been carried out, but some reasons for the rapid increase in domestic tourists may be enumerated from other sources (cited in Krieg 1993). As in most other societies, holidays and leisure travel were initially the privilege of the upper-classes. The upper-classes spent the hot season at summer residences in Chengde or, in more recent times, at the beach of Beidaihe. After the communist victory in 1949, Beidaihe became a popular destination for Communist Party functionaries and government officials. In pre-communist times, leisure travel for the common people consisted primarily of pilgrimages to Buddhist or Taoist temples. This was due to a lack of time and money, as well as strict government control over internal migration. Under the communist government of the PRC, leisure travel, until recently, has existed almost entirely in the form of organized events, including political indoctrination, scientific conferences, and group holidays for work units (i.e., government businesses and public agencies). This kind of travel still accounts for a significant part of the domestic tourism, especially to the most popular destinations.

It has been only since the socio-economic policies of Deng Xiaoping were introduced in 1978 that transformations in domestic tourism have taken place. These new policies, in particular, established designated vacation days for all workers and civil servants. Such vacation days can last up to two weeks if one accumulates additional vacation time by working overtime on Sundays. A large part of this new free time is used for hometown family visits during the Chinese New Year (which is based on the lunar calendar and typically takes place in February). During this time trains and buses are overcrowded, but few hotels are used. Besides Chinese New Year, there are other special holidays and events (such as a honeymoon or recognition for special achievements) that may warrant vacation leave. Trips made by university students and teachers during the summer holidays should not be underestimated. It is surprising how they manage to pay for lengthy summer journeys with their meager stipends and salaries. They can do this, in part, because the low cost of basic housing and foodstuffs in most of China provide surplus buying power that can be used for traveling. Increasing incomes, which enable more travel, have also resulted from the privatization of agriculture, handicraft industries, and service trades. In these areas there are already an estimated four million small-employers with some 100 million employees (*Frankfurter Allgemeine Zeitung* 1992).

Domestic Travel Destinations

At a 1987 national tourism conference in Tianjin, the importance of domestic tourism was emphasized and its further development was recommended (Gerstlacher, et al. 1991: 55). One reason cited for the lack of research and planning for domestic tourism in China is that the PRC government does not consider domestic tourism a contributor to the country's foreign exchange earnings. The role of domestic tourism in regional development, therefore, is overlooked. Tourism officials in Xian and Hangzhou estimate that there are at least twenty times as many domestic tourists as foreign visitors, and some provincial governments are already quite conscious of the importance of domestic tourism. In destinations that are less frequented by foreign visitors, this ratio is easily several hundred to one. In September, 1988 a large folklore festival was held in Kunming to promote the attractiveness of Yunnan. Besides foreign guests, more than 40,000 Chinese visitors filled the streets of the parade route for several hours to see the dress, music, and dance of the 24 national minorities in this province.

Estimates of regional domestic tourism patterns can be determined only through direct consultation with local authorities. While domestic tourists clearly outnumber international visitors in almost every destination in China, there are still considerable variations in visitation rates due to the tourism resources that each place has to offer.

The small, but well preserved town of Dali, on Erhai Lake in the highland of Yunnan, is known for its pleasant climate and has been a "secret tip" for backpack tourists since its official opening in May of 1984 (Hemberger 1990). Its most important tourism resource exists in the living culture of the Bai minority. Especially attractive are their rural settlements with artfully arranged courtyard houses, and the colorful everyday dresses of the Bai women. Along with the area's well-known marble products, these dresses, made of indigo batik and displaying fine embroidery, are popular souvenirs and a valuable source of income for the Bai people. In the years between 1984 to 1988, foreign arrivals here rose from 2,500 to 13,000. In the same period, compatriot visits (from Hong Kong and Macao) rose from 500 to 2,000 and domestic tourist visits increased from 22,000 to 45,000. Many domestic visitors were business people or conference participants. While the share of international tourists (foreign and compatriot) increased from 12 to 25 percent, their actual significance was even higher because they comprised 44,000 (36 percent) of the 121,000 overnight stays in 1988. In addition, foreign visitors must spend more per capita to stay in even a remote location such as Dali than do domestic holiday makers.

In contrast to Dali, which because of its remoteness and independent culture gives rise to comparably low interest among the majority Han Chinese, domestic tourism dominates almost completely in the 1,800 meter high mountains of Huang Shan (Anhui Province) (Tables 8.1 and 8.2). The most recent data on domestic visitors to Huang Shan is for 1987, when out of 1.6 million visitors only 15,144 (0.9 percent) came from foreign countries (Wagner 1990). More recently the number of foreign visitors has increased to 29,577 (1991), of which 57 percent are from Japan (YEARBOOK 1992). An additional 91,787 visitors in 1991 were compatriots. The attraction of Huang Shan is related to its amazing landscape of bizarre granite rocks, pines, and always changing clouds, as well as being a traditional place of Buddhist pilgrimage. Anhui's provincial government would, understandably, like to promote tourism and has invested considerable sums in the construction and repair of roads, a cable railway, and several hotels. The number of beds for foreigners increased from 1,506 to 6,636 between 1985 and 1990. In addition, there are many accommodation possibilities in hostels or private guest houses.

This remote, undeveloped rural area has had a long history of population outmigration due to a lack of economic opportunities. However, within the last few years it has experienced an enormous economic boom based largely on domestic tourism. Residents are participating in this, not only as employees in the predominantly state-owned hotels, but also by offering

TABLE 8.1 Accommodation Arrivals in Huang Shan, 1956-1987

Year	Domestic Arrivals	International Arrivals
1956	1,740	4
1960	8,941	8
1964	47,540	38
1968	27,140	-
1972	59,263	34
1976	190,645	42
1980	427,879	7,958
1984	1,183,570	16,416
1987	1,619,000	15,144

Sources: Wagner 1990; *Yearbook of China Tourism Statistics* 1992.

TABLE 8.2 Nationality of Tourists to Huang Shan, 1984 and 1991

Nationality	1984	%	1991	%
Total International	16,416	1.4	121,364	-
of which				
Compatriots[a]	11,986	73.1	91,787	75.6
Japan	1,215	7.4	16,786	13.8
USA	1,024	6.2	1,553	1.3
Singapore	572	3.5	1,843	1.5
Germany	334	2.0	331	0.3

[a] from Hong Kong, Macao, and Taiwan
Sources: Wagner 1990; *The Yearbook of China Tourism Statistics* 1992.

private accommodations and restaurants, and selling souvenirs and various other services. In 1988 there were, in the central part of this mountain region, 729 small-employers with 1,266 employees (Wagner 1990). These developments have resulted in a return migration of younger residents.

The environmental consequences of the mass tourism on the spatially limited summit/plateau of Huang Shan have been significant. The summit, which will be made even more narrow through planned hotel construction, must cope with more than 10,000 visitors on peak days. In 1984 the cable railway was not yet in existence, yet on May 1 more than 12,000 people climbed the mountain by way of kilometer long series of steps and stairways cut into the granite rock. Many of them had spent the night under the stars in order not to miss the sunrise. This natural spectacle is welcomed with loud cheers from the crowd of Chinese who cram themselves together in narrow open spaces. Together, they enthusiastically celebrate the birth of a new day. Like most Chinese holidays, it is a social event. In this respect the Chinese show a definite difference from the behavior of Western tourists, who tend to observe the sensation of scenic landscape individually.

In a similar way, masses of recreationists pack themselves on the beaches of China's large seaside resorts, such as Beidaihe. This impression is intensified by the fact that most Chinese cannot swim and therefore float around on air mattresses in shallow water. The rental of floating devises can be a very profitable business. Only well-protected bays are used whereas wide coastal areas, even in the surroundings of the seaside resorts, are almost undeveloped. Since its founding by an imperial edict in 1898, Beidaihe has been the most important holiday resort for prominent politicians and business people in Beijing, with which it is connected by several daily trains. In recent decades, it has been steadily expanded and finally supplemented by its southern neighbor, Nandaihe. Apart from several modern hotels, most accommodations are of medium quality and are owned by companies and government authorities who use them as holiday quarters for their employees. Many private guest houses for the ever-increasing number of individual Chinese travelers also exist.

According to estimates by the Beidaihe Statistical Bureau, the yearly arrivals of domestic tourists since 1984 were approximately four to six million, of which only 2,400 to 3,500 were international tourists (although a low of only 1,000 foreign visitors was recorded in 1989.) Apart from business travelers, these are mostly people who work for extended periods of time in Beijing and spend a few days vacationing on the coast. This pattern is also true for the other seaside resorts, including Dalian, Xiamen (Amoy), and Qingdao (the formerly German settlement, known for its *Tsingtao Beer*). All these places were founded by foreign traders in the 19th century at important harbors and have since been developed into modern resorts for the domestic Chinese population.

Large hotel complexes on the beaches of tropical Hainan Island are under construction as an important new resort, especially for the winter season. However, competition with established seaside resorts in Thailand, Indonesia, and the Philippines will probably limit foreign visitors to Hainan. It is, therefore, expected that compatriots from Hong Kong will predominate, as they already do in Haikou, the capital of Hainan Province. In 1991, 83 percent of the 118,107 recorded hotel arrivals in Haikou, and 86 percent of the 56,436 hotel arrivals at the main resort town of Sanya, were from Hong Kong. Visitors from Japan and Singapore are the only foreign visitors worth mentioning on Hainan, with 3 to 4 percent each. A considerable amount of the investment in Hainan comes from Hong Kong, along with direct flight connections that were established in 1988.

Contrary to the seaside resorts, Chinese cities that exhibit more of their traditional culture have many more international visitors. However, even here international visitors seldom reach even 10 percent of the number of domestic tourists. In Suzhou, the share of international tourists has increased from 1.1 percent (1978) to 5.2 percent (1990) due to a strong increase in foreign package holidays and a stagnation in domestic Chinese arrivals, which, nevertheless, has consistently been around five million in recent years (Table 8.3). These numbers are for overnight visitors. Day visitations by domestic tourists are probably considerable given the densely populated region of Shanghai-Jiangsu, where Suzhou is located.

Guilin (Guangxi Province) offers an interesting comparison to Suzhou (Table 8.3). Guilin is famous for its majestic towers of karst limestone peaks that have inspired Chinese landscape paintings for centuries. It shows a certain parallel with Suzhou in its growth rate in international arrivals, although in absolute numbers it receives over twice as many foreign visitors. The index values of domestic Chinese visitors, on the other hand, show a sharp rise in Guilin since 1978. A major factor responsible for this is the lower base value in the beginning year (1978) when access to the remote Guilin area was difficult for most domestic Chinese. Even today, the only easy access to Guilin is by air. An additional factor has been the effort of Guilin's tourism authorities to attract more domestic travel meetings in order to use their over built hotel capacity more efficiently. Consequently, while the total number of passengers on the popular Lijiang (Li River) day cruises has grown (Table 8.3), only 11 to 19 percent of the domestic Chinese to Guilin take this trip. The reason for this low participation rate is probably due to the high cost of the cruise or a lack of time. Instead, they are likely to visit the karst mountains and limestone caves within the city area that have been prepared for tourists to climb and explore. By comparison more than 80 percent of international visitors participate in the river trips.

TABLE 8.3 Tourism in Suzhou and Guilin

	Tourist Arrivals: Suzhou					Tourist Arrivals: Guilin					Lijiang River Cruise			
	International			Domestic		International			Domestic		International		Domestic	
	(1000)	%[a]	I[b]	(mn[c])	I	(1000)	%	I	(mn)	I	(1000)	I	(1000)	I
1978	27.7	1.1	15	2.5	39	48.2	4.6	14	1.0	22				
1979	50.2	1.4	28	3.7	58	87.2	5.7	26	1.5	33	30.5	9	134.5	18
1980	83.7	1.8	46	4.7	75	110.4	5.8	33	1.8	39	49.8	15	141.7	19
1981	110.9	2.4	61	4.6	73	147.3	5.8	44	2.4	52	151.4	46	256.5	34
1982	115.8	2.2	64	5.2	83	181.0	5.7	54	3.0	65	154.8	47	332.5	44
1983	130.4	2.6	72	4.9	79	200.6	5.9	60	3.2	70	166.0	51	383.3	51
1984	151.2	2.4	83	6.0	96	282.1	6.9	84	3.8	83	245.6	75	546.0	72
1985	181.8	2.8	100	6.3	100	336.4	6.8	100	4.6	100	327.7	100	754.8	100
1986	191.8	2.7	106	7.0	112	361.7	6.7	108	5.0	109	369.1	113	828.3	110
1987	186.4	3.3	103	6.5	105	455.1	7.8	135	5.4	117	422.6	129	1,019.9	135
1988	254.8	4.9	140	5.8	93	479.4	7.1	142	6.3	137	471.8	144	926.5	123
1989	159.5	3.9	88	4.8	77	306.6	5.8	91	5.0	109	330.5	101	760.2	101
1990	261.6	4.5	144	5.5	87	484.9	6.9	144	6.5	141	536.3	164	911.0	121
1991	227.7	4.5	125	5.1	81	429.1	5.9	128	6.8	148	488.1	149	1,135.6	150

[a]% Share of total arrivals
[b]I = Index (1985 = 100)
[c]mn = million (1,000,000)

Sources: Economic Research Center and Tourism Administration, Guilin; Statistics Bureau Suzhou, 1986, 1991 and 1992; Fieldwork with Xu Gang; Information of Garden Management Bureau, Suzhou, 1991.

Environmental Impacts

The most popular, and therefore most visited areas of China are all experiencing considerable degradation in environmental quality, which can be a hindrance to the further development of the country's tourism. Mass domestic tourism, in particular, leads to varied ecological distortions in the sensitive landscape budget. A serious lack of environmental awareness prevails among the large number of domestic Chinese visitors to classical gardens and other excursion sites (Li 1993). Much educational work will be necessary to create a better understanding of the complex ecological relationships that exist in these areas.

This is especially true for popular natural landscapes, including Guilin, the Changjiang (Yangtze River) Gorges, the Stone Forest near Kunming, and the various "holy mountains" of China. Huang Shan's cable cars attract many more domestic visitors than before they were built, making the crowded conditions of the past even worse today. The negative consequences for the environment on the narrow summit plateaus are obvious. While questionable state tourism projects are debated, even in the Chinese media, this seldom results in significant changes. For example, much criticism was directed against the construction of a cable railway on the Great Wall near Badaling because the crowds on the Wall there were already unpleasantly high (*China Daily* August, 1990). Despite this, construction of the cable car was completed in 1992. In addition, the alternate destination for the Great Wall near Mutianyu is already serviced by a cable railway (*Beijing Rundschau* 1992, 46: 29). Thus, domestic tourism is contributing, through the masses of people, to a critical environmental situation, while simultaneously providing an important economic boost for underdeveloped areas.

Conclusions

This analysis of the behavior of domestic Chinese tourists shows important differences in comparison to international tourists. For both groups, the most visited places include Beijing (and the Great Wall), Xian (and the ceramic army archeological site), and a few other outstanding places of the traditional Chinese culture. Domestic tourists, both local and regional, are more likely to predominate at Chinese traditional gardens, which are widely distributed in their original and carefully copied forms. Many monasteries have recently been renovated and are now major destinations for domestic tourists, as well as religious pilgrims. Understandably, only especially striking destinations are included in the programs of international tours, whereby the wealthy foreigner's access to airplanes and comfortable buses plays a decisive role. In many places, the initiation of tourism development took place with a specific orientation toward international tourism. However, today most of the visitors in every Chinese city come from China itself, and this often leads to an unbearable overburdening of facilities.

In contrast to this, the cultural and natural landscape peculiarities of the peripheral regions are strong attractions for foreign tourists. That domestic Chinese have less interest in these areas is not so much due to their remote location, but to a distinct belief in the superiority of Han Chinese culture. This is strengthened through the fact that for decades Han Chinese have lived and worked in the nominally autonomous regions as leading officials, civil servants, and professors at the universities. This has resulted in the mistrust of Han Chinese among the local population. Even the small number of foreign tourists that some of these areas receive contribute significantly to economic and societal changes.

Domestic tourism in China is a vast and complex force that is already taking on the appearance of being out of control. As with everything in China, the tremendous population base of 1.1 billion people makes all efforts at planning and development an awesome task. As the successes of China's economic development spread, so will the number of domestic tourists, and so will the enormous pressure they put on tourist destinations throughout the country.

Notes

1. Much of the information contained in this chapter comes from the author's personal observations and communications which he collected during six prolonged journeys to China between 1987 and 1993, as well as from a major research project on tourism in China that he is conducting with Martin Hübner, M.A. and Xu Gang, M.S., supported by the Volkswagen Foundation.

Please refer to Chapter 4, "International Tourism in China," for a detailed discussion of the accommodation and transportation sectors in China as they relate to both international and domestic tourism.

References

Beijing Rundschau (weekly review). Beijing.
Das neue China (quarterly review). Dortmund, Germany: Montania Verlag.
Gerstlacher, Anna; Renate Krieg; and Eva Sternfeld. 1991. *Tourism in the People's Republic of China.* Bangkok: Ecumenical Coalition on Third World Tourism.
Hemberger, Ralf. 1990. Tourismus in Dali. *Inst. für Tourismus, FU Berlin, Berichte und Materialen* 8: 169-77.

Krieg, Renate. 1993. Kommerzieller Tourismus in der VR China, Entwicklung mit Hindernissen. *Das neue China* 20(1): 10-4.

Li, Yuan. 1993. Massentourismus und Umwelt. *Das neue China* 20(1): 20-1.

Wagner, Susanne. 1990. Fremdenverkehr in den Bergen von Huang Shan. *Inst. für Tourismus, FU Berlin, Berichte und Materialen* 8: 157-68

The Yearbook of China Tourism Statistics (annual). Beijing: China Travel and Tourism Press.

9

The Chinese Landscape as a Tourist Attraction: Image and Reality

Ying Yang Petersen[1]

For many foreign visitors to China, the images that bring them to the East and the reality of their experience of the Chinese landscape seem unrelated. For thousands of years, the Chinese people have created their landscapes in relative isolation from the rest of the world. Between 1600 and 1800, when Grand Tour tourists were criss-crossing Europe, China was under its last empire, the Qing Dynasty, and its doors were closed to the world. In this century, improved transportation has broken many of the barriers between China and the Western world. However, conflicts between communism and capitalism continued to keep China out of the tourism limelight. Until 1978, few Westerners had traveled to China, while most Chinese citizens were forbidden to travel abroad. In 1978, with the establishment of an "open door" policy to promote economic reform, China began to embrace foreign tourists from the Western world.

The importance of the Chinese landscape in China's efforts to promote international tourism was recognized from the beginning. However, it was not supported by relevant research on the landscape itself. Instead, the economic aspects of tourism were emphasized, as a strategy to "accumulate funds for the Four Modernizations" (in industry, agriculture, science and technology, and national defense.) Tourism was initiated, structured, and conducted solely as an economic phenomenon. The Chinese government emphasized tourism as a clean and "smoke free industry." This perspective was understandable as the annual foreign currency gained directly from international tourism to China increased from US$262.90 million in 1978 to US$2,246.83 million in 1988.

This optimistic situation might have continued if it were not for the political unrest that occurred in 1989. On June 4 of that year, millions of people throughout the world were shocked to see Chinese tanks smash student demonstrations on Tiananmen Square. Immediately, the number of international tourists to China dropped from 32 million in 1988 to 24 million, while many deluxe hotels achieved only a 20 percent occupancy rate (Kristof 1991).

Several years after the crackdown, Chinese tourism is increasing through improved services, prices, and management. However, it is also true that the damaged human rights image of China poses a continuing challenge for Chinese tourism. Promoting the Chinese landscape allows China to emphasize apolitical aspects of its tourist attractions. Yet past neglect and a poor understanding of differences between Chinese and Western perceptions of landscape create further problems.

After over ten years of tourism practice, China is suffering from confusion in promoting its landscape images in international tourism. This study aims to develop an understanding of Chinese ideas about landscape based upon an analysis of the influence of Chinese philosophy on Chinese attitudes toward nature. The focus of this study is on the interpretations of Chinese landscapes in both the tourism industry and popular culture. It suggests that Chinese ideas about landscape are influenced by idealized images conceived in paintings and poetry. Typical Western perceptions of landscape, however, are divergent from the preconditioned "common knowledge" of the Chinese. With little knowledge about Western culture, decisions about tourist attractions are often made from the preconditioned and idealized Chinese point of view.

What is the image of China? How was it formed? In what way does it affect tourists going to China? All these questions seem fundamental, but they have not yet been adequately addressed by the Chinese. From the time when international tourism started in China in 1978 until June 4, 1989, Chinese tourism was a seller's market with more than a sufficient supply of tourists. The quality and variety of tourist attractions mattered little. According to officials of the National Tourism Administration of China (NTA), there had been no supporting research on either marketing or tourists in the first decade of Chinese tourism. Most of the decisions on selecting tourist attractions to open for foreigners were made either by copying patterns found in other countries (such as Spain and Mexico), or by best guess assumptions and common sense judgments.

How do Chinese authorities sell China to foreign tourists? For the most part this is done through images of China as a "mystical country." As Guo Laixi, a well known tourism geographyer in China, states:

China has always been considered a mystical place by the Westerners. Early in the Ancient Roman times, China was famed as a "Silk Country." In the Middle Ages, Marco Polo, a great traveler, described China as so magnificent a place that some people thought he was lying, therefore, they nicknamed him Marco Millions. But *the Travels of Marco Polo* had played a significant role in later great geographical discoveries. (Guo 1990: 123)

Tourism promotions adhere to China's traditional image. This image, however, is not based on sophisticated research of tourist markets or international visitors to China. While it may bring people to China, it does not necessarily reflect the visitor's true experience of the Chinese landscape. Unfortunately, the Chinese themselves have deeply held ideological preconceptions of what the Chinese landscape image is. These preconceptions make it difficult for the Chinese to see the landscape as the foreign tourist might.

The Common Landscape Knowledge of the Chinese People

To most Chinese people, including tourism planners and decision makers, the Chinese landscape is "common knowledge." Faced with volumes of Chinese tourist brochures, Westerners may find it difficult to identify the cultural roots of each idea or image. For a Chinese person, however, the association between promotional images and culture is just common knowledge.

Few Chinese people have traveled extensively, but most are familiar with the many famous places and landscapes in China through poetry and paintings. Different from Western literature and art, Chinese landscape poems and paintings are not portraits of the topography of real places. They are vehicles carrying Chinese philosophies and thoughts. Back to Confucius' time (c. 571-479? BC), Chinese philosophers possessed a consciousness to "seek ultimate truth from the landscape." (Ge 1991: 2). In the Yi-Jing (I-Ching), the bible of Daoism (Taoism), the basic elements of the universe are suggested as heaven, earth, thunder, fire, wind, marshes, rivers, and mountains. In Shi-Jing (Shih Ching), a collection of ancient odes by Confucius, the Chinese experienced expressions of grave sadness and delighted awareness in the beauty of the earth.

Chinese Landscape Poetry

In ancient landscape poetry, the harmonious relationship between people and nature formed the central idea. Many early landscape descriptions are actually found in *xuan* poetry, a mixture of Daoist discussion and landscape lyrics. When Chinese landscape poetry became independent from *xuan* philosophical discussions, marked by the poetry of Xie Ling-Yun (385-433), the expressions of Daoist meditation, harmony, and non-action still remained integral to Chinese landscape poetry.

Wang Wei (701-761) was the most famous landscape poet and painter of the Tang Dynasty (618-906). His landscape poems were not only popular in his time, but continue to be taught in Chinese schools today. Wang Wei's poems are inexhaustible expressions of the doctrines of Chan Buddhism, which is an interpretation of Buddhism in Daoist terminology.

> In middle years, I am attuned to Daoism,
> In late years, I made my home at the foot of Mt. Zhongnan.
> Whenever in the mood, I got there alone,
> The magnificent things, I, sure, have known.
> Walking to the place where the stream ends;
> Sitting to watch the clouds rise.
> --From *Retreat in Mt. Zhongnan*, translated by the author

This poem reveals the poet's sentimental attachment and meditation in front of a magnificent landscape. Besides enjoying the beauty of nature, Wang comprehended an ultimate truth of Buddhism through the landscape. The changing phases between stream and cloud suggest that everything in the world is no more than a rotation of life and death.

Wang Wei was also a painter. His landscape paintings, like his poems, are quiet, peaceful, and full of Chan Buddhist inspiration. Rather than portraits of landscape, they are expressions of his thought and interpretations of nature. One of the paintings by Wang Wei has a banana palm growing in the snow. This does not mean that Wang Wei ignored the accordance of seasons and plants, but instead suggests that he interpreted the unpredictable and sometimes incomprehensible forces in the natural world (Bush and Shih 1985: 100).

Tang poetry has had deep and continuing influence in Chinese culture. The spirit of the Tang Dynasty is identified by its glorious aspiration and cosmic view. Compared with Wang Wei's quiet and unaffected attraction, Li Bai (Li Po, 701-762), another famous Tang poet, moved China by his overflowing enthusiasm. Li Bai enjoyed sharing his freedom, passion, and wine with friends and nature. His sincere feelings of glorious landscapes have impressed the Chinese for hundreds of years. A farewell poem states:

> I saw my old friend off at the Yellow Crane Terrace,
> On his way to Yangzhou in the mists and flowers of March.
> While the shadow of his lonely sail was fading in the blue sky,
> Only the river was flowing toward heaven.
> --From *A Farewell to Meng Hao-Ran*, translated by the author

Li Bai's unlimited encouragement and panoramic view of the world influenced the whole nation. The places and images portrayed in Li Bai's poems became destinations for pilgrims in the past and tourists today. For example, since Li Bai's poem cited above, the Yellow Crane Terrace has had enormous sentiment and popularity among the Chinese people (Figure 9.1).

In China, poetry has actually taken on the function of religion (Lin 1935: 241). The Chinese have come to worship Li Bai in temples. His point of view toward landscapes, in particular, has always been held in highest respect.

FIGURE 9.1 Li Bai's poem "A Farewell to Meng Hao-Ran on His Way to Yang-Zhou" in a children's book, 1990.

Chinese landscape ideas mirror a long succession of idealized images and visual bias perceived through poetry and painting. Until Guo Xi's treatise *The Lofty Message of Forest and Stream* was compiled and released in the eleventh century, only the elite of Chinese would know how artists interpreted landscapes and why the Chinese are so deeply attached to certain landscapes. With a deep understanding of life and landscape, Guo Xi said:

In what does a gentleman's love of landscape consist? The cultivation of his fundamental nature in rural retreats is his frequent occupation. The carefree abandon of mountain streams is his frequent delight. The secluded freedom of fishermen and woodsmen is his frequent enjoyment. The flight of cranes and the calling of apes are his frequent intimacies. The bridles and fetters of the everyday world are what human nature constantly abhors. Immortals and sages in mists and vapor are what human nature constantly longs for and yet is unable to see. (Bush and Shih 1985: 151)

In history, however, only the small elite of Chinese society could successfully have identified themselves with nature as Guo Xi describes. Most of the masses of the Chinese population had been held to the village and city by filial and feudal ties. Forests and streams, and nature-spirits and fairies, could only be conceived in their dreams and imaginations. For these people, Guo Xi notes,

It is now possible for subtle hands to reproduce them (landscapes) in all their rich splendor. Without leaving your room you may sit to your heart's content among streams and valleys. The voices of apes and the calls of birds will fall on your ears faintly. The glow of the mountain and the color of the waters will dazzle your eyes glitteringly. Could this fail to quicken your interest and thoroughly capture your heart? This is the ultimate meaning behind the honor which the world accords to landscape painting. (p. 151)

To be able to take a trip without leaving home and enjoy mists and vapors through images suggest a subtle communication between Chinese artists and their audience. This communication was almost entirely a function of shared culture experiences, and this kind of journey is dramatically framed by artists and poets through their own interpretations. Although this spiritual journey promised no authentic travel experiences, it has been fairly popular and accepted among Chinese people.

Chinese Landscape Painting

The special correlation between landscape images and actual travel experiences is a direct consequence of the influences of landscape representation in China. The literati in China played an important role in the development of landscape literature and art. The literati class consisted of a group of scholars who studied the classics and composed paintings and poetry during their spare time. They believed that "painting is a creation of the mind and intrinsically a superior art." This became particularly important in the Song (Sung) Dynasty (960-1279).

A literati painting is identified as an expressive outlet of a scholar--his mind, his created world, and his personality. Compared with professional paintings, literati paintings are eccentric and non-profit, while professional painters were considered no more than "craftsmen." Most literati painters were amateurs who often used deliberately amateurish-looking techniques in order to reach pure arbitrariness.

Since the literati art was initiated for self-expression, the meaning of paintings could be partially or wholly free from what the objects represent. They could deliberately serve many purposes besides art. For example, plums, orchids, bamboo, and chrysanthemums are frequently found in literati works. They respectively symbolize loftiness, modesty, unyielding, and aloofness. Because of these symbolic metaphors, the significance of many natural objects is defined by their cultural associations in Chinese society.

The emphasis on spontaneity and delight rather than the pure experience of landscape is the central idea of literati paintings. In literati eyes, landscape is timeless and placeless. Therefore, paintings are not obligated to display geographical facts or the formal likeness in nature.

The tradition of the Song Dynasty was carried on, but taken to extremes, by Yuan Dynasty artists (1250-1368). Where Song paintings were focused on meanings through the abbreviated rendering of forms, Yuan paintings were simple and direct sketching of ideas beyond the forms of nature. To express emotions, painting was considered simply an ink play. Ni Zan (1301-1374), the most sensitive and unconventional landscape painter in the Yuan period, wrote a colophon to describe his own art:

> What I call painting does not exceed the joy of careless sketching with the brush.
> I do not seek for formal likeness; I do it simply for my amusement. (Sirén 1958: 110)

Ni Zan spent most of his life traveling in fishermen's boats and resting in Buddhist temples, and his art was an intimate expression of the poetry of loneliness. No people are shown in Ni Zan's cool and chaste landscapes. What Ni Zan was interested in painting is not the actual world, but images of his mind. The purity and loftiness of Yuan painters made them the historical model for Chinese scholars.

The legendary styles of the Yuan period, as an ideal of literati art, have been carried on to recent times. But paradoxically, in the Ming Dynasty (1368-1644) and the Qing (Ch'ing) Dynasty (1644-1912), the same scholars who believed in natural genius and effortlessness in art were also found searching intensely for other models and styles from the past. This incongruity first appeared in the ink bamboo and plum blossom albums of the Yuan, then followed by the Ming's imitations of the ancient masters, finally resulting in orthodoxism in the Qing Dynasty period. From then on, the creation of landscape paintings in China simply became a process of copying and rearranging model mountains and rivers from ancient masters' works in an aesthetic layout.

Image and Reality in the Chinese Landscape

Artistic and poetic landscapes directly affect the perception of landscapes in reality. The idealization of landscape representations can enhance the differences between images and reality. In China, the original mission of searching for purity and simplicity in the physical landscape has been replaced by a search to uncover the historical associations and cultural symbolism of places based upon literature and art. To most Chinese, including overseas Chinese, picturesque Guilin mountains, Suzhou gardens, old capital cities and palaces, and sacred mountains are considered more attractive because they constantly appear in poems and paintings. Other places, such as the Gobi Desert, the highlands of Tibetan, and the bare Loess Plateau, are less attractive, since the dominant images associated with these places are wars, lack of civilization, and famine.

For most Chinese people, their individual and collective impressions of landscapes are rarely derived from direct physical contact. The environments and landscapes they are experiencing are often unapproachable, and many are entirely fictional. Surrounded by a gulf of literary and visual landscape images, it is impossible, sometimes, for Chinese to distinguish their own feelings about the landscape from the impressions derived from others. Generally speaking, ordinary Chinese are exposed to landscape images much more than having real experiences of varied habitats and environments. Without paying much attention, ideas and impressions of famous landscapes have been absorbed naturally because their cultural influence is everywhere in China. Through thousands of years of cultural demonstrations, the Chinese seem inclined to appreciate landscape through images illustrated in literature and art.

Today, modern technology is enabling more people to experience the fact and reality of landscapes directly. The traditional association of certain places with Li Bai's poetry or Wang Wei's paintings, however, gives Chinese visitors greater spiritual satisfaction than would the landscape's scenery in itself. To the Chinese people, visiting a scenic spot or a historical place is always attached to sentimental expectations. In order to watch the sun rising over Mt. Tai, for example, many old and young Chinese wait in the chilly darkness for hours. What they are really looking for is not simply the scene of the sun rising from the clouds, but the experiences and reflections which have been memorialized again and again in Chinese poetry.

The famous poetry and art of the Tang and Song Dynasties are introduced regularly through Chinese elementary school textbooks as part of literature and patriotic education. In addition, every year, millions of copies of calendars bearing the prints of famous landscape paintings or photo images are sold to Chinese families as popular household decorations. Part of the common knowledge among educated Chinese people is to recognize representations of the picturesque hills of Guilin, the sea clouds of Mt. Tai, the Three Gorges of the Changjiang (Yangtze) River, the water falls of Mt. Lu, and the elegant gardens of Suzhou. These images bring spiritual unity to the Chinese people, even though most have never actually visited them. When they do visit, the importance of these images is reinforced even more.

Since the individual knowledge of landscapes is seldom the result of travel or personal experiences, it actually promotes the functional usage of images in Chinese society. In order to further enhance the awareness of traditional landscapes among the Chinese population, 93 million stamps with the Guilin landscape were published in 1980, 51 million with Mt. Huang in 1981, and 41 million with the Zhuozheng Garden in Suzhou in 1984 (Figure 9.2). These efforts aside, the role of landscape knowledge in Chinese society is poorly understood. Because of the existential nature of the Chinese people's common landscape knowledge, the power of these images in the thoughts and behavior of Chinese people has not yet been studied in China.

Chinese Landscapes and Tourism

Since it is hard to separate the influence of images from Chinese people's lives, it is also hard for Chinese to appreciate landscape without preconditioned thought. When Westerners look at the Changjiang (Yangtze) River, they may only see a large waterway; when Chinese look at it, however, they see a poem. This preconditioning has become a serious problem for Chinese tourism. The judgments and decisions on tourism development and promotion are generally made to reflect Chinese values, which includes preconditioned "common knowledge" about foreigners and

(Mt. Huang)

(Guilin)   (Suzhou Gardens)

FIGURE 9.2 Chinese Landscapes on Government Postage Stamps

their tastes of landscape. Because of their cultural bias, decision makers can easily overlook the reality of a landscape.

A significant difference exists between the destinations of international tourism in China and those of Chinese domestic tourism. Although big cities are often visited by both groups, each is usually motivated for different reasons. The international visitor's trip is often arranged (and even dictated) by the China International Travel Service (CITS). The domestic visitor's motivation is a voluntary cultural decision, which is more akin to a pilgrimage to historical, cultural and political centers. Western tourists are also more frequently directed to visit minority frontiers because Westerners are seen to be more adventurous and interested in exotic attractions than the Chinese. Chinese tourists, on the other hand, prefer to validate the poetic knowledge of places such as the gardens of Suzhou. From the statistical data in 1989, among visitors to Tibet, 99 percent were Westerners.

The absence of Chinese visitors to Tibet shows the cultural influence of the domestic tourist's perception of remote places. It also reflect the disdain for minorities among the dominant Han Chinese.

Conclusions

The arrival of international tourism has changed China in many ways. China is no longer an isolated territory. It is open to the whole world. And people from all over the world are interested in seeing China. After more than a decade of international tourism, however, China has not yet been able to bring in as many tourists as it has hoped. This has been due to both political instability and a lack of alternatives and flexibility in tourism. The sharp decline of international tourists after the Tiananmen Square Incident in 1989 has profoundly damaged Chinese tourism. The number of international tourists to China has recently increased. However, the lost market of Western tourists has merely been replaced by Taiwanese and overseas Chinese from Southeast Asia. These new markets tend to prefer low prices and service, while the wealthy, upscale market of the West remain tenuous.

The incident in Tiananmen Square in 1989 was a catalyst that accentuated many more problems in Chinese tourism which have been accumulating over a long period of time. In order to confront these problems, China has to make an endeavor to win back the trust from the world. In fact, starting in 1992, China began a program to introduce greater variety in its tourist product "to enrich the experience for overseas visitors ... and to suit their individual particular interests" (NTA 1992). Fourteen special interest tours and 113 festival tours were introduced in the form of "mini-packaged tours." These mini-tours complemented the major packaged tours and were specifically designed for small groups of tourists. Surprisingly, while most of the new tours, such as the Ma'anshan International Poetry Recitation, the Folk Song Festival, and the Scholar-Tree Festival have attracted large numbers of domestic tourists, they have had little impact on international tourism. Other problems with the mini-package tours for international visitors were their high cost and a lack of adequate assistance in booking them.

What has been left out of all the "sound good" ideas and plans that have been promoted so unsuccessfully in China? It is this author's opinion that sensitivity to cultural diversity is a key element lacking in China's tourism efforts. As cultural landscapes have been converted into tourist attractions and replicated as tourist products, the economic value of international tourism has been emphasized over its cultural aspects (Lanfant and Graburn 1992: 94). As a result, local interests and government plans have leaned toward quantity instead of quality in tourism development. At the same time, most of the research on tourism has focused on its economic and political (i.e., government policy) significance. This pragmatic intensity not only blurs the cultural problems behind the statistical data, but also discourages necessary social and cultural studies on tourism.

Although a greater variety of tourist attractions has been introduced, the separation between the promotional images and the reality of the Chinese landscape is still found. This is true for both the newly staged festivals and the showcases of ancient relics. "Chinese culture" is still narrowly defined in Chinese tourism. The Chinese landscape is presented either as one of ancient history or one of minority ethnic cultures (Figure 9.3). This point of view has been directly responsible for limiting the expansion of the market for Chinese tourism in the past decade, and it will probably still take some time for Chinese authorities to realize that Western tourists are not only interested in China's past but also the current lives of Chinese people.

The future success of Chinese tourism is full of challenges. There is not only a need for better research on the unique situation of Chinese tourism, but also a need for a deep rethinking of Chinese ideology and the development of more objective attitudes toward other cultures. Since landscapes comprise a main attraction in tourism to China, studies on the image and reality of Chinese landscapes are important in order to cope with the changing demands of the international market. The challenge of Chinese tourism in the future will not be simply to choose either mass or alternative tourism, but to initiate tourist attractions on the basis of mutual understanding between hosts and guests.

Tourism is different from cultural education. It is not just a showplace for idealized images. It is a contract between insiders and outsiders. To successfully target international tourism, Chinese decision makers will have to step away from traditional Chinese thinking. Tourism marketing is not local but global, and highly competitive. A narrow definition of "Chinese culture" will limit opportunities for expanded tourism.

While modern Chinese may wish to maintain their traditional ideals, international tourists are more pragmatic. Without having been nurtured in the same cultural environment, it is difficult for foreign tourists "to completely understand an insider's full experience of a place" (Lew 1992: 46). Chinese tourism cannot provide a fulfilling and satisfying experience to foreign tourists by changing the physical appearance of landscapes, but it can be done through proper education, promotion, and other forms of communication, both literary and visual. In order to attract more people, China has to seek out what visitors want directly from tourists themselves, instead of telling them what they should want.

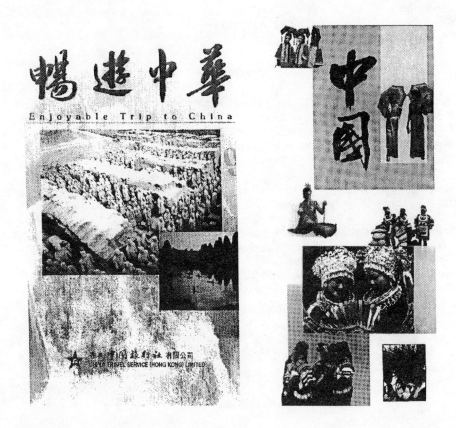

FIGURE 9.3 Chinese Government Tourist Brochures

Notes

1. This research owes acknowledgment to Professor David Hooson, Professor Nelson Graburn, and Professor Robert Reed who offered substantial advice and encouragement. The author also thanks Professor Ge Xiao-Yin and Mr. Liang You-Quan for their support and help during the research.

References

Bush, Susan and Hio-yen Shih, eds. 1985. *Early Chinese Texts on Painting*. Cambridge, Massachusetts: Harvard-Yenching Press.

Ge, Xiao-Yin. 1991. The Transformation of *Xuan* Nature toward Landscape Aesthetics in East Chin Dynasty. Unpublished paper, Beijing University.

Guo, Lai-Xi. 1990. A Study of China's Tourist Resources and their Development. *GeoJournal* 21(1/2): 123-6.

Kristof, Nicholas D. 1990. China Tries to Win Back Tourists. *New York Times* (Jan. 20).

Lanfant, Marie-Francoise and Nelson H. H. Graburn. 1992. International Tourism Reconsidered: The Principle of the Alternative. In V.L. Smith and W.R. Eadington, eds., *Tourism Alternatives*, Philadelphia: University of Pennsylvania Press, 88-112.

Lew, Alan A. 1992. Perceptions of Tourists and Tour Guides in Singapore. *Journal of Cultural Geography* 12(1): 45-52.

Lin, Yu-Tang. 1935. *My Country and My People*. New York: The John Day Company.

National Tourism Administration of the People's Republic of China (NTA). 1992. *Visit China '92*. Beijing: NTA.

Sirén, O. 1958. *Chinese Painting, Vol. II*. Hong Kong: Hong Kong University Press.

10

Overseas Chinese and Compatriots in China's Tourism Development

Alan A. Lew

There exists a China other than the People's Republic of China (PRC). This "other China" is more than just the Republic of China (ROC) in Taiwan. It consists of over 50 million ethnic Chinese around the world who are not under the direct rule of the PRC. These include "compatriots" in Hong Kong, Macao, and Taiwan, and overseas Chinese elsewhere in the world. Most of the citizens of this other China maintain strong personal and cultural ties to their motherland. Most of them have also experienced economic success in their adopted lands. It is impossible to understand the dynamics of tourism development in China without including consideration of the other China.[1]

Ethnic Chinese who live outside the PRC are a major force in the country's tourism development. They form the majority of travelers to China and are the principal foreign investors in its tourism industry. The desire to visit China stems from a history of well maintained familial and cultural ties, despite many years of separation. Investment in China's hotels and resorts by ethnic Chinese residing outside the PRC reflects these close personal ties. Such investments also reflect the personal wealth accumulated by Chinese who have been living in capitalist societies. Through the combination of these factors, the other China provides the PRC with a development resource the likes of which few countries can compare.

A Brief History of the Chinese Diaspora

For most of its recorded history, emigration from China proper has been minimal. By the 3rd century A.D. (the Three Kingdoms period), expansion out of the north China cultural hearth had extended the area of Han Chinese settlement into what is today central and southern China. While China became a major trading nation in the Indian Ocean during the Tang Dynasty (618-906), emigration during this and subsequent periods was both illegal and generally not on a large scale. Most of the emigration that did occur consisted of traders (actually pirates) from the southern coastal province of Fujian.

The first major period of emigration beyond China proper occurred in the late 14th and early 15th centuries, and again in the 16th century (during the Ming Dynasty) when Chinese traders and naval vessels again traveled the southern seas as far as Africa (Lyman 1974: 3). These travelers encountered scattered Chinese settlements founded on the pirating and smuggling activities of previous centuries (Pan 1990: 4-6). Throughout the Ming Dynasty large numbers of Chinese traders migrated and settled in the Philippines, the Malacca Strait area, and the islands of Indonesia. The fall of the Ming to the Manchurian Qing Dynasty in 1644 resulted in yet a larger wave of emigration to Taiwan and Southeast Asia. In 1712 the Qing, fearing revolutionary influences, made the return of Chinese from abroad punishable by death.

It was not until the mid-nineteenth century that treaties forced on China by European powers during the Opium Wars changed Qing Dynasty policy to legally allow emigration (Pan 1990: 48,51). The colonial powers sought Chinese "coolie" laborers to work in Southeast Asia and the Americas. Chinese workers willingly sought these opportunities, in part to escape natural and manmade disasters that plagued their homeland in the 19th century (Lyman 1974: 3; Pan 1990: 13). The vast majority of Chinese who took advantage of these opportunities were from the southern provinces of Guangdong and Fujian. Emigrants from this period were the original settlers in most of the Chinatowns found throughout the world today. Indeed, Lyman says that "Nineteenth century China is more alive in twentieth-century American Chinatowns than in the contemporary villages of Kwangtung [Guangdong] and Fukien [Fujian]" (1974: 6). It is the culture of the overseas Chinese from southern China that has largely defined the traditional relationship between China proper and the ethnic Chinese in Southeast Asia and the Americas.

The most recent wave of Chinese emigration began with the liberalization of mainland Chinese society in the late 1970s.[2] While southern Chinese still predominate, in general this new group of overseas Chinese comprises a broader mix of people from different parts of China than had previous periods of emigration. Economic motivations, however, remain the dominant force in their decision to emigrate to their preferred destinations of the U.S., Canada, and Australia.

Taiwan has periodically experienced lengthy periods of independence from mainland China. It was occupied in the seventh century by Chinese agriculturalists who migrated seasonally to Formosa and the Pescadore Islands (Lyman 1974: 3). When the Ming Dynasty temporarily banned overseas trade in 1433, Formosa became a haven for Chinese pirates. Ming Dynasty loyalists fled to the island in 1644 to escape the conquering Manchurians (Qing Dynasty). The Ming maintained a separate Chinese state there until 1683 when they were overcome by Qing forces. Japan controlled Taiwan from 1895 to 1945. A repeat of the 17th century scenario occurred in 1949 when some two million Nationalist Chinese government officials, soldiers, and sympathizers fled to Taiwan, leaving the mainland to the Chinese Communist Party. Although voices calling for the formal independence of Taiwan from China have existed since at least the 1940s, both the Nationalist and Communist governments of China consider Taiwan an integral part of the mainland (Andrews 1992a).

It was the last period of separation from the mainland that caused contemporary differences between Taiwan and the PRC to develop. Cold War politics intensified divisions between the Nationalist ROC government on Taiwan and the Communist PRC government on the mainland. Economic and cultural ties were nonexistent as both sides sought the support of the Chinese outside of East Asia. This situation changed considerably with the liberalization of the mainland society and the death of the old Nationalist leaders in Taiwan. Today, visitors and investments from Taiwan play a major role in China's tourism development.

The Ming Dynasty ceded Macao to Portugal in 1557 as a gift for assistance in fighting pirates along the south China coast. The mainland Chinese government, however, has always had considerable say in the policies of the tiny colony that will return to PRC administration in 1999. No other European power was able to make significant inroads into trading and colonizing China, until the start of the Opium Wars in 1841. By this time, Great Britain had become the major European colonial power in Asia, and opium from India had become the major product being traded for Chinese goods. In an effort to stop the opium trade, the Chinese government confiscated European opium caches in Guangzhou. British traders responded by calling on the English Royal Navy to attack the coast of China. Hong Kong was subsequently ceded to the British government in a treaty signed while British gunboats threatened to destroy the coastal cities of China.

The population of Hong Kong grew rapidly as large numbers of Chinese from neighboring Guangdong Province migrated to the colony. Hong

Kong received a major influx of Shanghai industrialists and capital when the communists came to rule the mainland in 1949. British colonial policies were based on liberal economic theory and Hong Kong developed into the epitome of laissez faire capitalism at the same time that mainland China sought to epitomize the communist ideal under the leadership of Mao Zedong. In the early years of communism, the door between mainland China and Hong Kong was wide open. By the mid-1950s, however, a "bamboo curtain" was raised preventing mainland Chinese from migrating to Hong Kong and Macao. Although Hong Kong will come under PRC administration in 1997, its economic and social policies, and its relationship to the mainland are scheduled by treaty to remain unchanged for 50 more years.

One important part of the relationship between Hong Kong and the mainland has been that even with the Bamboo Curtain, Hong Kong and Macao Chinese have always been able to travel easily into the PRC. This special access to mainland China has given Hong Kong Chinese an advantage over all other groups, making them the single largest investor in China's tourism industry and the largest visitor group by far to the PRC.

Tourism and the Existential Tie to China

The strong sense of nostalgia that Chinese of the other China feel toward their ancestral land is particularly pronounced among those who reside the farthest away from it. Today, this feeling consists of sentiments that both pull them to China as a place where they feel a sense of belonging, and push them toward their adopted lands as a place where they prefer to physically live and work. While the following discussion focuses on the overseas Chinese experience, the mixed emotions that all Chinese have as descendants of China extends to Taiwanese and Hong Kong Chinese, as well.

Historically, the overseas Chinese experience has been described as one of a "sojourner." For the Chinese sojourner, the basic motivation for leaving home was to seek opportunities to increase one's status at home. This was usually accomplished through increased economic opportunities in another place. Unlike the economic immigrants of today, the sojourner had no intention of remaining in the host place. While this situation has changed for overseas Chinese over the years, the sojourner model describes a basic foundation that explains how overseas Chinese today continue to relate to their motherland.

Woon (1984) has identified several reasons for sojourning (i.e., working away from home and returning home to retire.) These include:

1. The importance of the extended family and a feeling of insecurity in a place without the extended family reference group. A Chinese proverb says that "Being away from home only one li [about one-third mile] is not as good as being home." Unlike northern China, most of the villages in southern China are patrilocal, clan communities, with everyone in the village related by male lineage and marriage (Pan 1990: 18; Woon 1983). Southern Chinese, in particular, identify themselves to one another in terms of the village or group of villages from which they descend. Even when direct ties to home village relatives are severed, overseas Chinese will find comradeship with other Chinese from their home county or who have the same surname. Surname-based associations often replaced village-based networks for Chinese when they arrived in a foreign land.

2. Group pressure from villagers to return home and acceptance upon returning home, despite having left. A strong sense of filial piety, expressed in terms of caring for both aged parents and the graves of ancestors, is reinforced by village relatives on those who are working away from home. In areas of southern China where ties between the home villagers and overseas sojourners were strong communist collectivization efforts in the 1960s were less successful (Peterson 1988). In return for remittances for overseas relatives, villagers made every effort to maintain the property rights of sojourners. Despite over 40 years of communist rule many of the Chinese who left before 1949 still maintain ownership of their village homes.

3. The existence of an open class society allowing upward socioeconomic mobility, particularly for males. Southern China has been referred to as a "cultural borderland" (Pan 1990: 13). The Chinese of the south have a greater diversity of language and genetic influences than elsewhere in China. A dominant Confucian land owning class was also less pronounced in the clan villages of southern China, and an openness to new ideas was more common. The idea that one could leave China was, therefore, more accepted, as was the concept of an economic-based social class system.

While away from home, the overseas Chinese sojourner gained prestige among fellow sojourners based upon these same values. The more trips home one could make before retirement increased one's prestige. So did the amount of money sent home to relatives, and the amount donated for public works projects for the villages (e.g., schools, roads, and bridges.) Saving a large amount of money to bring back to China also increased the sojourner's prestige. If a sojourner died while away, he typically was buried for several years, after which his bones would be dug up and sent back to the village for a proper reburial (Pan 1990: 55).

Unfortunately, the unsettled political situation in China in the first half of the 1900s made it increasingly difficult for overseas Chinese sojourners to return. The victory of the communists in 1949 all but closed the country to return migration. In the 1950s anti-Chinese movements in Southeast Asia did result in some 50,000 ethnic Chinese returning to China to settle, but most of these were distrusted by the government and encouraged to leave in the early 1970s (Godley 1989). The vast majority of the world's overseas Chinese sojourners became resigned to remaining in their host country permanently.

The sentiments and ties to China of the earlier sojourner period, however, remained strong. Money continued to be sent back to the village throughout the Maoist period, and this continued to be a source of prestige among overseas Chinese. When China reopened to tourism in 1978, a new form of returning "sojourner-tourist" quickly developed.

For overseas Chinese, China is an "existential home." It serves as the center of their personal and social value systems, which are based on the extended family. Though they cannot live in China, it remains the place where they feel most at home. Relph refers to this experience as "existential insideness," which includes the experience of permanent residents of a place (1976: 55). Cohen, in describing different modes of tourist experiences, refers to the "existential tourist" as one who is *spiritually* alienated from their place of physical residence and *physically* alienated from their spiritual center (1979). The "spiritual center" may be either elective or ancestral. Cohen argues that existential tourism is increasing as forced and voluntary emigration has increased in recent decades.

There are many reasons why overseas Chinese find existential tourism preferable over sojourning. The decades during which China was closed to most of the world fostered a greater degree of assimilation of overseas Chinese in their host society than in earlier periods. When restrictions on return migration occurred among Southeast Asian Chinese in the 15th and 16th centuries a distinctive Southeast Asian Chinese culture developed, known as "Peranakan Chinese" culture in Malaysia and Singapore (Clammer 1980). Nineteenth and twentieth century emigrants faced a similar situation after the communist victory in 1949. Greater assimilation contributed to a permanent state of sojourning.[3] Continuing difficulties in China made contributions sent home ever more valued. This in turn relieved the pressure from home villagers for sojourners to return permanently. When China became more open to tourism, returning overseas Chinese found that their status was greatly enhanced. They were, however, expected to bring monetary gifts for all villagers on their visits. (For some overseas Chinese, this expectation has actually limited the number of return trips they have chosen to take to their village.) The rural areas of Guangdong and Fujian Provinces, where an estimated half of all overseas Chinese originate, are today among the wealthiest areas in China due to these continuing remittances (*The Economist* 1992: 22).

Pan has described the experience of the overseas Chinese tourist succinctly:

> Each time they visit they ask themselves, 'Why are we here? Why do we keep coming back?' Why must they return to this cruel, tormented, corrupt, hopeless place as though they still needed it? Could they never achieve immunity? And yet had China meant nothing to them, any other place thereafter would have meant less, and they would carry no pole within themselves, and they would not even guess what they had missed . . . yet they realize that they could never live there. Deep in their hearts they know that they love China best when they live well away from the place. (1990: 379)

The existential overseas Chinese tourist, therefore, can enjoy the benefits of two worlds. Tourism allows them to strengthen their ties to the extended village and to pay proper respects to the ancestors. This, in return, strengthens their personal self esteem by giving them a broader perspective of their place in the world. It also increases their prestige among other overseas Chinese residing abroad. In fact, the acceptance and value placed on ancestral-based existential tourism to China today has lessened the pressure for younger people to stay in the village and increased their propensity to seek opportunities abroad.

With each succeeding generation, direct ties to the village become weaker and weaker. This is particularly true as a family becomes more assimilated into their new society. In recent years, special offices in the major overseas Chinese areas of Guangdong and Fujian Provinces have been established to help second and third generation overseas Chinese find their ancestral villages. However, even those who have lost all connections to China cannot avoid a sense of existential belonging when they visit, even if it based largely on racial grounds. Even Hong Kong and Taiwan compatriots have a nostalgic preference for a single China that includes Hong Kong, Taiwan, and the PRC over the current divisive situation. However, like the overseas Chinese, compatriots have grown too accustomed to their current governments to readily return to living under the rule of the PRC. As with overseas Chinese, visiting relatives in China is also the principal motivation of compatriot visits to the mainland (Lee 1982).

Economic Impacts on Tourism in China

The economic impacts of the other China on tourism and travel in the PRC are twofold. The first is in terms of visitations to China. The second is in the area of foreign investments in tourism. In both of these areas, Chinese living in the other China have been the dominant force in the development of international tourism and travel in the PRC. However, it is first necessary to clarify the terms used to identify the different groups that comprise the other China.

Defining the Overseas Chinese

There exists two major categories of Chinese who reside outside of the PRC. In addition, each of these has some significant subclassifications. The first category consists of Chinese living in Hong Kong, Taiwan, and Macao. The PRC considers each of these places an integral part of China proper and officially refers to their citizens as "compatriots." However, none of the three compatriot places has experienced direct rule under the communist government of China. Indeed, they have often represented the very antithesis of the political and economic policies of the PRC. While significant visa differences do exist, compatriot Chinese who visit the PRC experience similar border formalities as do other visitors. There are two major types of compatriot Chinese: those from the British colony of Hong Kong and the Portuguese colony of Macao, and those from the ROC on the island province of Taiwan.

The term "overseas Chinese" refers to ethnic Chinese who live beyond the areas claimed as territory by the PRC. Overseas Chinese reside on every continent, although the vast majority are in Southeast Asia, followed by North America (Table 10.1).[4] The history of overseas Chinese in Southeast Asia dates back to at least the pirate traders of the 13th century, while many of those in other parts of the world trace their migration back to the Opium Wars of the mid-1800s. Despite being separated from China for many generations, overseas Chinese still maintain close cultural and, for more recent immigrants, familial ties to their ancestral land. In the following discussion, the overseas Chinese are classified into three types: those residing in Southeast Asia, many of whom are descendants of early emigrants from China's Fujian Province; those who reside in North America (American Chinese); and those who live elsewhere in the world. Most of the Chinese now residing in the U.S. and Canada trace their immigration from Guangdong Province in the 19th and 20th centuries. Chinese residing in the rest of the world are widely scattered and are not discussed in detail here.

One problem in using the term "overseas Chinese" is due to the way the classification of "Overseas Chinese" is used in China's tourism statistics. For

TABLE 10.1 1990 Compatriot and Overseas Chinese Populations

	Number of ethnic Chinese (in millions)	
Indonesia	7.2	
Thailand	5.8	
Malaysia	5.2	
Singapore	2.0	
Burma	1.5	
Philippines	0.8	
Vietnam	0.8	
Southeast Asia Total	23.3	
USA	1.8	
Canada	0.6	
Latin America	1.0	
Americas Total	3.4	
Rest of Asia and the Pacific	1.8	
Europe	0.6	
Africa	0.1	
OVERSEAS CHINESE TOTAL		29.2
Hong Kong	5.9	
Macao	.5	
Taiwan	20.7	
COMPATRIOT CHINESE TOTAL		27.1
WORLD TOTAL		56.3

Source: Kao 1993; *The Economist* 1992.

official purposes, "Overseas Chinese" (upper case "O") refers to persons who hold a mainland Chinese passport, but live outside of China. Visitors to China with these characteristics are significant only in Indonesia, where 1.5 million (1982) Chinese hold PRC citizenship, and in Thailand with 300,000 (1980) PRC citizens (Poston and Yu 1990). In 1991, China recorded 133,427 "Overseas Chinese" visits (Sun 1992). However, the vast majority of overseas Chinese, as the term is used in this chapter, do not hold a Chinese passport. These visitors are officially classified as "Foreign Visitors," along with non-ethnic Chinese travelers. Thus, almost all of Singapore's 98,097 visitors in 1991 (Sun 1992) were considered Foreign Visitors in China's tourism statistics, despite the fact that 77 percent of the population of Singapore is ethnic Chinese. A method to estimate the actual number of overseas ethnic Chinese visitors to China from around the world is introduced below.

Chinese Tourist Travel to China

Fortunately, compatriot visitations to the PRC are recorded and published on an annual basis, although like many numbers from China, especially in the past, these may be inflated. The total number of annual compatriot Chinese trips to China has consistently been more than 20 million since 1986, and reached almost 34 million in 1992 (Table 10.2; see also Table 1.1 in Chapter 1). Most of these visits are to see friends and relatives and for leisure travel (Chow 1988). The city of Guangzhou, for example, claims to have 679,843 residents with close relatives in Hong Kong or Macao (*Guangzhou Economic Yearbook* 1984, cited in Chow 1988). Family-oriented holidays, such as the Chinese New Year, witness large numbers of Hong Kong Chinese crossing into China. An increasing number of compatriot business trips are also part of the PRC's total visitor arrivals.

In 1992, the nearly six million residents of Hong Kong made 21.5 million visits across the border into the PRC (SCMP 1993). Hong Kong compatriots are not required to have a visa to visit China--they only need to show a travel identity card. In addition to family visits, many leisure travelers from Hong Kong visit resorts in the neighboring Shenzhen and Zhuhai Special Economic Zones (Table 10.3). These are areas of China that border Hong Kong and Macao, respectively, and in which liberal economic policies (similar to those in Hong Kong) prevail. Hotels and full featured resorts have been built in these areas, making for an easily accessible vacation destination for urban Hong Kong compatriots (Chow 1988; Lew 1987). Visits to these destinations are also organized by schools, workplaces, and other organizations in Hong Kong. Such groups also organize longer tours of China.

Taiwanese visits to the mainland have increased dramatically since the Taiwan government relaxed its restrictions on such visits in November 1987 (Andrews 1992b). Illegal visits had been taking place through Hong Kong since the mid-1980s, when China began admitting Taiwanese without stamping their passports. A rapid increase in Taiwanese visitors occurred just in time to help compensate for part of the decline in tourism to China that resulted from the Tiananmen Square Incident in 1989 (Chang 1992; He 1991; Zhang 1990). A peak of 1.5 million was reached in 1993. The 1994 figures are likely to be considerably lower following the the robbery murder of a Taiwanese tour group in Hangzhou and subsequent travel restricts enacted by the government of Taiwan (Mark 1994a; 1994b).

Although the Taiwan government initially stipulated that travel to the PRC would only be allowed to visit relatives, this condition was gradually dropped (Andrews 1992). Increasingly, these visits have included large numbers of business travelers. Limited visits by mainland Chinese to Taiwan have been allowed since 1990, the same year that Taiwan sent a

TABLE 10.2 Compatriot and Overseas Chinese Visitor Arrivals to China

			Overseas Chinese	
	Hong Kong and Macao	*Taiwan*	*Number*	*% Foreign Visitors*[a]
1987	25.09 million	<2,500	202,155	11.7
1988	29.34 million	437,700	320,544	17.4
1989	22.43 million	541,000	270,279	18.5
1990	24.68 million	947,600	277,823	15.9
1991	29.56 million	946,632	409,225	15.1
1992	32.63 million	1,317,800	n/a	n/a
1993	35.18 million	1,526,969	n/a	n/a

[a]The percent of foreign visitors that ethnic overseas Chinese comprise is the mean of an estimate high and an estimated low for each year using the method described in the text for 1991.

Source: He 1991; *The Yearbook of China Tourism Statistics* 1992; Xiang 1991; Ministry of Public Security 1994.

TABLE 10.3 Major Cities visited by Compatriots and Foreign Visitors, 1991[a]

	Compatriot Chinese	*Foreign Visitors*
Shenzhen SEZ (Guangdong)	1,704,807	108,379
Guangzhou (Guangdong)	1,473,721	444,555
Zhuhai SEZ (Guangdong)	433,076	24,124
Beijing	381,707	913,887
Shanghai	331,783	612,723
Hangzhou	229,690	136,809
Quanzhou (Fujian)	220,902	7,286
Guilin	207,556	199,159
Xiamen (Fujian)	135,324	66,816
Nanjing	121,921	96,803
Shantou (Guangdong)	114,229	76,705
Fuzhou (Fujian)	110,113	34,656
Suzhou	103,262	116,294
Kunming	100,713	57,539
Xian	68,943	237,824
TOTAL	30,506,231	2,710,103

[a]This table is extracted from a list of 53 cities. All cities which received 100,000 or more compatriot or foreign visitors in 1991 are shown. The city counts are from the National Tourism Administration. SEZ stands for Special Economic Zone.

Source: The Yearbook of China Tourism Statistics 1992.

large delegation to the Asian Games held in Beijing. Taiwan, however, still bans direct air and sea links to the mainland, although it may be only a matter of time before this restriction is liberalized, as well.

Southeast Asian Chinese also helped to compensate for the decline in tourist visits to the PRC in 1989 and 1990, though the numbers were less significant than among the Taiwanese. Part of the reason for the Southeast Asian increase was due to new laws adopted by Southeast Asian countries making travel to China more accessible (Zhang 1990). As in Taiwan, mainland China had become the new place to go for the more wealthy of Southeast Asia. In 1991, China received 104,791 foreign visitors from the Philippines, making it the fourth largest market behind Japan, the U.S., and the U.K. (Sun 1992: 24-5). The small city-state of Singapore was China's fifth largest market with 98,097 visitors. Germany was slightly ahead of Thailand, which was China's seventh largest market at 88,624 visitors.

The per capita expenditures of Hong Kong Chinese, Taiwanese, and Southeast Asian Chinese are much lower than that of other international visitors, including American Chinese and overseas Chinese elsewhere in the world. Compatriot and Southeast Asian Chinese are more likely to stay with relatives or in inexpensive Chinese hotels rather than in international hotels, while Taiwanese have received special incentive prices that cut into profits. The rise in tourists from among these groups has provided a new market for the older Chinese hotels in the PRC (Zhang 1990). It has also resulted in an increase in the production of rosewood furniture, screens, and calligraphy art which are popular among these groups.

As discussed above, estimating the total number of overseas Chinese visitors is difficult due to the way in which China collects tourism statistics. One method of estimating the true number of overseas Chinese visitors to China is to compare the number of foreign visitors from each country that are serviced by the China Travel Service (CTS). CTS primarily handles the travel arrangements of ethnic Chinese living outside the PRC.[5] In 1991, CTS serviced 225,036 foreign visitors (Sun 1992). This amounted to 8.3 percent of all foreign visitors and 21.9 percent of foreign visitors who traveled under the auspices of one of China's major travel agencies.[6] (It is possible to travel without using a major travel agency by being on government business or as guests of trade associations, schools, and other organizations that provide their own travel agency-type services.) Because most of the travel agencies that are not listed individually in the NTA statistics primarily handle non-ethnic Chinese visitors, a safe assumption is that about 15.1 percent of foreign visitors to China in 1991 were overseas Chinese. (The figure of 15.1 percent is half-way between the low of 8.3 percent and the high of 21.9 percent.) Using this estimated percentage, the total number of ethnic Chinese that comprise China's foreign visitor count in 1991 would be 409,225.

While low in comparison to compatriot visits, the number of ethnic Chinese is a good proportion of the total foreign visitor count. In addition, since the majority of overseas Chinese come from localized areas in Guangdong and Fujian, they frequently include these provinces on their itinerary. Their concentration in these areas is a major source of income and economic development for rural southern China.

Table 10.2 shows the estimated number of ethnic overseas Chinese visitors dating back to 1987. The low percentage of 11.7 in 1987 reflects restrictions on travel to China that were still in existence then in many Southeast Asian countries. This began to change in 1988, while the high of 18.5 percent in 1989 accurately shows the importance of ethnic Chinese in supporting China's tourism economy when visitors from most Western countries canceled their visits following the June 4th Tiananmen Square Incident.

It should be cautioned that these are rough estimates. With the liberalization of travel services in China, CTS has started to handle larger numbers of non-ethnic Chinese visitors. Using CTS as a guideline in the future will be more difficult. In 1991, however, CTS was still the dominant travel agency for overseas ethnic Chinese. This can be seen in the statistics for Singapore, where 77 percent of the population is ethnic Chinese. In 1991, 88 percent of the Singaporeans who came to China under the auspices of one of the country's two major travel agencies used CTS, while only 12 percent used CITS. For Thailand, another major source of overseas Chinese visitors, 90 percent used CTS. By contrast, only 16 percent of visitors from Japan, and 13 percent of those from France, used CTS in 1991.

Tourism Investment in China

It is estimated that the liquid assets of the 50 million overseas and compatriot Chinese worldwide are between $1.5 and $2 billion (*The Economist* 1992). On a per capita basis, this amount is higher than the approximately $3 billion in liquid assets held by Japan's 124 million people, and is far higher than any of the other countries in the world. This personal wealth was built on the same traditions of family ties and economic mobility which drives overseas Chinese tourism to China today. Family-owned businesses, combined with social and business networks built through larger family associations, enabled overseas Chinese communities to become dominant economic forces in many countries (Kao 1993; Sender 1991). The reestablishment and strengthening of direct ties to China since 1978 has also worked through these traditional business networks.

The government of China has encouraged foreign investment to rapidly bring the country into the global economic system. Outside interests invested approximately $11 billion in China in 1991, and 1993 saw that amount more than double to $25 billion in pledges in the first quarter alone (although only $3 billion was actually spent during that period) (*The Economist* 1992; Koan and Kaye 1993). While Japan is the main source of loans to China, Hong Kong and Taiwan comprise about two-thirds of the actual direct investments. Some of this amount is in wholly foreign owned enterprises.   However, the vast majority (about 95 percent of all investments) are as "equity joint ventures" (*hezi jingying*) and "cooperative or contractual agreements" (*hezou jingying*) (Leung 1990: 406; Thoburn, et al. 1990: 16-7). For both of these arrangements, foreign investors and local Chinese government entities or state companies share the cost, management, and profits of a factory or hotel.

Most Hong Kong compatriots speak the same language as in neighboring Guangdong province where they have placed 80 percent of their investments in China. Hong Kong accounts for approximately two-thirds of all foreign investments in Guangdong Province (Thoburn, et al. 1990: 1). Hong Kong developers are also leading the way in real estate investment in the PRC, and in particular in the development of resorts and golf courses (Karp 1992; PB 1993; Ross and Rosen 1992). Along with the good, Hong Kong Chinese have also been involved in criminal activity, such as prostitution, in Guangdong Province (Mosher 1992).

In the early 1980s, Taiwan businesses, eager to become economically involved in the PRC, began to set up "paper" companies in Hong Kong which they used as a trans-shipment point to export goods to China (Kao 1993). This growing practice lead to a relaxation of ROC regulations governing investments in China in 1987. By 1992, Taiwanese had officially invested $9 billion in the mainland (P. Liu 1993) (although unofficial estimates placed the number at two to three times the official amount.) Most of the Taiwanese investment has gone into neighboring Fujian Province, where people speak a dialect of Chinese that is closely related to Taiwanese. Mandarin is also more widely spoken in Taiwan than in Hong Kong, giving the island a potential edge in northern China. Taiwanese have been particularly adept at working with China's bureaucracy (Flannery 1991). Kentucky Fried Chicken, for example, uses Taiwanese managers extensively in its many branches in mainland China (Goldstein 1992).

Southeast Asian Chinese direct investment accounts for 10 to 15 percent of all foreign investment in China. The potential, however, is much greater given the large number of overseas Chinese in Southeast Asia and their tremendous wealth (Sender 1991). With approximately US$3 billion in two-way trade, overseas Chinese dominated Singapore accounts for 44 percent of all trade between the PRC and Southeast Asia (Stoltenberg 1990).

Thailand, Malaysia, and Indonesia each traded close to US$1 billion with China in 1989. Singaporeans and Thais (mostly Chinese businessmen) have invested the most in China among Southeast Asians.

The cultural advantage that overseas and compatriot Chinese hold has provided them with access to relatively safer investments than other foreign investors, including the Japanese. Investments by American Chinese and Chinese from other parts of the world have occurred to a much lesser degree. These overseas Chinese are more likely to limit their financial contribution to remittances for building schools, hospitals, roads, and other public facilities in their home village areas.

Between 35 percent and 40 percent of direct foreign joint venture investments in China have been in property development, including hotels, luxury resorts, golf courses, apartments and condominiums for foreigners, and office space (Leung 1990: 407; Asiaweek 1990; Associated Press 1993). An additional 5 percent has been in transportation, restaurants, and related services. Most of the five-star hotels, and many four-star hotels in China were built under provisions of the 1979 Joint Venture Law (with subsequent revisions in 1983 and 1986) (Pearson 1991). By 1991, there were a total of 202 joint venture hotels in China (Sun 1992: 86). This was an increase of 16 percent over the previous year (He 1991: 82). In addition, four hotels were solely foreign owned and 215 hotels were operated under cooperative agreements. While joint venture hotels are located throughout the country, the latter categories are almost entirely in Guangdong and Fujian Provinces, reflecting their exclusively overseas and compatriot Chinese influences.

A typical joint venture hotel has an upper management staff from a major international hotel chain based in Hong Kong. This staff would normally include the general manager, financial manager, rooms manager, executive housekeeping, and head chef. All other employees would be local Chinese. Joint venture agreement consists of ten to twenty year leases (although a few couple have fifty year leases), after which the foreign partner will either renegotiate the agreement or withdraw leaving the facility to the local Chinese partner. China's first joint venture hotel, the Jianguo opened in Beijing in 1982. It took only three years for foreign investors to recoup their costs and start earning a profit (Gerstlacher, et al. 1991: 39). However, increasing competition and sluggish growth in attracting high-end international visitors has created problems for joint venture hotels in recent years. The overall occupancy rate in 1991 was only 52.35 percent for joint venture hotels, compared to 59.58 percent for cooperative hotels and 63.47 percent for state-owned hotels (Sun 1992). Cooperative and state-owned hotels tend to be of a lower caliber than joint venture hotels.

The PRC government levies a Joint Venture Tax of 33 percent on all foreign-generated income, with an additional 10 percent on income that is exported out of China (although many tax breaks also exist.) Unlike joint venture hotels, cooperative hotels are managed entirely by the Chinese side, which also provides land and labor. The foreign investor provides capital, equipment, and technology, in return for a share of the profits (or losses). To further encourage foreign investment, China's National Tourism Administration (NTA) announced in late 1992 the establishment of eleven "tourist zones" where special tax incentives will be provided to encourage foreign investment in resort and hotel development, and in travel agencies and taxi services (PB 1993).[7]

Few other countries in the world have the kind of financial and managerial resources that China has in its compatriot and overseas Chinese. When the PRC first opened its doors to tourism in 1978, accommodations were woefully lacking in both number and quality. Through joint ventures, the quality of hotel services in China is finally beginning to reach international standards. On the down side, some of China's cities are starting to experience an overcapacity in hotel rooms for the first time. The economic experience, managerial knowledge, and financial resources of compatriot and overseas Chinese have clearly been important factors in modernizing (and internationalizing) tourism in China.

Conclusions: The Future of the Other China

There are five basic subdivisions of the other China: Hong Kong and Macao compatriots, Taiwan compatriots, Southeast Asian overseas Chinese, American overseas Chinese, and other overseas Chinese. Each of these groups relates in their own way to mainland China. The overseas Chinese sojourner experience helped in understanding the existential relationship that Chinese everywhere have with China. Compatriot Chinese, however, have had the greatest overall economic impact on the PRC.

Being farther removed from their homeland, the overseas Chinese are more likely to find themselves belonging to two very disparate worlds: that of their adopted land and that of their ethnic heritage. First generation sojourners typically maintained close contact with their home villages. There was always the possibility that they would return some day and in some way. For many, that way is as an existential tourist. This has been especially true for overseas Chinese living outside Asia. A large number of overseas Chinese in North America trace their origins to Guangdong Province, which has developed a rural culture built largely around their remittances. Southeast Asian Chinese, like Taiwanese, have closer ties to Fujian Province where they send remittances and invest in development projects.

Hong Kong compatriots have had the closest ties to the mainland and are the most influential in its tourism development. Their interests and influence are concentrated in Guangdong province, although in recent years they have increasingly invested in other parts of the country (Engardio 1992). Taiwanese are rapidly pursuing opportunities in China as their legal access to the PRC has increased. Much of their influence has been in neighboring Fujian Province where the language dialect is more closely related to that of Taiwan. In time, they are likely to venture further into the mainland, as well.

In recent years, several trends have been developing which will further complicate the scenario described here. The first is the imminent return of Hong Kong and Macao, and projected future return of Taiwan, to mainland Chinese control. Many foresee the development of a "greater China" in which the differences among these three entities gradually disappear. In the near term, business people in Taiwan and Hong Kong see themselves as leaders in the development of a major economic trading center that includes coastal mainland China (Einhorn 1992). Alternatively, the fear is that over investment in the mainland could allow the PRC government to hold the economies of Hong Kong and Taiwan hostage to their policies. It appears, however, that culture and ethnicity are driving Hong Kong and Taiwan to become ever more closely tied by economics to the PRC. As this process continues, the compatriot Chinese, as an external force in China's tourism development will cease to exist. In the future we will be talking of domestic travel between the mainland provinces and the provinces of Taiwan and Hong Kong.

A second trend is the gradual progression into second, third, and succeeding generations of overseas Chinese. With each generation the direct ties to the home village become weaker. Language is more difficult to maintain and familiar faces become fewer and fewer. Remittances to the village fade away as the values of the adopted land overshadow those of the original homeland. The children and grandchildren of the permanent sojourner are not themselves sojourners. However, they remain ethnically and racially Chinese. A link still exists, upon which tourism can occur. As this group of descended sojourners grows larger and wealthier over time, they will offer new opportunities for mainland Chinese tourism and economic development. Some areas are already taking advantage of this by offering services to visitors who are tracing their genealogy. More of this type of service will be needed in the future, especially in the overseas Chinese areas of Guangzhou and Fujian Provinces.

A third trend is the new wave of emigration from China that has occurred in the 1980s and 1990s. Large numbers of Chinese have both legally and illegally emigrated from China. Their preferred destinations are the U.S., Canada, and Australia. Like the last sojourners to leave China after World

War II and before 1949, they sense that they will probably never permanently return to their homeland. In all likelihood, however, they will maintain some of the traditional ties to their homeland that characterized the sojourners of old. One major difference is that the new emigrants are more likely to be from urban areas and more likely to come from a variety of regions in China. The traditional social organization of rural southern China does not exist for them, and just how they organize themselves in their adopted lands, and how they ultimately relate and contribute to their homeland remains to be seen.

All of these trends point to a transformation of the other China. They also indicate that the other China will continue to exist for a long time to come. And it will continue to play an important role in the development of tourism in China.

Notes

1. The "other China" should not be confused with "outer China." Outer China typically refers to the western peripheral regions of China where ethnic Han Chinese are non-indigenous and often a minority group. The term "other China" has been a sensitive one for the PRC government because it may imply that Taiwan and Hong Kong are not part of China proper. This connotation is not intended in this present discussion. Kao (1993) refers to the other China as the "Chinese commonwealth." This term has problems too, in that it may imply imperialistic desires on the part of the PRC, especially in Asian countries where ethnic Chinese loyalties are often distrusted. The term "greater China" has also been used, but is typically limited to the overseas Chinese presence in East and Southeast Asia only.

2. From 1981 through 1990 some 298,900 people emigrated legally from the PRC to the U.S. (U.S. Immigration and Naturalization Service, cited in several *World Almanacs*.) To this can be added an additional 98,200 from Hong Kong, 47,800 from Taiwan, and many overseas Chinese among the 549,000 immigrants from Philippines and 281,000 from Vietnam. An estimated 100,000 Chinese from the PRC are believed to have entered the U.S. illegally in 1992 alone (Mooney, et al. 1993). Southern China, in particular Fujian Province, is the main source of illegal Chinese emigrants (M. Liu 1993).

3. The assimilation for overseas Chinese was never complete. In Southeast Asia it sometimes turned into mass violence and death (*The Economist* 1992; Godley 1989). In North America, a period of violent anti-Chinese campaigns in the 19th century resulted in immigration restrictions (Lyman 1974: 55). Since World War II, however, American Chinese have gained the status of an upwardly mobile minority group, and are actually envied by Southeast Asian Chinese (Gibney 1993).

4. The estimates in Table 10.1 from Kao (1993) and *The Economist* (1992) are originally from the *Overseas Chinese Economy Yearbook*, which is published by the Chinese Traders Convention, Taipei, Taiwan. Estimating the number of overseas Chinese is not an easy task. Poston and Yu (1990) compared published data from Taiwan (which these authors regard as somewhat overstated) with actual census data

from around the world to estimate the 1980 overseas Chinese population. Giving priority to census data, their growth rates would give a 1990 overseas Chinese population total of 31.6 million (including compatriot Chinese). Poston and Yu, however, did not consider a major increase in emigration from China in the 1980s. The estimates provided by *The Economist* are primarily used in Table 10.1 because the financial arguments made by that publication, and presented in this chapter, were based on these numbers.

    5.   The China Travel Service (CTS) also handles travel arrangements for compatriots and Chinese nationals living abroad. These numbers, however, are not included in the figures in this chapter. CTS will also service a very small number of non-ethnic Chinese visitors.

    6.   The counterpart of CTS for non-ethnic Chinese visitors is the China International Travel Service (CITS). CITS also handles a few ethnic Chinese foreign visitors who are on standard non-Chinese tours. CITS has decentralized in recent years, with many local offices now granted considerable autonomy. The third major Chinese travel agency is the China Youth Travel Service (CYTS) which handles arrangements for youth tour groups.

    7.   The eleven zones include Taihu (in Jiangsu Province), Dianchi (in Yunnan Province), Nanhu (in Guangzhou), Shilaoren (in Qingdao), Jinshitan (in Dalian), Hengshadao (in Shanghai), Zhijiang (in Hangzhou), Wuyi Mountain and Meizhoudao (in Fujian Province), Yintan (in Guangxi Province), and Yalong Bay (in Hainan Province) (PB 1993).

References

Andrews, John. 1992a. A Question of Identity. *The Economist* 325: survey 7-9.

_____. 1992b. China Fever. *The Economist* 325: survey 15-7.

Asiaweek. 1990. Open Doors, Empty Rooms. *Asiaweek* (September 22): 70-1.

Associated Press. 1993. Rapid Development Spurs China to Curb 'Stir-frying Real Estate.' *The Arizona Republic* 104 (August 14) 88: A18.

Chang, Parris H. 1992. China's Relations with Hong Kong and Taiwan. *The Annals of the American Academy of Political and Social Science* 519 (January): 127-39.

Chow, W.S. 1988. Open Policy and Tourism between Guangdong and Hong Kong. *Annals of Tourism Research* 15: 205-18.

Clammer, John R. 1980. *Straits Chinese Society*. Singapore: Singapore University Press.

Cohen, Erik. 1979. A Phenomenology of Tourist Experiences. *Sociology* 13: 179-201.

The Economist. 1992. The Overseas Chinese: A Driving Force. 324 (July 18): 21-2,24.

Einhorn, Bruce. 1992. Mainland Fever Hits the Island. *Business Week* (August 10): 38.

Engardio, Pete. 1992. Mainland Mania in Hong Kong. *Business Week* (August 17): 48.

Flannery, Russell. 1991. The Merger of the Decade: Taiwanese Business Involvement in China is Ballooning. *Asian Business* 27 (August): 42-4.

Gerstlacher, A.; Kreig, R.; and Sternfeld, E. 1991. *Tourism in the People's Republic of China*. Bangkok: Ecumenical Coalition on Third World Tourism.

Gibney, Frank B. 1993. The American Connection. *Harvard Business Review* 71 (March-April) 2: 30-1.

Goldstein, Carl. 1992. Strait Talking. *Far Eastern Economic Review* 155 (December 3) 48: 46-8.

Godley, Michael R. 1989. The Sojourners: Returned Overseas Chinese in the People's Republic of China. *Pacific Affairs* 62: 330-52.

He, Guangwei, ed. 1991. *The Yearbook of China Tourism Statistics 1991*. Beijing: China Travel and Tourism Press.

Karp, Jonathan. 1992. Greens for the Reds: China Discovers the Golfing Boom. *Far Eastern Economic Review* 155 (October 29) 43: 74,76.

Kao, John. 1993. The Worldwide Web of Chinese Business. *Harvard Business Review* 71 (2): 24-7,30-5.

Koan, A. and Lincoln Kaye. 1993. Feeling the Heat (Economic Monitor: China). *Far Eastern Economic Review* 156 (June 24) 25: 24.

Lee, Fong Mo Kwan. 1982. *Enhancing Shenzhen's Environment For Tourism*. Hong Kong: Geographical Research Centre, Chinese University of Hong Kong (June).

Leung, Chi Kin. 1990. Locational Characteristics of Foreign Equity Joint Venture Investment in China, 1979-1985. *Professional Geographer* 42 (4): 403-21.

Lew, Alan A. 1987. The History, Policies and Social Impact of International Tourism in the People's Republic of China. *Asian Profile* 15 (2): 117-28.

Liu, Melinda. 1993. The Capture of a Gang Leader, Chinatown: The Underworld of Alien Smuggling. *Newsweek* (September 13): 42.

Liu, Phillip. 1993. Mixed Diagnosis for Mainland Fever. *Free China Review* 43 (9): 42-7.

Lyman, Stanford M. 1974. *Chinese Americans*. (Ethnic Groups in Perspective series, Peter I. Rose, series editor.) New York: Random House.

Mark, Jeremy. 1994a. Suspicions about Deaths of 24 Tourists Drives Wedge between Taiwan, China. *Wall street Journal* (April 12): A15.

_____. 1994b. Taiwan Curtails Trade with China in Tourist Death. *Wall Street Journal* (April 13): A10.

Mooney, Paul; Changle; and Melena Zyla. 1993. Braving the Seas and More: Smuggling Chinese into the US Means Big Money. *Far Eastern Economic Review* 156 (April 8) 14: 17-9.

Mosher, Stacy. 1992. No-man's Land: Chinese Municipality Prospers as Hongkong's Partner in Crime. *Far Eastern Economic Review* 155 (16 July) 28: 32-3.

PB. 1993. China Opens Tourism Industry. *The China Business Review* 20 (Jan-Feb): 4.

Pan, Lynn. 1990. *Sons of the Yellow Emperor: A History of the Chinese Diaspora*. Boston: Little, Brown and Co.

Pearson, Margaret M. 1991. The Erosion of Controls Over Foreign Capital in China, 1979-1988. *Modern China* 17 (1): 112-50.

Peterson, Glen D. 1988. Socialist China and the Huaqiao. *Modern China*. 14 (3): 309-35.

Poston, Dudley L. Jr. and Yu, Mei-yu. 1990. The Distribution of the Overseas Chinese in the Contemporary World. *International Migration Review* 24 (3): 480-508.

Relph, Edward. 1976. *Place and Placelessness*. London: Pion.

Ross, Madelyn C. and Kenneth T. Rosen. 1992. The Great China Land Rush. *The China Business Review* 19 (Nov-Dec): 51-2.

Sender, Henny. 1991. Inside the Overseas Chinese Network. *Institutional Investor* 25 (September): 37-42.

SCMP (South China Morning Post) 1993. Hong Kong 'Immune' to Easing of Controls on Yuan Flow. (June 22): 8.

Stoltenberg, Clyde D. 1990. China Links to Southeast Asia. *China Business Review* 17 (May-June): 33-8.

Sun, Gang, ed. 1992. *The Yearbook of China Tourism Statistics 1992*. Beijing: China Travel and Tourism Press.

Thoburn, J.T., H.M. Leung, E. Chau, and S.H. Tang. 1990. *Foreign Investment in China*

PART FOUR

Outer China

China is far from being a homogeneous nation-state. Vast regions in the north, west, and south of the country are populated by non-Han Chinese minority groups. The following essays presents the tourism development experiences in three of these minority regions of China. In these areas, the dominant Han Chinese are as much of an outsider-tourist as is the foreign devil from overseas. All three of the essays in this part of the book are based on extensive fieldwork in China.

The first essay is an inventory and assessment of tourism development in the Xinjiang Uygur Autonomous Region, an Islamic area of China. In addition to discussing the variety of fascinating attractions that this region has to offer, Stanley Toops provides considerable insight into the politics of how remote towns and regions are "opened" to tourism. He shows how infrastructure is used by the Chinese authorities to create touristic places in minority regions.

The second essay is a case study of tourism in Guizhou Province. Timothy Oakes examines the historical relationship between the dominant Han Chinese society and the minority groups of Guizhou. His research findings indicate that the colonial policies of the past are still clearly seen in the dominance of Guizhou's tourism industry by the core economic centers of eastern China, as well as urban centers within the province. How the minority groups in Guizhou manage within this system is a particularly interesting story.

Margaret Swain reports on the artisan production of handicraft souvenirs in Yunnan in the third essay. She compares the production and sale of minority ethnic souvenirs in state factories versus private household enterprises. She shows that the state, actually has considerable influence over production, income, and artistic expressions in both settings. She also sheds considerable light on the organization and livelihood of the souvenir hawkers who seem so ubiquitous in tourist China.

11

Tourism in Xinjiang:
Practice and Place

Stanley W. Toops

This chapter examines tourism in the Xinjiang Uygur Autonomous Region (XUAR). Xinjiang is a minority border area of fifteen million people, 47 percent are Uygurs, a Turkic Muslim group. Only 37 percent of the population in XUAR are Han Chinese. Located in China's Great Northwest (Da Xibei), the region covers an area of 1.66 million square kilometers, three times the size of France (see Figure 11.1).

The practice of tourism in Xinjiang is examined here through the touristic system. The touristic system is composed of raw material, tourist market, and infrastructure. This concept is used to discuss tourism development in six cities: Urumqi, Turpan, Kashgar, Kuqa, Korla, and Gulja. In each city, a touristic place is created through the touristic system.

As an organizing framework, tourism operates through three components -- raw materials, infrastructure, and markets (Figure 11.2). Smith and Eadington (1992) identify these as raw material, framework, and tourists, respectively. Nash (1992: 217) has defined the touristic process as

> originating with the generation of tourists in some society, continuing as these tourists travel to other places where they encounter hosts with a different culture, and ending as the give-and-take of the encounter affects the tourists, those who serve them, and the various societies involved.

This touristic process works through the touristic system. The touristic system interlinks societies as tourists are brought to a host country. The raw material and market components of the touristic system are connected

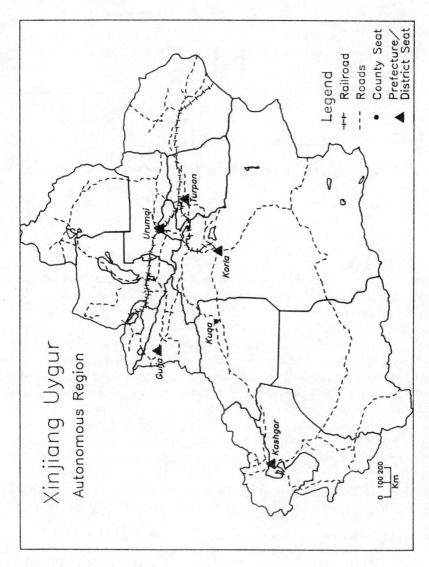

FIGURE 11.1 Xinjiang Uygur Autonomous Region Map

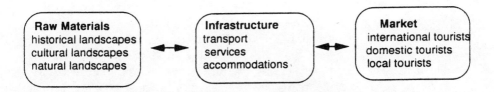

FIGURE 11.2 The Touristic System

through the infrastructural component. Infrastructure is developed later to meet the needs of the tourist rather than to meet the needs of the host area (Smith and Eadington 1992).

In Xinjiang, tourism functions through these three basic components also. Raw materials are the supply, the tourists are the demand, and the infrastructure is the means of conveyance of the tourism process.

The Raw Material of Xinjiang's Tourism

A base component of tourism is a destination--a place constructed and formed through tourism. Elements of this component are historical, cultural, and natural landscapes. Historical landscapes include museums and relics of religious, trade, or political significance show past lives and livelihoods. The cultural offerings show tourists contemporary society and its lifestyles. The built environment, celebrations and festivals, markets and bazaars, and art and music create the cultural landscape. The natural landscape is the basis for much resort tourism, be it the beach or mountain. The intricate beauty of the natural environment is a major attraction. Within Xinjiang, the most attractive cultural offerings are in Kashgar and Turpan. Historical sites are rich in Turpan and Kuqa. Diverse elements of the natural landscape are present around Urumqi (mountains) and Turpan (desert).

Xinjiang's historical sites are an important touristic resource. Xinjiang was a crossroads for religious, cultural, and economic communication between east and west. Trod by Marco Polo, and the famous Chinese monks, Fa Xian and Xuan Zang, the Silk Roads linked China to India, Persia, and Europe. The many ruins of long forgotten kingdoms are evident in the landscape and are the heritage of Xinjiang's people. Xinjiang has been called Serindia, the land between China and India. Important historical centers were Kashgar and Turpan.

Xinjiang's cultural offerings attract international tourists. The Uygurs, concentrated in the south, have a sedentary lifestyle in the oases of the Tarim Basin. Their language is Turkic, their script is Arabic, their religion is Islam. The Uygurs have lived in these oases for centuries, engaging in trade on the Silk Road and serving as cultural transmitters between East and West. The Kazaks, living in Dzungaria and the Ili Valley, lead a nomadic lifestyle. The traditional lifestyles of the Kazaks and the Uygurs are important cultural resources for tourism in Xinjiang.

Xinjiang's natural landscapes provide additional attractions for tourists, encompassing mountains, lakes, deserts, and steppe. The Tian Shan range, dotted with lakes, bifurcates Xinjiang. On the south, Xinjiang's Kunlun Mountains are the locale for K-2 (also known as Mt. Godwin-Austen), the second highest point on the surface of the earth. The second lowest point on the surface of the earth is at Ayding Lake in the Turpan depression. Taken together these elements of the natural landscape challenge international tourists with a rugged and fierce beauty.

International tourists who have already made a China trip often wish to go to places like Xinjiang to experience a different side of China. However, they tend to be concentrated in relatively few areas (Urumqi, Turpan, and Kashgar), which are most accessible, but not the richest in tourist resources. Table 11.1 lists the major tourist destinations in Xinjiang.

Xinjiang's Tourism Market

The tourists themselves are the second component of the touristic system. They are the market. As Harrison (1992) and Smith and Eadington (1992) have noted, international travel volume has been enormous in the world in

TABLE 11.1 Xinjiang Tourist Destinations and Visitors, 1991

Destination	International Visitors[a]
Urumqi	54380
Kashgar	34425
Turpan	13600
Gulja	4364
Kuqa	3032
Korla	3000
Xinjiang Total	134100

[a]International Visitors include foreign tourists, overseas Chinese nationals, and compatriots from Hong Kong, Taiwan, and Macao.
Source: Xinjiang Nianjian 1992.

recent years. As more leisure time and more discretionary income has become available, the world has seen more and more tourists. While the developed world is both the origin and destination for most international tourists, increasing numbers are turning to the unfamiliar developing world. Among the developing countries, China is a major destination.

Sources of tourists and their motivations pose major research questions (Harrison 1992; Crick 1989). Different tourists (from different sources) create different geographies of tourism across the globe (Toops 1992b). The motivation for tourism, to escape the usual and seek pleasure from the unusual (but with appropriate comforts), stimulates the touristic system. The different kinds of tourist in the system have been examined by many including Cohen (1972), who found four, and Smith (1977/1990), who identified seven. These range from mass tourists, who are more sedentary and recreation oriented, to alternative tourists, who are more exploratory and risk oriented in their activity.

The tourist market of Xinjiang is as complex as any other. Xinjiang's international tourism began in 1978 when it was first open to foreigners. In that year, 88 international tourists visited Xinjiang. A decade later over 50,000 tourists visited Xinjiang (Figure 11.3). There was a major decline in 1989 with the Tiananmen Square Incident, but recovery was complete by 1990 as the upward trend resumed. By 1991 nearly 134,100 international tourists visited the region (*Xinjiang Nianjian* 1992).

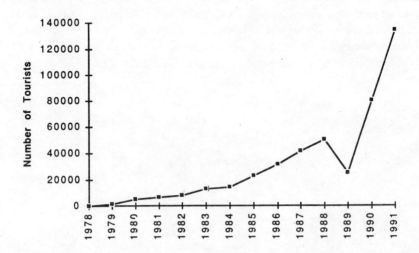

FIGURE 11.3 Tourists to Xinjiang, 1978-1991. *Source:* Hu 1984; *Xinjiang Ribao*, March 30, 1986; *Xinjiang Nianjian* 1988; *Xinjiang Nianjian* 1990; *Xinjiang Nianjian* 1991; *Xinjiang Nianjian* 1992.

Although tourists to Xinjiang come from many countries, most of the foreign tourists are from Japan and the United States (Figure 11.4). The graph shows a breakdown for 1981, when 5586 visitors arrived in the region. Japan is a chief source of foreign tourists because of its identification with Buddhism and interest in the historic sites of the Silk Road. Americans going to Xinjiang are attracted to both the natural environment as well as its cultural distinctiveness. Europeans travel on the Silk Road and recall explorations at the turn of the century by Sven Hedin and Aurel Stein. Visitors from Hong Kong and Taiwan accounted for the largest number of tourists in Xinjiang in 1981. By 1990, however, this group made up about 20 percent of the tourists to Xinjiang. For visitors from Hong Kong and Taiwan, all elements of the landscape serve as attractions, plus these tourists can negotiate the landscape in Chinese (Hu 1984: 431, 439; *Xinjiang Tongji Nianjian* 1991).

In general Xinjiang attracts tourists of two types. At the lower end of the economic scale, the backpacker tourist spends a long time in the area but does not spend a lot of money per day. At the other end of the scale are those who spend $10,000 over a period of a few weeks. These upscale package tour travelers are the "golden rice bowl" for China International Travel Service (CITS) and the newer travel services of the region. Both types of tourists, however, seek the exotic. Their goal is the same destination, but they reach it by different routes.

Increasing numbers of tourists have meant an increase in revenues for Xinjiang. In 1988 Xinjiang received FEC¥ 68.11 million from tourism--the travel services accounted for FEC¥18 million, or 26 percent of the total. A sharp decrease in all categories is marked for 1989. By 1991, tourism had recovered from the Tiananmen Square Incident and Xinjiang gained FEC¥ 116.46 million from international tourism (Figure 11.5). Visitors spent

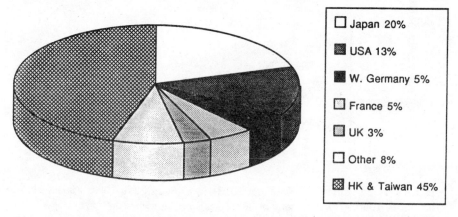

FIGURE 11.4 International Tourist Origins for Xinjiang, 1981. *Source:* Hu 1984.

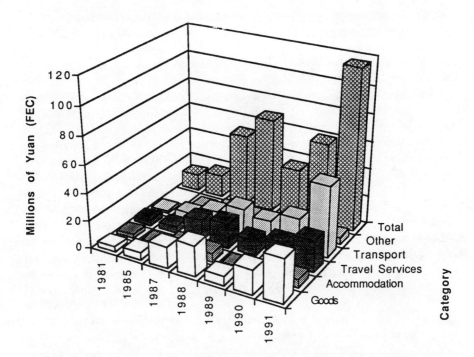

FIGURE 11.5 Tourism Expenditures in Xinjiang. *Source:* Hu 1984; *Xinjiang Ribao*, March 30, 1986; *Xinjiang Tongji Nianjian* 1989; *Xinjiang Tongji Nianjian* 1990; *Xinjiang Tongji Nianjian* 1991; *Xinjiang Tongji Nianjian* 1992.

more on tourist goods and souvenirs and transport also generated more income (Hu, 1984; *Xinjiang Ribao*, March 30, 1986; *Xinjiang Nianjian* 1988: 390; *Xinjiang Nianjian* 1992).

Infrastructure and Xinjiang's Tourism

Infrastructure provides the conveyance for tourists to accomplish their touristic project. While infrastructure is a gateway, it also functions as a refractive lens that conveys a touristic image to the tourist. Who develops this infrastructure is as important as how the infrastructure is provided. Today, entrepreneurs and governments, both local and national, may provide the services. Foreign companies also have a major role to play (Sinclair, et al. 1992; Crick 1989).

Transportation is a major element of the infrastructural framework. Transportation affects the location, distribution, and seasonality of tourism.

A poor infrastructure (accommodations and transportation) may deter
tourists from visiting magnificent sites. Additionally, interpreters, guides,
drivers, and coordinators have an infrastructure role in the touristic system.
They serve as cultural brokers between the hosts and the guests (Cohen
1985; Bowman 1992; Crick 1992).

Infrastructural development has taken place in both the number of beds
and travel service personnel. In 1986, of Xinjiang's nearly 2400 standard
beds (in rooms with attached bath) over 1000 were in Urumqi, 600 in
Kashgar, and 450 in Turpan. By 1992 small increases in the number of
beds were registered for all areas but Urumqi (Figure 11.6). Urumqi
gained 1500 beds with the opening of two joint venture hotels, the Holiday
Inn and the World Plaza Hotel (NTA 1990; Xu 1992).

Among service providers, CITS had focused on foreign tourists (non-
ethnic Chinese), while the China Travel Service (CTS) focused on overseas
Chinese tourists and those from Hong Kong, Macao, and Taiwan. The
lines of distinction are now becoming blurred, however, and ticketing can
now be done by either. In 1989, employees of the international tourism
industry in Xinjiang numbered 6520 including 5715 at hotels, 510 at travel
services, 106 at coach and cruise companies, and 174 at tourism
administration organs. By 1992, there was a proliferation of new travel
services including Nature Travel Service, Xinjiang Cultural Travel Service,
Western Regions Travel Service, Rail Travel Service, Oasis Travel Service,
Desert Travel Service, and Tianshan Travel Service (Bi 1986; *Xinjiang
Nianjian* 1988: 390; NTA 1990: 70-1, 74-5; Xu 1992).

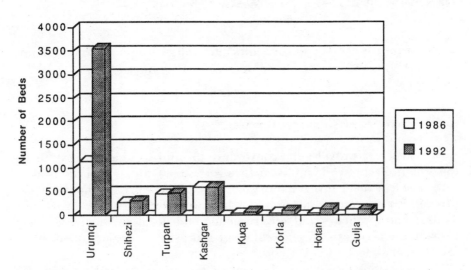

FIGURE 11.6 Standard Hotel Beds in Xinjiang. *Source:* Interviews 1986; Xu 1992.
Standard hotel beds are those in rooms with an attached bath.

A significant determinant of Xinjiang's tourism is its location. Xinjiang is not an easy place to get to--the tourist expends four hours by jet or four days by train from Beijing to reach Urumqi. Once there, visitors must cover long distances by road and air to visit sites. Although the journey is part of the value of the Xinjiang experience, it also limits the number who are willing and able to participate in this experience.

The distribution of tourists is affected by location and transportation. In 1987 Urumqi attracted 63 percent of the visitors to Xinjiang, while Kashgar and Turpan each attracted about 45 percent of all tourists in 1987. By 1991, Kashgar was attracting more tourists than Turpan due to the open route over the Karakoram Pass. Many tourists are centered in Urumqi because of its transportation facilities. During the peak season, when many of those tourists head to the cool waters of nearby Tian Chi (Heavenly Lake), the concentration of tourists is extreme. (Hu 1984: 440; *Xinjiang Nianjian* 1988; *Xinjiang Nianjian* 1992).

The seasonality of tourism is also related to the availability of transportation. Xinjiang's tourist season is busiest in the late summer-early fall (Figure 11.7). The peak month is August with almost 25 percent of the total tourist arrivals in 1981 (Hu 1984). In recent years, visitors in September and October have grown, effectively extending the high season into the shoulder season. During the off-season, tourism personnel prepare for the next year.

Tourism and Place in Xinjiang

What follows is a discussion of tourism in six places: Urumqi, Turpan, Kashgar, Korla, Kuqa, and Gulja. The analysis shows how tourism is organized in each place. The infrastructure of tourism creates these touristic places out of the raw materials of tourism. Two of these places (Kuqa and Gulja) were closed to tourism in 1986, when the analysis here begins. By 1992 all of these places were open to tourists with new and expanded infrastructure supports. The focus in this section is on the infrastructure of tourism in Xinjiang. Specifics on the tourist offerings of each of these places are found in Toops (1992a). Managers at all the major tourism sites were interviewed in 1986, providing a local perspective on the tourism industry. Subsequent observations in 1988, 1990, 1992, and 1993 have allowed a deeper understanding of Xinjiang's tourism system.

One method of measuring the impact of tourism in an area is the Tourism Intensity Rate (TIR) (Harrison 1992). The chief purpose of this rate is to provide a context by which to compare tourist arrivals, by also considering the size of the population This rate is calculated with the following formula.

$$\text{Tourism Intensity Rate (TIR)} = \frac{\text{Tourists in a given year}}{\text{Population in a given year}} \times 100$$

In Table 11.2, Kashgar and Turpan show the largest impact from tourism. While Urumqi receives the greatest number of tourists, the TIR suggests that the impact of those tourists is lower. A small town like Kuqa sees a significant impact even with its small number of tourists. Of course, this measure does not consider financial or socio-cultural impacts of tourism. Although the tourism flow into Xinjiang is not large now, if the increase continues unabated, the impacts of tourism will increase rapidly.

Urumqi: Locus of Xinjiang's Tourism

According to Samalgaski, "Urumqi is an interesting place, but it's got to be one of the ugliest cities on the face of the earth" (1988: 769). While Samalgaski's description is harsh, this capital city of 1.2 million has become the locus of Xinjiang's tourism. Urumqi's best offerings are the natural landscapes outside the city. Its most significant draw for the visitor is the natural landscape of the nearby Tian Shan mountain range and Tian Chi (Heavenly Lake). Urumqi has so few sites of significant historical or cultural value that it was not on the historical map of Serindia. While tourists can see examples of Uygur culture at the Erdaoqiao Bazaar or at the mosques, Urumqi is mostly a Han Chinese city. With limited tourist sites, but an excellent infrastructure, Urumqi is a fine example of an infrastructure-created tourist place.

While Urumqi was opened to tourists in 1978, they did not come in any numbers until 1980. In 1991 foreign visitors numbered 54,380, of which 42,789 were foreigners (the remainder being compatriots, mostly from Hong Kong). Urumqi receives more tourists than any other city in Xinjiang, because of its dominant position within the transportation network of Xinjiang (Bi 1986; *Xinjiang Nianjian* 1988; *Xinjiang Nianjian* 1992).

TABLE 11.2 Tourist Impact Measurement in Xinjiang 1990

Destination	TIR	Rank
Kashgar	15.2	1
Turpan	6.3	2
Urumqi	4.7	3
Kuqa	3.0	4
Gulja	1.7	5
Korla	1.2	6
Xinjiang	0.9	--

Source: Xinjiang Nianjian 1991.

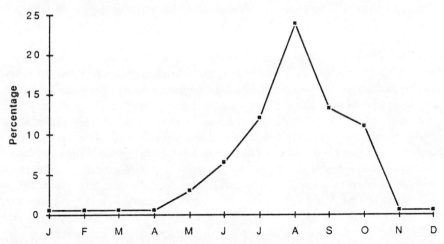

FIGURE 11.7 Monthly Distribution of Tourists in Xinjiang, 1981. *Source:* Hu 1984.

In 1989, Japan, the Commonwealth of Independent States (CIS), and compatriots from Hong Kong and Taiwan were the principal sources for Urumqi's tourists (NTA 1990). The tourists from the CIS are unlike other international tourists. They are economic tourists engaged in an informal trade network. They are composed of Uygur, Kazak, and Kirgiz traders with family connections in Xinjiang, and thus have people in their network who speak one or more of the Turkic languages plus Chinese and Russian. Of all the international tourists, this group is the closest in proximity and culture to Xinjiang (Figure 11.8).

Urumqi makes a significant contribution to Xinjiang's tourism statistics. For Xinjiang, Urumqi continues to be the leader in garnering the tourist dollar. In 1990 Urumqi pulled in FEC¥49,300,000 or just under US$9,000,000 (*Xinjiang Nianjian* 1991).

Accommodations are a major part of the infrastructure that creates a touristic place. By 1992, there were nine hotels of one-star quality and higher with a total of 3548 standard beds (NTA 1990; Xu 1992). A profile of the Overseas Chinese Hotel and the Urumqi Holiday Inn shows the variety of accommodations available to tourists. The Overseas Chinese Hotel (Huaqiao Bingguan) is under the administration of the Overseas Chinese Affairs Office of Xinjiang. A two-star hotel with 500 beds, its purpose is to serve the needs of the overseas Chinese community visiting Xinjiang. One of the hotel buildings was built in the 1950s and the other, the tallest building in Urumqi until the construction of the Holiday Inn, was completed in 1986. There are over 250 employees. A Uygur and a

Chinese restaurant as well as a rooftop buffet and gift shops complete the offerings of the hotel (Lan 1986; 1992).

The four-star Urumqi Holiday Inn (Xinjiang Jiari Dajiudian) the newest hotel in town, is a joint venture operation between the Xinjiang Hotel Corporation Limited and Holiday Inn Management Group. This 25-story hotel, now the tallest in Urumqi, has the best location in downtown Urumqi, just opposite Hong Shan (Red Mountain), a large glacial outcrop that dominates the skyline. The hotel has 700 beds and was developed with Hong Kong backing. It has Swiss management and Uygur workers, although most of the nearly 1000 employees are Han Chinese. These young workers, recruited in Xinjiang, underwent intensive Holiday Inn training. The hotel has Chinese, Western, and Muslim restaurants, English and Japanese-style bars, a discotheque, shops, and a well-equipped business center. The 383 rooms are all equipped with satellite televisions, Western-style bathrooms, international direct dial phones, and refrigerators. In short, this is the most prestigious hotel in Urumqi and in Xinjiang (Holiday Inn staff 1992; 1993; Xu 1992).

These two hotels are a study in contrasts. When the Holiday Inn supplanted the Overseas Chinese Hotel, the touristic landscape was altered. A joint venture rather than a local hotel became the favored site for international interaction. Holiday Inn has the better location, close to Urumqi's centers of power and business activities. Holiday Inn definitely has more creature comforts, creating an island of international touristic space in the midst of Urumqi. The Overseas Chinese Hotel is more representative of what Xinjiang is really like. For example, this hotel has much better Uygur food than the Holiday Inn. Although few of the staff know English, they more accurately reflect Xinjiang's reality. The Urumqi Holiday Inn compares quite favorably to other four-star hotels in China. The corporate decision makers who planned this hotel sought a location on the frontier of China and advertise the hotel as being in the middle of Asia, which is essentially correct.

Travel services are another element in the infrastructure of the touristic system. Two Urumqi services are profiled here. Founded in 1979, the Xinjiang CITS (formerly the Urumqi branch of CITS) is connected with the Tourism Bureau of Xinjiang, and is fortuitously located next door to the Holiday Inn. From 1980 to 1992, the company received over 200,000 visitors. It employed over 120 people by 1992, about half of whom were engaged as translators or guides. Japanese, English, and German speaking guides were available. While most guides are Han, six other ethnic groups are employed including Uygur, Kazak, Hui, Xibo, and Kirgiz (Bi 1986; Xu 1992).

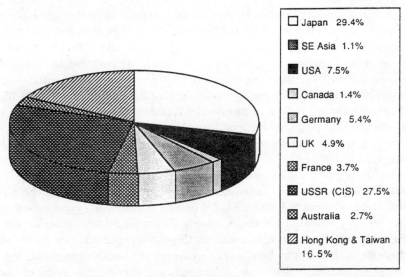

☐	Japan 29.4%
▨	SE Asia 1.1%
■	USA 7.5%
☐	Canada 1.4%
▨	Germany 5.4%
☐	UK 4.9%
▨	France 3.7%
▨	USSR (CIS) 27.5%
▨	Australia 2.7%
▨	Hong Kong & Taiwan 16.5%

FIGURE 11.8 Origins of Tourists in Urumqi, 1989. *Source:* NTA 1990: 46-47.

The Urumqi CTS office is situated on the grounds of the Overseas Chinese Hotel. Fifty employees include six guides and twenty drivers. Though lacking the language skills of the CITS guides, CTS guides focus on quality individual service. Guides are required to know the history, economy and culture of Xinjiang (Rixit 1986).

The number of employees in Urumqi's international tourism industry increased steadily during the 1980s. By 1989 there were 3400 employees in hotels, travel services, transport companies, and tourism administration. Not included in these numbers are those employed by Air China, the railways, and tourist shops (NTA 1990: 72-3).

Urumqi has been the site for much investment in the transportation element of Xinjiang's tourism infrastructure. Long distance bus service connects Urumqi with all of the major cities in Xinjiang. Daily train service out of Urumqi links Xinjiang to six major cities in China. By 1990 train service was extended to the Alataw Pass leading to the country of Kazakhstan, with one train leaving daily from Urumqi (*Xinjiang Nianjian* 1991). Urumqi has the only international airport in Xinjiang. The airport was refurbished in 1992 and 1993. Air China and Xinjiang Airlines operate flights from Urumqi to the major cities of China. Within Xinjiang, Air China has daily connections to Kashgar and Gulja and at least weekly connections to eight other cities in Xinjiang. International connections are available to Kazakhstan (Almaty, formerly Alma Ata), Pakistan (Karachi), and Turkey (Istanbul) (Liang F. 1987; Xu 1992).

The management of local tourist sites, especially Heavenly Lake (Tian Chi), has been a source of recent concern. Tian Chi is heavily used during the summer months. The site was designated as the Tian Chi Scenic Area (Tian Chi Fengjing Qu) in 1981 because of the diversity of wildlife. However, in 1985 the area received 15,000 visitors (this figure would be much larger today) (*Xinjiang Ribao*, August 25, 1985: 2). Historically the area was used as a summer pasture by Kazaks. During the summer, many of the Kazaks work as informal guides of the lake basin rather than as herders, thereby changing the area's economic landscape (*Xinjiang Ribao*, August 13, 1983: 1).

Urumqi plays a key role in the tourism industry of Xinjiang. Even though the city does not have many touristic sites, its position as the political and economic center for the XUAR means that tourists are focused on the city as they enter and leave Xinjiang. Two points characterize this city. First, Urumqi does not have much in the way of touristic raw material and, therefore, has less to be concerned about problems of maintaining local culture. Touristic activities in Urumqi are directed away from the city proper, toward Tian Chi or the city of Turpan. Cultural interactions between tourists and locals are limited to service personnel. This mitigates cultural influences on the wider local populace.

Second, Urumqi's role as hub of the tourism industry is based upon its crucial position within Xinjiang's infrastructure, mirroring the political economy of Xinjiang. Priorities for the tourism industry in Urumqi are continued development of the transportation and accommodation elements of the touristic infrastructure. The number of hotels is certainly more than sufficient as the construction boom has expanded room capacity to the desired level. With the expansion of international flights and railway routes, Urumqi's position as international transportation gateway to Xinjiang will continue (Bi 1986; Liang F. 1987).

Turpan: Heritage Tourism in an Oasis

When Marco Polo passed through here during the reign of the Great Khan Kubilai, Turpan was the capital of Uygurstan, a region of well developed laws and traditions, including Buddhism and Nestorian Christianity (Polo 1982). Now Turpan is only one of the smaller districts of Xinjiang, no longer a great capital. Tourists visit the 18th century Emin Minaret, the ruins of the Uygur capital Kara Khocho (7th to 11th century), the Bezeklik Buddha Caves (4th to 13th century), and Yarkhoto, a military outpost of the Han Dynasty and of Uygur Kingdoms. The district relies on its historical heritage as the basis for its tourism. Cultural offerings include the city bazaar and staged musical performances. In August, Turpan sponsors a Grape Festival. Grapes are grown using a karez irrigation system, similar to that in the Middle East. Tourists also visit the desert in this hot spot of China.

Turpan city has a population of just over 200,000. Located south of Urumqi, in 1991 it hosted almost 14,000 tourists (*Xinjiang Nianjian* 1992). Turpan, half open in 1978, has steady growth in numbers of tourists. Tourists come from Japan, the U.S., France, Germany, Italy and Canada. The Japanese have been the most numerous. The busiest months are in July, August, and September when the grapes are ripe (Keyum 1986; Xinjiang Nianjian 1988).

The Foreign Affairs Office at Turpan operates a CITS office with about 50 employees, including 20 translator/guides who speak English or Japanese. Translator/guides have to pass an examination before acquiring a "guide certificate" indicating their language competency. CITS Turpan has about 25 vehicles, including sedans, vans and buses. As several historic sites are over 40 kilometers away and no public transport is available, CITS has several do-it-yourself tours, which require hiring drivers and cars. Another option for the closer sites (Yarkhoto or Emin Minaret) is to take the Turpan "taxi," the donkey cart. Young boys do a brisk business during the summer taking the tourists on a bumpy ride through the back streets of the oasis.

The rail station is 45 kilometers away at Daheyon. The public bus takes two hours, so CITS also provides transport service for tourists to and from the rail station. Six trains ply the Urumqi-Lanzhou route daily, all of which stop at Daheyon. Turpan has no airport, so most tourists come by train or CITS vehicle from Urumqi. Construction of an airport would definitely increase visitation to Turpan.

The Foreign Affairs Office operates two hotels, the older Turpan Hotel and the Oasis Hotel, constructed in 1985. In total, 450 standard beds and 250 nonstandard beds are available in Turpan. The older hotel has a grape arbor covered interior courtyard at which a song and dance troupe, sponsored by the Foreign Affairs Office, performs nightly during the tourist season. The newer hotel, built under a joint contract with a Hong Kong developer, combines ethnic stylings with modern conveniences.

Several beautification actions have been undertaken to increase the appeal of Turpan. The rebuilding of the Turpan bazaar has provided the tourists with an interesting facility, while locals have benefitted too from the cleanliness of the new stalls. In 1985 Turpan built eight kilometers of grape arbors covering the sidewalks of the town. These arbors linked the two hotels with the bazaar downtown, encouraging tourist circulation within the oasis (Keyum 1986).

Local officials have been concerned primarily with promoting tourism in Turpan, rather than the possible deleterious effects of the industry.

Preserving local traditions and customs was not considered a big problem, because tourists are insulated from the locals (other than those in the tourism industry). Most tourists confine themselves to their hotel and the established attractions, supplemented with a walk to the bazaar. The historical sites will continue to be a draw for tourism, though Turpan has a competitor in Kashgar.

Kashgar: Cultural Tourism on the Frontier

Marco Polo noted that the Kashgaris live by trade and industry, marketing their wares over all the world (Polo 1982). The main draw for tourists to Kashgar is the culture. Its major sites are the Sunday bazaar and the central bazaars where the crafts and produce of Kashgar are on display. The Id Kah Mosque and Tomb of the Appak Khoja are deeply connected to the daily life of Kashgar's people, transcending the historical nature of these offerings. Outside of Kashgar, hardy tourists can take the Khunjerab Pass to Pakistan, which passes Mt. Muztagata, and crosses the Karakoram mountain range. There is a saying in the region: "You haven't been to Xinjiang, until you have been to Kashgar" (He 1988).

Modern Kashgar, the administrative and cultural center for Southern Xinjiang, began to see a small number of invited foreign guests in 1982 when the city was still closed to tourism. When Kashgar was opened in 1984, there were no direct connections to any city in China (or elsewhere) except, through Urumqi. The Khunjerab Pass between Pakistan and China was opened to foreigners in May 1986, offering an alternative route to Kashgar and doubling the volume of visitors to the city. As in Turpan, most tourists visit between June and September. Japanese, British, American, and Australian tourists predominate. Kashgar City, with a population of 225,000, saw about 34,000 tourists in 1991 (Xinjiang Nianjian 1992, Xinjiang Nianjian 1988: 644; Mao 1987; Wang 1986). This figure includes a large number of Pakistani traders who are essential to the city's economy.

Kashgar District has emphasized its development effort in the production of tourist goods. Purchases by tourists totaled over RMB¥739,000 in 1985. These tourist articles include hats, musical instruments, earthen pots, carpets, felts, embroidery, clothing, jewelry, cloth, and knives. This side of tourism, commercial goods rather than services, has been a neglected aspect of tourism in Xinjiang in the past (Xinjiang Ribao, December 27, 1985; Toops 1993).

Twenty-five people work at the CITS branch office in Kashgar including translators, guides, and chauffeurs. CITS Kashgar in 1986 had 13 vehicles to transport tourists -- five vans, four Landcruisers, two buses, and two sedans. In 1986 the XUAR government allocated money to buy five

Landcruisers. Because of the rugged terrain on the Karakoram Highway, Landcruisers are the preferred vehicle. When the Khunjerab Pass opened in 1986, the demand for vehicles increased. Transportation options include weekly public bus service to Khunjerab, as well as daily buses and flights to Urumqi.

The primary accommodation in Kashgar is the New Kashgar Hotel located on the eastern end of town. The Seman Hotel is located on the grounds of the former Russian Consulate. Together these two hotels provide 600 standard beds (in rooms with bath). Other possible accommodations are at the Chini Bagh Hotel, the former British Consulate, and the Tian Shan Hotel for a total of 350 beds (with public bath). Some 450 service personnel work at the hotels.

As viewed by the Office of Foreign Affairs, problems related to the tourist industry include tourists wandering into closed areas and the thriving black market. Routes along the Southern Silk Road (beyond Hotan) are still closed to tourists, yet these areas have a certain attraction to those seeking an off-the-beaten-track experience. In 1985, one tourist died of illness and exposure in the mountainous Aksai Chin area near the Tibet/India border. The black market is growing in the area--the dominant activity involves the exchange of U.S. dollars and of Foreign Exchange Certificates (FEC¥) for Chinese renminbi (RMB¥). Stricter supervision of locals in the hotel areas or bazaars is the primary means of enforcement.

Maintenance of the historical sites of Kashgar is the job of the Cultural Relics Bureau. Much work on the refurbishing of the sites had to be accomplished before Kashgar became an open city in 1984. Renovation of such sites as well as the bazaar is a part of the general program before a city can become open. The bazaar is both a locus of local commerce and a touristic place. At the Sunday bazaar a new building was constructed at the entrance to the bazaar. Renovation of the bazaars benefits both tourists and locals (*Xinjiang Ribao*, January 16, 1984).

Kashgar's attraction to tourists derives from its significance on the Silk Road and the predominantly Uygur character of the area. The essence of Uygur culture dominates the landscape of this modern-day city on the Silk Road through its bazaars, mosques, tombs, architecture, foods, and products (Wang 1986; Mao 1987).

Kuqa: Rich Heritage and Cultural Resources of a County Seat

When the Chinese Buddhist monk, Xuan Zang, visited Kuqa on his journey to India in the 600s, he noted that the manners of the people were honest and that they excelled in music and art (Waley 1952). This county in southern Xinjiang, with the treasures at Kizil Buddhist Caves, Subash, and the Kizil Kara caves, has a deep historical heritage. Kuqa, being a small county seat, has maintained a traditional Uygur lifestyle in its bazaar, crafts, and mosques (Toops 1993). Here is much potential for tourism as both cultural and historical sites abound. Yet administration of such cultural and historical resources is difficult for a rural county.

Kuqa began receiving invited guests in 1978. By 1984 the number of foreign visitors increased as Kashgar was opened, although many visitors to Kuqa were only in transit to Kashgar. Because Kuqa was still closed, they could only stay in town or be taken to the historical sites managed by the Kuqa Cultural Relics Bureau, which did not include the Kizil Buddhist Caves. By 1985 the official tourist groups consisted mostly of Japanese. These were usually specialty group tours emphasizing photography of the Kizil Caves. Americans, West Germans, French, and visitors from other countries comprised the small number of individual tourists who had gained permission of the Urumqi Public Security Bureau to visit Kuqa. A growing occurrence were specialty tours of Muslims from Pakistan, Saudi Arabia, or Turkey who may have relatives in Xinjiang. In general most tourists visit April through August. By 1991, this 'closed' town of less than 100,000 had over 3000 tourists per year (*Xinjiang Nianjian* 1992; Imimjan 1986).

The Kuqa Foreign Affairs Bureau includes the four CTS guides. One guide was studying Japanese in 1986. The primary difficulty for Kuqa is language training for the guides. CTS has three cars: one jeep, one four-wheel drive Toyota Landcruiser, and one 20-passenger van. The Foreign Affairs Bureau has three Chinese sedans. The Kuqa Hotel, constructed in 1985, has fifteen double rooms with bath, a souvenir kiosk, and a Uygur restaurant. Weekly air flights are available to Urumqi and Korla.

In 1986 Kuqa applied to be an open city, but this request was denied. The tourist sites were there, but accommodations and personnel required further expansion. Kuqa's administrative status as a county seat rather than a district seat also hindered its upgrade to open status (Imimjan 1986). By 1992 Kuqa was an open city. With this administrative hurdle crossed, a new touristic landscape was created. A new hotel, the Silk Road Hotel was constructed with 70 beds available. More staff and vans were added to CTS Kuqa and more Japanese tourists came to Kuqa. CTS Kuqa can look for even more tourists in the coming years. The Kizil Caves and Uygur folkways make Kuqa an interesting alternative destination (Ahmetjan 1992).

Gulja: Cultural Tourism with the Nomads on the Frontier

A daughter of a Han Dynasty (202 B.C.E. - 220 C.E.) Emperor was married, for political reasons, to the king of the Wusun, a nomadic people of this district. She wrote a poem saying that this place was the "world's end," with "only mutton for food and the milk of mares" (Wu 1940: 201). Tourists may no longer feel they are at the world's end in Gulja, but they are certainly at the frontier of China's touristic system. These pastures along the shores of Sayram Lake and the Ili River were the historical cradle of Central Asian nomadic groups. The Kazaks are only its most recent residents. Tourists come to see the pastoral nomadism of the Kazaks in this frontier of China. This type of cultural resource/attraction is very limited as fewer and fewer Kazaks live a traditional nomadic life.

In 1985, about 1000 tourists came to Gulja, which is located on the border with Kazakhstan. A large group, led by Jules Verne Travel, embarked on a Silk Road tour through Turkey, the Soviet Union, and China by rail. From Almaty (formerly Alma Ata) the group crossed into China at Korgos by bus, overnighted at Gulja, and then went onto Urumqi by bus via Sayram Lake. This sort of expensive travel group is welcomed by Gulja. Most of the tourists to Gulja, though, are from Hong Kong (Mao 1990). Gulja was opened to tourists in 1991. As the administrative center of the Ili Kazak Autonomous Prefecture, it had none of the difficulties of Kuqa in being opened. In 1991 this city of 260,000 received 4300 tourists. Most of these were from Hong Kong as before, but a growing number are from the CIS. The CIS visitors actively trade in Gulja and the nearby border town of Korgos.

The Ili District Foreign Affairs Office manages CTS which employs several guides, one of whom speaks English. The centrally located Ining Hotel has 120 beds in rooms with baths. The hotel is on the grounds of the former Russian Consulate. Two new hotels are under construction on the western side of town. Various guesthouses, at Sayram Lake and in town, are available, as well, although none of these have rooms with attached bath. There are flights six times weekly to Urumqi. CTS has several jeeps and sedans available for visitors.

From Gulja to Sayram, there exists a variety of ethnic cultures, historic places, and beautiful natural scenery. The Ili Kazak Autonomous Prefecture may play a major role in the future of Xinjiang's tourism. However, without much infrastructural development, tourism in the near future will remain fairly limited in Gulja (Chen 1985; Bonavia 1988: 116-22; Liang A. 1987: 56-68; Ren 1986.)

Korla: Tourism and Administrative Status

Korla is the capital of the Bayingolin Mongol Autonomous Prefecture in Xinjiang. The largest prefecture in all of China, Bayingolin is roughly the size of California. The population of Korla is mostly Han Chinese with a small Mongol minority. Ethnic groups, including Mongol or Uygur, generally live in the rural areas of this prefecture. There is nothing to see in Korla as it is mainly an administrative center. Korla will probably never become a major stop on the tourist itinerary given the relative paucity of its attractions. It may, however, develop into a gateway for the Takla Makan Desert and the towns of southern Xinjiang. Korla is, at present, the railhead of the Nanjiang railway, which runs through the mountainous region south of Urumqi. The route, a minor engineering feat, is very scenic with many bridges and tunnels. The timetable puts the most scenic section of the route in darkness, however.

The total number of tourists in Korla was just over 1000 (including foreigners and overseas Chinese nationals) in 1985. Of the foreigners, the Japanese and the British were the most numerous. Mountain climbing parties also arrived in 1985. May through September are the peak months. In 1985, groups planning to tour the area had to be approved by the Foreign Affairs Office of the Autonomous Region, one to two months in advance. Individual tourists that arrived were out of luck since the Bayingolin Foreign Affairs Office had limited facilities. In 1991, this administrative center of 250,000 received 3000 tourists (*Xinjiang Nianjian* 1992).

The Bayingolin Foreign Affairs Office has available to it several cars for transporting tourist and only a few personnel deal with tourists. Bayingolin Hotel, built in the 1980s, had 50 beds in rooms with attached baths and another 50 without. That hotel was torn down and the New Bayingolin Hotel opened in 1992. This new one-star level hotel has about 100 standard beds. Planes fly weekly to Urumqi and Kuqa. The train runs daily to Urumqi.

In 1985 Korla applied for open tourist status. With its transport and administrative status, Korla was an open city by the end of 1986 even though its tourist offerings were not well developed. The new Bayingolin Hotel shows further how administrative status can create a touristic place in a city without attractions and even without tourists (Sun 1986; *Wen Hui Bao* 1986).

Urumqi, Turpan, Kashgar, Kuqa, Gulja, and Korla all have different potentials for tourism. All have different capacities for tourism. All are different places, created by tourism. All combine to make up Xinjiang.

Conclusions: Issues for Xinjiang's Tourism Industry

As tourism continues to develop in Xinjiang, several issues confront the region. These include cultural transformation, economic growth, and infrastructure.

A major concern for the Chinese government is how to provide a product that is consonant with the requirements not only of tourists but also of China. One of China's goals for tourism, beyond that of foreign exchange, is to allow foreign travellers to see and view China and to return home with a good impression. For Xinjiang, the government's policy on the minority nationalities is a part of the showcase, especially for tourists from Islamic countries. Xinjiang shows these tourists how China deals with its own Muslim minorities.

The product, structure, market, and returns of tourism in the developing world must be in sync to ensure that tourism preserves places rather than destroys them (de Kadt 1979). A major issue is how places are transformed through tourism. There will be changes, but will these changes be good for the locality (Harrison 1992)? In areas where tourism focuses on the cultural landscape, does tourism change and challenge local culture (Rossel 1990)? In areas of historical tourism, does tourism preserve or protect historical sites (Urry 1990)? In regions of natural landscape tourism, does tourism encourage or minimize environmental degradation (Pigram 1992)?

Xinjiang's major issue is the cultural and economic impact of tourism. As the tourism industry developed in Xinjiang, different problems have surfaced. During the early stages of development in Xinjiang (1979-1982), those in the industry felt there was not enough capital for investment and not enough souvenirs for tourists (*Xinjiang Ribao*, January 28, 1982: 1). A major concern for the tourism industry is sustaining the growth of tourist arrivals. A recent addition in Xinjiang has been tourists from the states of the ex-Soviet Union. The Chinese from Hong Kong have been a mainstay for Xinjiang's tourism and Taiwan will be another important new source for tourism. But the largest potential is found in China's domestic tourism. As the Chinese economy improves, individuals will have more discretionary income for touring their country. This may well be one of the mechanisms for capital transfers from the coast to the interior of China.

Xinjiang tourism managers have identified infrastructural issues as foremost in their concern. Hotels can be built, roads can be paved, buses can be bought, personnel can be trained--all with relative ease assuming the capital is available. If the tourists come, that demand will generate capital to fund the needed infrastructural improvements.

A major question is the presentation or preservation of touristic resources. When tourism works well, the presentation is balanced with preservation. A dysfunctional tourism is one that does not present the tourist sites well or fails to preserves the raw material of tourism. The people of Xinjiang and their place, its landscape and its images, are the raw material of its tourism. Preservation and presentation should be the priority not only of the managers or practitioners of tourism, but also of the tourists and of the people of Xinjiang. The tourists are guests, while the people of Xinjiang are the hosts. Both hosts and guests need to take responsibility for the outcome of the tourism.

The distinctiveness of Xinjiang derives from the characteristics of place, in particular, places like Urumqi, Kashgar, Turpan, Kuqa, Gulja, and Korla. These touristic places were created by the touristic process. In Urumqi, the state structures a transportation network that has created a tourism center. Kashgar, on the frontier, has access to international tourists in Pakistan for its cultural tourism of an Islamic region. Turpan and Kuqa have developed a heritage tourism that preserves and presents the Buddhist past of Serindia. Administrative status has been a factor in holding back Kuqa's tourism, while enhancing tourism in Korla and Gulja. The biggest change to come will be in Gulja, when international tourism networks in Kazakhstan completely extend across the border.

As the tourism industry grows, Xinjiang needs to emphasize the preservation of its historical, cultural, and natural landscapes. Tourism has been considered a valuable resource in Xinjiang (Lu 1985). Rational development of such tourism resources can only be accomplished by coordinated action by the Xinjiang Tourism Bureau and the Cultural Relics Bureau, and with the involvement of the local people. Urumqi emerges as the center of Xinjiang's tourism in terms of the PRC's policies of economic development and political integration. Growing centers for the tourist industry are found in Kashgar and Turpan with possible development sites in Gulja and Kuqa. Thus the present and future economic landscape of tourism in Xinjiang mirrors the past cultural landscape of Serindia, the land between China and India. The needs of the locals and the tourists can be accommodated only with rational and cautious planning.

References

Ahmetjan. 1992. Interview with Ahmetjan of the China Travel Service in Kuqa (October).

Bi Yading. 1986. Interview with Bi Yading of the Urumqi Tourism Bureau (May 20).

Bonavia, Judy. 1988. *The Silk Road*. Hong Kong: Passport Books.

Bowman, Glenn. 1992. The Politics of Tour Guiding: Israeli and Palestinian Guides in Israel. In David Harrison, ed. 1992. *Tourism and the Less Developed Countries*. New York: John Wiley, pp. 121-134.

Chen Zhenbin, ed. 1985. *Ili Hasake Zizhizhou Gaikuang* (Ili Kazak Autonomous Prefecture Outline). Urumqi: Xinjiang Publishing House.

Cohen, Eric. 1972. Towards a Sociology of International Tourism. *Social Research*. 39 (1): 164-182.

_____. 1985. The Tourist Guide: The Origins, Structure and Dynamics of a Role. *Annals of Tourism Research*. 12 (1): 5-29.

Crick, Malcolm. 1989. Representations of International Tourism in the Social Sciences: Sun, Sex, Sights, Savings, and Servility. *Annual Review of Anthropology*, 18: 307-44.

_____. 1992. Life in the Informal Sector: Street Guides in Kandy, Sri Lanka. In David Harrison, ed. 1992. *Tourism and the Less Developed Countries*. New York: John Wiley, pp. 135-147.

Harrison, David. 1992. International Tourism and the Less Developed Countries: The Background. In David Harrison, ed. 1992. *Tourism and the Less Developed Countries*. New York: John Wiley, pp. 1-18.

He Lin. 1988. Kashi Diqu de Luyou Ziyuan (Kashgar District's Tourist Resources). *Ganhanqu Dili* (Arid Land Geography), 11 (3): 61-66.

Holiday Inn staff. 1992. Interviews with Urumqi Holiday Inn staff (October).

Holiday Inn staff. 1993. Interviews with Urumqi Holiday Inn staff (October).

Hu Zuyuan. 1984. Luyouye (Tourism). In Chen Hua, ed. *Xinjiang Jingji Gaishu* (An Outline of Xinjiang's Economy), Urumqi: Xinjiang People's Publishing House, pp. 431-443.

Imimjan. 1986. Interview with Imimjan, the Kuqa Foreign Affairs Bureau Director (April 29).

de Kadt, Emmanuel. 1979. *Tourism: Passport to Development?* New York: Oxford University Press.

Keyum Rozi. 1986. Interview with Keyum Rozi, Chief of the Foreign Affairs Office in Turpan (June 4).

Lan Yunyuan. 1986. Interview with Lan Yunyuan, the Overseas Chinese Hotel Manager (May).

_____. 1992. Interview with Lan Yunyuan, the Overseas Chinese Hotel Manager (June).

Liang Aili, et al. 1987. *Xinjiang Daoyou Tuce* (A Guide to Xinjiang). Hong Kong: Xiangbali International.

Liang Feng, ed. 1987. *Wulumuqi Luyou* (Urumqi Tourism). Urumqi: Xinjiang People's Publishing House.

Lu Yun. January 7, 1985. Xinjiang—A Centre for Future Development. *Beijing Review* 28 (1): 27-34.

Mao Baodi. 1987. Kaifa Nanjiang Luyouye Chuyi (My Humble Opinion on Developing Tourism in Southern Xinjiang). *Xinjiang Shehui Kexue* (Xinjiang Social Science) 4: 44-46.

Mao Baodi, et. al. 1990. Tourist Resources and Tourism Development in North Xinjiang, *GeoJournal* 21 (1/2): 161-165.

Nash, Dennison. 1992. Epilogue: A Research Agenda on the Variability of Tourism. In V. Smith and W. Eadington, eds. *Tourism Alternatives: Potentials and Problems in the Development of Tourism*. Philadelphia: University of Pennsylvania Press, pp. 216-225.

National Tourism Administration (NTA). 1990. *Zhongguo Luyou Tongji Nianjian 1990* (The Yearbook of China Tourism Statistics 1990). Beijing: China Travel and Tourism Press.

Pigram, John. 1992. Alternative Tourism: Tourism and Sustainable Resource Management. In V. Smith and W. Eadington, *eds. Tourism Alternatives: Potentials and*

Problems in the Development of Tourism. Philadelphia: University of Pennsylvania Press, pp. 76-87.

Polo, Marco. 1982. *The Travels.* Translated by Robert Latham. New York: Penguin.

Ren Yuandi. 1986. Interview with Ren Yuandi, the Ili District Foreign Affairs Bureau Director (June 2).

Rixit Niyaz. 1986. Interview with Rixit Niyaz, CTS Urumqi Director (May 27).

Rossel, Pierre. 1988. Tourism and Cultural Minorities: Double Marginalisation and Survival Strategies. In Pierre Rossel, ed. *Tourism: Manufacturing the Exotic.* Copenhagen: International Work Group for Indigenous Affairs., No. 61, pp. 1-20.

Samalgaski, Alan, et al. 1988. *China: A Travel Survival Kit.* Victoria, Australia: Lonely Planet.

Sinclair, M. Thea, et. al. 1992. The Structure of International Tourism and Tourism Development in Kenya. In David Harrison, ed. 1992. *Tourism and the Less Developed Countries.* New York: John Wiley, pp. 47-63.

Smith, Valene, ed. 1977/1990. *Hosts and Guests.* Philadelphia: University of Pennsylvania Press.

Smith, Valene and William Eadington, eds. 1992. *Tourism Alternatives: Potentials and Problems in the Development of Tourism.* Philadelphia: University of Pennsylvania Press.

Toops, Stanley. 1992a. Tourism in Xinjiang, China. *Journal of Cultural Geography* 12(2): 19-34.

_____. 1992b. Tourism in China: The Impact of June 4, 1989, *Focus* 42(1): 2-7.

_____. 1993. Xinjiang's Handicraft Industry. *Annals of Tourism Research* 20(1): 88-106.

Urry, John. 1990. *The Tourist Gaze.* London: Sage.

Waley, Arthur. 1952. *The Real Tripitaka.* London: George Allen and Unwin.

Wang Jiangong. 1986. Interview with Wang Jiangong, Foreign Affairs Office Director, Kashgar District (May 5).

Wen Hui Bao. 1986. Zhongguo Zai Kaifang 192 ge Shi Xian (China Opens 192 more Cities and Counties). *Wen Hui Bao* (Compilations Daily), (December 4). Hong Kong: American Edition.

Wu, Aitchen K. 1940. *Turkistan Tumult.* London: Methuen.

Xinjiang Nianjian (Xinjiang Yearbook). 1988 to 1992. Compiled by the Xinjiang Weiwuer Zizhiqu Difangzhi Bianji Weiyuanhui (Xinjiang Uighur Autonomous Region Gazetteer Editorial Committee). Urumqi: Xinjiang People's Publishing House.

Xinjiang Tongji Nianjian (Xinjiang Statistical Yearbook). 1989 to 1992. Compiled by the Xinjiang Weiwuer Zizhiqu Tongji Ju (Xinjiang Uygur Autonomous Region Statistics Bureau). Urumqi: China Statistics Publishing House.

Xu Jinfa. 1992. *Xinjiang Luyou Zhansheng* (A Guidebook to Xinjiang Tourism). Urumqi: Xinjiang University Press.

12

Tourism in Guizhou: The Legacy of Internal Colonialism

Timothy S. Oakes[1]

Debates over the geography of post-Mao development in China have often focused on whether or not economic reforms are creating greater regional disparities by encouraging decentralized markets and local specialization (see Yang 1990; Prime 1991). Cannon and Kirkby (1989: 17), for example, have suggested that policies which allow certain households to "get rich quick" are also relevant on a regional scale, "and it is therefore likely that regional differentials in economic growth will, in the medium term, at least, become more pronounced." Though the evidence of this remains inconclusive, the Chinese state is concerned with presenting the deployment of market mechanisms as a truly socialist endeavor. Thus, strategies to develop poor regions and mitigate the uneven accumulation of wealth are highly publicized to reassure people that the state remains committed to social equality, if not complete equity. Officials, academics, planners, and propagandists in China actively discuss policies and strategies for developing poor (usually ethnic and mountainous) regions. In some regions, tourism has become an important component of these strategies; it is promoted as a catalyst for reducing the isolation and lack of integration which afflict poor regions.

This chapter explores the role of tourism as a development and modernization strategy in Guizhou Province, long stigmatized as one of China's most backward and impoverished regions. In particular, it examines how tourism is promoted as part of broader efforts to commercialize the rural economy in Guizhou. Although tourism-enhanced commercial development in remote rural areas offers a practical solution to rural Guizhou's lack of economic integration, a lingering political economy of internal colonialism is, in many ways, being reinforced by tourism development. This can be illustrated on two levels. On one level, we find an economic environment which encourages the geographical concentration of tourism income in urban centers. The tourism industry in Guizhou is almost entirely state-owned, and locally initiated commercialism, particularly in rural areas, remains undeveloped, due to powerful urban-bureaucratic control of tourism planning, investment, and development. This has helped fuel a continuing urban-rural sector gap in which rural peripheries find it difficult to realize the economic benefits needed to stimulate local commercial transformation. On another level, tourism involves a process whereby particular images and experiences of places are constructed and sold to the tourist. In Guizhou, these images are often informed by dominant representations inherited from the region's internal colonial and frontier histories. They are representations which convey a remote, backward, culturally exotic, even erotic place. How these images are accommodated or resisted by locals will also condition the benefit they derive from tourism development.

Given the significance of Guizhou's history to its contemporary tourism development, the following section traces the historical patterns of both the internal colonial legacy and the post-Mao reforms as they have affected Guizhou's society and economy. This is necessary before going on to exploring Guizhou tourism in detail, for it brings to light many of the difficulties currently being faced among those counting on tourism to help drive the region's commercial development.

Guizhou's Internal Colonial Legacy

The province of Guizhou straddles the rugged, rain-drenched eastern half of the Yun-Gui Plateau in China's culturally diverse southwest. It is primarily a landscape of karst-limestone topography, significantly eroded by the high rainfall (up to 60 inches annually). The province boasts the least amount of flat land of any region in China--moreover, the leached soils are generally unproductive. Though this riverine land of sinkholes, caves, subterranean rivers, canyons, and waterfalls is now admired by a growing number of tourists, Guizhou's harsh landscape was long avoided by Chinese settlers. The air was malarial, fertile valleys were few and far between, rivers were unnavigable, and it was populated by hostile, rebellious natives. As surrounding lands were gradually brought under the direct administration of the empire, much of Guizhou remained a contentious frontier for the Chinese, even into the 20th century. The story of Guizhou's colonization is a long and complex one, and cannot be done justice here. But a few key points should be considered.

Internal colonialism in Guizhou was manifest primarily in terms of increasing in-migration, a vulnerable and unstable economy based on resource extraction, and repressive administrative rule and taxation. Migration, both government sponsored and independent movements of land hungry peasants from nearby provinces, led to much indigenous land alienation.[2] Arable land was the most precious of Guizhou's resources, and even landowners had difficulty surviving. Unnavigable rivers and mountainous terrain inhibited transport and trade, and rural markets were undeveloped since few products could bear the cost of transport. Increased debt among farmers, especially during the turbulent 19th and early 20th centuries, led to concentrated land ownership among the upper classes, higher rates of tenancy, and impoverishment for subsistence producers (Spencer 1940). During the 19th century, modern industrial production along China's coast was causing Guizhou's rural household industries to wither, and prompted more land to be devoted to cash crops like raw cotton, medicinal products, tung oil, and opium poppy.[3] Timber and mineral extraction also intensified. As a result, sites of capital accumulation were increasingly found not at the place of extraction, but in the production and processing areas beyond the province's boundaries (see Qiandongnan G.E.B. 1986: 29-32). Conflicts with local chieftains (known as *tusi*) were endemic as Han settlement and economic changes intensified. Late-imperial Guizhou became a highly militarized frontier landscape of walls, towers, garrisons, and social repression. Few autonomous social institutions developed beyond those controlled by the military and the government--it became a region well suited to unchecked warlord power, and remained only tenuously under imperial control.[4]

As with colonial experiences around the world, Guizhou's colonization was cultural as much as political and economic. The militarized frontier landscape of Southeast Guizhou (Qiandongnan), for example, was legitimized in cultural terms by emphasizing differences between the civilizing Chinese and primitive indigenous people (cf. Harrell 1993a). Ethnic identities were largely conditioned by the unequal economic exchanges and landscapes of political and military control which characterized Guizhou's internal colonialism. Miao identity, for example, was associated with wilderness--they were the stubborn, tenacious antithesis of civilization (Diamond 1993). Evidence of this was most often represented in highly gendered ways. For example, women were depicted as having loose sexual morals and pursuing everyday activities thought to be improper for women (such as drinking in public and engaging in business) (Diamond 1988). Much of Guizhou came to be identified as a 'Miao Pale' (*Miao Jiang*), a wilderness of quintessential 'Miaoness', remote, hostile, and impenetrable. The cultural legacy of internal colonialism was thus one of defining indigenous people according to their temporal and spatial distance from the Chinese center. Although that distance was accepted in *a priori* terms by the colonizing Chinese, it was in fact a distance constructed by colonialism itself. The boundaries of Miao identity were drawn according to social distinctions engendered through aspects of the colonial experience, such as land alienation, onerous taxation, new divisions of labor based on cash crop production, and especially the harsh implementation of direct rule. Those identified as Miao were generally those who were most disadvantaged through this experience (Oakes n.d.).

Maoist Period: The Great Leap and Third Front

During the late 19th century, the Qing government gradually abandoned Guizhou as imperial finances withered and unrest increased. The succeeding Republicans were unable to counter this trend. Visitors, like Hosie (1890) and Spencer (1940), were impressed by Guizhou's abject poverty and lawlessness. The Communists were likewise impressed as they passed through during the Long March in 1934-5.[5] Yet, while the Long March may have heightened the Communists' awareness of Guizhou's poverty, regional development policies during the late 1950s, 1960s, and early 1970s were probably dictated more by security concerns than the egalitarianism which the Maoist leadership was long praised for. The professed goal of regional parity, moreover, was inadequately provided for by a strategy which stressed heavy industrial development, regional economic autarky, and high rates of investment in production at the expense of services and basic infrastructure. By stressing regional self-sufficiency and massive industrial development projects in the interior which lacked integration with local economies, the state only generated a levelled-down, center-dependent regional parity. While this resulted in phenomenal economic growth at a national scale, it was achieved through unsustainably high investment rates. Little was achieved in the way of encouraging fully integrated regional economies, nor were the needs of poverty stricken areas adequately addressed.

After a relatively calm period during the early 1950s, in which Guizhou's new leadership began to reestablish social order and rejuvenate food production, Maoist China was soon caught up in the Great Leap Forward (GLF). Guizhou, with its vast coal and iron ore reserves, quickly became the center of extraction for fueling rapid industrial development throughout Southwest China. Nearly all state investments were diverted to mining and mineral processing, the result being a decrease in agricultural productivity, and an increased dependence on central financial assistance. Ironically,

Guizhou's leaders perceived the GLF as a turning point in provincial integration, and welcomed it as an opportunity for Guizhou to cast off its colonial status. Guizhou was even promoted as a model of the virtues of having been "poor and blank" (Goodman 1983: 111). Ultimately, however, rapid collectivization of agriculture and the excessive investment focus on extractive industry only led to economic and political chaos in Guizhou. Unable to implement national policies and disabled by ethnic tensions resulting from the campaign against 'local nationalism', Guizhou's entire leadership was dismissed in 1965 and replaced by functionaries from Sichuan (Goodman 1986). It would be 15 years before a Guizhou native would once again serve among the province's leaders.

This situation set the stage for probably the most significant factor in Guizhou's development during the Maoist period: the 'Third Front' (*di san xian*) policy. This was largely a defense related plan which began in 1964 when Mao called for a reemphasis on state investments in basic industry over consumer goods, as well as the relocation of coastal industry to the interior. The Third Front was highly centralized and required enormous state investments. Two-thirds of the central state's entire industrial budget went to Third Front development during its peak (Naughton 1988: 365). The plan was characterized by the rapid design and construction of large scale, remotely located factories which offered little for developing local economies. While Guizhou no doubt enjoyed massive investments during this period, the Third Front served to render the province's economy even more vertically oriented and dependent on the center. Poorly planned and nearly inaccessible factories rarely generated a profit, and most operated well below their designed capacity, while whole cities were built to house workers, most of which were not native to the region. Inefficiency was the rule. For example, though fixed assets for industrial enterprises in Guizhou during this period were 27 percent higher than in Beijing, Tianjin, Shanghai, Jiangsu, and Liaoning, labor productivity remained 56 percent lower than in these coastal areas (He 1988: 65). Many projects, in fact, were never completed, as international political tensions eased through the 1970s, and the government realized that Third Front investment was unsustainably high.

Post-Mao Period: Bureaucratic Centralism vs. Comparative Advantage

By 1978, Guizhou's lack of development was not so much due to the long history of 'self-sufficient economies,' which some analysts point to as the cause of continued uneven development (see, for example, Li 1990), but more from an entrenchment of its internal colonial status. If Guizhou's economy was ever self-sufficient, it was during the short-lived leniency of the early 1950s. But overall, the Maoist period left a legacy of increased dependence on the center, low agricultural productivity, heavy industrial inefficiency, poor infrastructure development, and inadequate attention to local conditions on the part of leadership. Post-Mao economic reforms, however, were not undertaken with a comprehensive plan in mind for addressing these problems. Rather, the primary concern was the overall inefficiency of the economy--only in an *ad hoc* way have reforms been dismantling the structure of the Maoist system, leaving significant gaps between the increased incomes being realized on the one hand, and prospects for comprehensive economic development in impoverished regions on the other. The incremental nature of reforms may thus be a problematic factor in Guizhou's ability to cast off its internal colonial status.

Echoing the new emphasis on regional comparative advantage, officials in Guizhou seek to promote the region's (1) rich variety of plant and animal resources, which flourish in a favorable sub-tropical climate and in a wide variety of vegetation zones provided by mountains which cover 87 percent of the province, (2) mineral wealth, especially coal and iron ore, and (3) tourist resources as a place of scenic beauty and local ethnic color (*minzu fengqing*) (Yi 1989). In prioritizing the development of "all aspects of the rural economy," Guizhou's leaders heavily stress the development of a township and village consumer goods economy consisting of three components: cash crop production (such as rapeseed, tobacco, and tung oil); traditional specialties (such as liquor, cigarettes, and ethnic textiles); and light industrial production focusing on local consumer goods and export items (ethnic handicrafts, textiles, and cheap appliances) (Chen and Wang 1990). In addition, strategies also call for an increase in the local services sector, and this is to play a particularly important role in tourism development.

Light industrial production in rural Guizhou has grown considerably, especially during the early 1980s, with output value from 1979 to 1986 far surpassing the entire three decades preceding the reforms (GPRCC 1987: 458). These developments, however, have generally taken place only on the fringe of major urban centers like Guiyang and Liupanshui (He 1988: 490), leading some officials to look toward household level commercialism to stimulate more remote regions. Such a strategy relies on the improved circulation of and access to capital, labor, and information. Yet Guizhou's history of internal colonialism has left a legacy of vertical dependency which persists to this day. This is often referred to as the *"tiao tiao kui kui"* problem, in which the state's bureaucratic and fiscal structure cannot adequately adapt to a relatively autonomous, decentralized economy. Inter-regional trade is thus inhibited by local bureaucratic control of commercial development, often in the form of territorial protectionism. Guizhou suffers a chronic shortage of local capital. According to a source cited by Yang (1990: 225), Guizhou in 1984 *exported* over 700 million yuan (RMB¥), "virtually equal to the total financial subsidies from the central government!" Outside capital is thus desperately sought for investments in less lucrative projects like infrastructure (which is crucial for tourism development).

Guizhou's development is being carried out by a government which is trying to unleash a decentralized commercial economy to improve living standards, while at the same time continuing to reserve its diminishing investment resources for traditional heavy industrial, mining, and mineral processing sectors. Commercial, agricultural, and rural industrial sectors are thus largely left to themselves for capital inputs. It is in this light that we approach the issue of tourism development, for tourism is not only promoted as a potential earner of income but as a catalyst for a much broader process of commercial development and 'modernization' (*xiandaihua*). Tourism, it is hoped, will not only attract investment in rural industry, commerce, and infrastructure, but will stimulate a transformation in traditional thinking from subsistence to commercial-oriented activity. However, given the lingering political economy of internal colonialism and local bureaucratic control, tourism development has significant obstacles to overcome if it is to generate locally initiated economic change. The problem is symbolically most evident in the fact that it is the colonial representations of local culture as remote, wild, and primitive, which remain the most enticing images to draw on in the marketing of tourism in ethnic regions of Guizhou.

Tourism Development in Guizhou

Background

The emphasis of tourism development in Guizhou has been on the scenic attractions of the province's predominantly karst landscape, and on the cultural attractions of minority groups which make up over one-third of Guizhou's population. Two separate tourist routes (*luyouxian*) have been opened, with the bulk of investments and tourists being funneled to the western route. Western sites--including Huangguoshu Falls, Longgong Cave, Hongfeng Lake, Zhijin Cave--are easily accessible from Guiyang (the provincial capital). They are primarily scenic attractions. The eastern route, focusing on Qiandongnan Miao and Dong Autonomous Prefecture, is more remote from Guiyang, with poorer roads, more rainy days, and fewer scenic sites. While the western route has nine state-level scenic and cultural sites, the eastern route only has two. While this difference is significant in terms of which route receives the most funding, accessibility to Guiyang has been the principle factor conditioning the geography of Guizhou's tourism development.

The eastern route was actually established at the same time as the western, in 1982, but clearly lags behind in development. Qiandongnan is promoted primarily as a region rich in minority culture (*minzu fengqing*). It has only been fairly recently, however, that tourism promoters in Guizhou have recognized the culture of minority nationalities as a tourist attraction. With ethnic culture now seen as one of Guizhou's most lucrative tourist resources as well as one of its most colorful attractions in improving its 'comparative advantage,' more and more funding has gone into promoting ethnic tourism as a foundation of Guizhou's tourism development, especially along the more accessible western route. This has brought about some interesting developments regarding tourism's relationship to commercial development in ethnic minority regions of Guizhou.

Numerous proponents of tourism development in the mountainous and ethnic regions of Guizhou argue that tourism is a form of social, cultural, and economic exchange, and that through tourism, 'modernization' can be brought to remote areas (He 1986; Liang 1990; Liao 1986; Wang 1985; Wu 1987). Instead of the massive development projects of the Maoist era (such as the Third Front) which had little to offer local economies, tourism is seen as a gradual catalyst for changing "traditional thinking" and enabling locals to "grasp" the market incentive and understand the importance of diversification.[6]   He (1986) comments that in Guizhou, isolated mountainous regions lack capital, locals don't understand the meaning of 'commodity economy' (*shangpin jingji*), and have little comprehension of the outside world. This attitude is compounded by policies which prioritize grain self-sufficiency over commercial rural development projects in these poor regions, since grain-rich regions are now selling surplus grain on the open market instead of having it redistributed to poorer regions. Given this situation, He expects tourism to be a significant agent of change in these areas, and that its development will not be a drain on local resources since metropolitan tourists will naturally flock to exotic cultural sites expecting a primitive experience.

This latter point represents an interesting twist on tourism as 'modernization', since ethnic sites are to be promoted as exotically 'un-modern.' Mindful of Guizhou's poor infrastructure, proponents of ethnic tourism in Guizhou hope that tourists will in fact be lured by the possibility of a primitive experience, and that they will not mind the temporarily poor quality of the facilities and services if these are cloaked in an ethnic style. As Swain (1990, 29) puts it, "ethnic tourism is intended to be used economically, as a temporary cultural phenomenon, not as a vehicle for ethnic group sustainability." This approach is revealed in the saying, *luyou datai, jingmao changxi* ("economic trade performing on a stage built by tourism"). Thus, ethnic tourism is supposed to stimulate commercial activities and services as local entrepreneurs provide for the tourist's exotic experience. It is unclear, though, what kind of modernization will result. Representations of ethnic and cultural differences have long played a role in the outsider's perception of Guizhou as a remote, hostile, and backward place. As discussed above, the history of Guizhou's internal colonial development has been one of constructing these differences, rather than erasing them, as China's modernization strategy is expected to do.

By 1994, Guizhou had established at least 20 officially recognized ethnic tourist villages. These are easily accessible places, which offer an 'on-demand' cultural experience for group tourists. Originally, these villages were found primarily in Qiandongnan along the eastern route, but recently, in an effort to expose more tourists to Guizhou's ethnic culture, a number of villages along the western route have recently been opened, and it is these villages which now receive the most tourists. Officials in Guizhou's tourism industry regard these villages as important components of a poverty alleviation program, and expect more and more villages to be opened as the number of tourists in Guizhou increases.

Beyond these special sites where an entire experience is staged, ethnic commodity production is stressed. By 1988, 63 township and village enterprises (*xiangzhen qiye*) had been established as 'tourist product factories' (*luyou pinchang*) in Guizhou. Over half of these were producing specifically ethnic textiles and handicrafts (GPTB 1988: 707). Most of these products are actually sold outside of the province in busier tourist centers, such as Shenzhen, Guilin, and Xian, where a consistent market can be found. In Guizhou itself, selling ethnic handicrafts is generally carried out informally at tourist sites. Festivals are also promoted as ideal settings for the direct cultural and financial exchange between hosts and guests which tourism is supposed to encourage. Officials make a point of stressing that some 440 festivals and public rituals are held in Guizhou each year. These serve as ready-made experiences which simply need to be opened to tourists. For example, promoting tourism at the Dragon Boat Festival (*Longchuanjie*) in Shidong (along the eastern route) has encouraged locals to put on a gala event which has become a significant generator of revenue for the local region (Schein 1989: 208).[7]

However, tourism development strategy in Guizhou is shifting more towards staged villages. Festivals occur on fixed dates and are thought of as risky ventures for drawing tourists, while staged villages provide an 'on-demand' environment more to the convenience of tourists. MacCannell (1984: 386) has argued that ethnic tourism offers little commercial benefit to locals since very little of the tourist's money is spent at the actual site. While this is true in Guizhou, the real issue is not economic but geographic. Staged villages do experience a dramatic increase in income in a very short time.[8] As an agent for commercial transformation, tourism in these villages is, in fact, quite successful. But tourist villages remain geographically concentrated around Guiyang, Kaili, and a few other scenic regions. Contrary to the expected spread of this kind of tourism throughout Guizhou's minority regions, current patterns indicate an increasing concentration of tourist investments and revenues along the western route corridor between Guiyang and Huangguoshu Falls, and to a lesser extent around Kaili in Qiandongnan.

Assessment

Two major issues are evident in Guizhou's tourism development. First, despite the increased opportunities which economic reforms have brought to Guizhou's rural populace, tourism is still largely conditioned by a state structure which controls investments, the choice of sites to be promoted, as well as the flows of tourist expenditures. This is true for China as a whole. But in Guizhou, the relationship between the state and those whose lives are in various ways affected by tourism must be viewed in the historical context of internal colonialism to fully understand the patterns and potentials of (especially ethnic) tourism development. Second, the images of exotic ethnicity, which are increasingly pervasive in Guizhou's tourism, need to be understood in a similar context. That is, tourism is part of an on-going process of the reproduction of cultural difference. This reproduction occurs among a complex of various actors (from village heads to foreign travel agents) and is by no means under the control of one particular monolithic force (such as "the tourism industry"). The ways locals accommodate and/or resist this process will significantly affect the patterns of tourism development, and the potential benefits from it.

The effects of state control over tourism development in Guizhou can be seen in several ways. The state is generally a centralizing force in Guizhou's tourism development. State-run travel agencies, hotels, and souvenir manufacturers are concentrated overwhelmingly in Guiyang, with an additional few in the satellite cities of Anshun and Kaili (regarded as the centers of the western and eastern routes, respectively). In 1992, Guiyang accounted for 72.4 percent of Guizhou's tourist receptions, while Anshun accounted for an additional 21.4 percent. Revenues were even more concentrated, with Guiyang retaining 94.1 percent of the tourist income, and Anshun another 4.6 percent. Spending among domestic tourists shows a similar pattern, with Guiyang retaining 94.3 percent of domestic tourism revenues (TYEC 1993: 217). As tourism in Guizhou has increased over the past few years, Guiyang's proportion of total revenues has likewise increased.

Thus, a geographical hierarchy is evident when we examine patterns of tourist spending in Guizhou. The picture is so skewed because there remain few opportunities for commercial contact between rural locals and tourists in anything other than informal sales of handicrafts in the staged settings afforded by ethnic tourist villages and scenic sites. Trips to ethnic villages and scenic sites are usually arranged for one day only, taking guests from hotels in Guiyang, Anshun, or Kaili, to a village and a cave or waterfall, and returning them again safely before nightfall. At festivals, tourists often sit in cordoned-off enclosures and stay in barricaded guesthouses. While minimizing contact may be undertaken with the good intentions of reducing the shock of tourists intrusions in a relatively impoverished region, it reserves the opportunities of commercial benefit for agents and entrepreneurs in urban areas who control lodging, transport, and other commercial services.

With the power to retain the most income at the urban top of this hierarchy, localities resort to territorial protectionism in competing for the remainder. Counties which share one scenic area--such as the Wuyang River which is split between Shibing and Zhenyuan counties--are thus developing parallel and competing tourist development projects for attracting tourists rather than creating an integrated plan (*Guizhou Ribao*, Aug. 11, 1993). Ethnic tourist villages are similarly established by each county seeking direct access to Guiyang, rather than cooperating to form a regional network of tourist resources which could be tapped for commercial development based locally rather than in Guiyang. Such geographical protectionism is a familiar scenario among other Third World countries promoting tourism (see Britton 1982; Lea 1988). Oudiette (1990: 130-1) has made similar observations regarding competition between China's provincial travel agencies. As she argues, tourism offers an interesting perspective on the contradictions of a decentralizing economy which remains subject to bureaucratic manipulation.

The structure of tourist commodity production further concentrates tourist revenues in regional and international urban centers. While the proportion of revenues generated from the purchase of commodities declines as tourism expands (3.4 percent in 1992 down from 10 percent in 1988), successful producers are forced to market their goods in other parts of China. State-owned urban enterprises have much greater success in this than local workshops. Thus, a situation is developing in which tourist commodity production is concentrated in Guiyang, Anshun, and Kaili, with more labor-intensive aspects of handicraft manufacturing (such as indigo dying of batik and embroidered patches for wallets) contracted out to villages on a piece-work basis. This provides cash income to villagers and helps prevent traditional skills from dying out, but also serves to maintain an urban-rural gap in which rural producers have no systematic means of generating indigenous commercial enterprise. This trend is definitely on the increase in Guizhou, heralded by Western consumers under the banner of 'cultural survival.' In general, travel services are beginning to create specialized itineraries for international ethnic textile collectors and wholesalers. One American company has been contracting with villagers for embroidery and batik work to then be assembled in town workshops into Western-style clothing to be marketed in North America and Europe. The company's partner in Guizhou has been the province's largest travel agency.

Patterns of domestic tourists are also conditioned by the centralized state bureaucratic structure. This is most profoundly seen in the large proportion of China's domestic tourists travelling ostensibly on official business. As noted by Schein (1993), Xijiang, a large Miao settlement in Qiandongnan, has become famous as a 'typical' (*dianxing*) Miao village. Its model status attracts numerous official visitors on trips arranged by various bureaus of the local state. Official tourism in Guizhou (that is, for conferences and meetings) is thus channeled toward a specific set of model tourist villages, as well as a newly constructed set of replica Miao, Yi, Dong, and Bouyei villages on the shores of Hongfeng Lake, a state-level scenic area a mere half hour from Guiyang. Beyond this 'state-sponsored' version, domestic tourists in Guizhou remain profoundly concentrated in the scenic sites of the western route, and, as the above figures have indicated, spend most of their money in Guiyang.

In terms of state tourism investments, it appears that as these increase, resources continue to be channeled toward the more accessible western route scenic sites. The 7th Five Year Plan (FYP) saw a dramatic increase in state tourism investments in Guizhou (from 28.37 million yuan during the 6th FYP to 75.29 million yuan during the 7th) (GPTB 1988: 704; GPRCC 1991: 649). An even sharper increase is expected for the 8th FYP, which emphasizes SW China as a major development front in China's national tourism strategy (TYEC 1991: 358). The bulk of these investments go to Guizhou's five state-level scenic sites, four of which are found along the western route. This has led to a burst of activity in developing ethnic tourist villages near these western route scenic sites, which serves to further concentrate investments geographically and maintain Guiyang's dominance rather than encourage the spread of tourism-inspired commercialism. It also is having the effect of rendering the more isolated ethnic villages of Qiandongnan more authentic, exotic, and culturally distant in the eyes of Guizhou's urban-based tourist industry. Related construction investments further this trend--Guizhou's first and only divided highway (completed in December, 1991) links Guiyang directly with Huangguoshu Falls, providing easy access to nearly all western route sites, none more than three hours from Guiyang.

TABLE 12.1 Tourism Characteristics in Guizhou, 1991-1993

	1991	1992	1993
Total International Receptions	37,462	76,293	102,483
Hong Kong, Macao	8,634	14,854	13,087
Taiwan	18,367	42,405	45,701
Foreigners	10,362	18,706	42,570
Total Group Receptions	19,402	43,682	70,117
Hong Kong, Macao	n/a	6,334	7,925
Taiwan	n/a	25,947	25,612
Foreigners	n/a	11,401	35,791
Total Individual Receptions	18,050	32,611	32,366
Hong Kong, Macao	n/a	8,520	5,162
Taiwan	n/a	16,458	20,089
Foreigners	n/a	7,300	6,977
Length of Stay (days):			
Total average	1.80	1.72	1.93
Foreigners	2.24	2.19	2.06
Foreign Exchange Earnings (US$)	3,037,500	6,861,300	10,494,500
Domestic Tourist Earnings (RMB¥)	n/a	271,899,300	n/a

Sources: TYEC 1993; GPRCC 1993; Guizhou Provincial Tourism Bureau.

TABLE 12.2 Origins of International Visitors to Guizhou, 1992-1993

	% of Total Foreigners Received	
International Origin	1992	1993
Regional:		
Asia (not including Compatriots)	63.5	77.8
Europe	14.8	9.2
North America	8.4	5.5
Pacific Region	4.4	5.8
Other	8.7	1.7
National (top 6):		
Singapore	31.2	41.2
Malaysia	5.8	9.3
Japan	16.4	7.0
Thailand	4.8	4.7
USA	6.6	4.2
France	n/a	2.9

Sources: TYEC 1993; Guizhou Provincial Travel Bureau.

TABLE 12.3 Breakdown of Foreign Tourist Spending, 1992

Expenditure Category	%
To tourist organizations	73.03
To other services	26.97
including:	
air travel	19.3
commodities	3.4
rail travel	3.0
post/telecommunications	0.9
other	0.4

Sources: TYEC 1993.

Guizhou has seen an average 35 to 40 percent increase in international tourists each year since 1989 (see Table 12.1 and 12.2). But along with this increase, as mentioned above, tourist related commodity purchases have declined proportionally, even as they become more concentrated geographically. Total foreign exchange earnings have increased even more rapidly than the numbers of tourists. The jump of 123.5 percent in foreign exchange earnings from 1991 to 1992 was China's largest for that year. Yet it seems that these increases don't translate into benefits for local suppliers (Table 12.3). Most of the increase is coming from group tours, which do provide a consistent supply of tourists to rural ethnic villages and generate cash income for locals in these settings, but which also serve to further the systematic concentration of tourism income in Guiyang and bypass whatever incipient local commercial endeavors there may be beyond Guizhou's few urban centers.

Besides the issue of geographic concentration of income and a history of unequal urban-rural exchange, Guizhou's internal colonial history has left a legacy in which the state participates in a process of selective extraction. State control over tourism development in many ways reflects the continuation of this process, by providing a hierarchical, urban-biased structure which determines the flows of tourist investments and expenditures, and prioritizes tourist activities which are kept separate from the majority of the rural populace. Potential rural benefits are minimized and tourism-enhanced commercialization remains elusive to those who the state claims need it most. But for those whose lives *are* affected by the increasing numbers of tourists passing through their towns and villages, the colonial legacy is even more profoundly experienced in another way: through representations which maintain their distance from the world of the tourists. Schein (1993) has called this "Internal Orientalism."

Tourism is playing a role in which Qiandongnan is promoted as a hearth of Miao culture and identity, creating a contemporary 'Miao Pale.'[9] As such, it attracts outsiders who come not simply for travel but for research, filming, artistic, and other purposes for which Miao culture has become attractive. Promotional materials from the tourist bureau and CITS in Kaili present the local Miao as tourists expect to see them: bedecked in colorful costumes, singing and dancing, sexually promiscuous and uninhibited, and 'savage' yet 'noble' (see Oakes 1992: 11-2). As Schein (1993) points out, these representations are highly gendered--women are objectified as the sexualized embodiment of Qiandongnan's ancient remoteness. As she also argues, the construction of these images for the tourist market is a highly complex process, and is played out according to local power dynamics all the way down to the village level. A local elite, for instance, may play a major role in serving up local women as tourist attractions (thereby reducing its own distance from the tourists while reinforcing that distance for the women). But the women themselves may complicate this by their reluctance to cooperate with the local elite's planned activities. For many women, successful employment in tourism-oriented services, such as at the *Minzu Binguan* (National Hotel) in Kaili, may hinge on their willingness to perform as bearers of a selected and officially recognized Miao tradition. That this becomes something of a paradox in their quest for modernity, Schein reports, has not been lost on many of these "custodians of Miao authenticity." The local politics of representation, in other words, significantly conditions the benefits of tourism as a modernization strategy.

A similar paradox is found at ethnic tourist sites throughout the province. Several of Guizhou's tourist villages are officially recognized by the provincial cultural bureau as 'preserved open-air museums,' repositories of authentic minority culture to be enjoyed by tourists and studied by scholars. In one, a Bouyei village near Huangguoshu Falls which is recognized as the 'home of batik' (*laran zhi xiang*), locals have put together a plan to build a small batik factory, recognizing that they currently have no regular means of accumulating a tourism income other than the informal sale of household batik textiles to tourists. But the county government won't fund it and the villagers can't get a loan, despite official 'allowances' which are supposed to encourage this kind of locally initiated commercial development. County officials consider the village's plan to be unfeasible and, economically speaking, they're right. But it is ironic that the 'home of batik' can't scrape together the capital to build its own batik factory. In their quest for modernization, it remains their role to be the quaint, handicraft village seen in post cards.

Conclusion

Tourism in Guizhou is still in its incipient stages. One can only speculate at this point about future developments as tourism increases rapidly throughout Southwest China. However, it seems clear that tourism as a state-sponsored modernization strategy is, in many ways, being channeled by the historical political economy of internal colonialism. For the state, 'modernization' entails very specific and limited goals, ranging from a more 'civilized society' (*wenming shehui*) to a stronger army. Yet, it is increasingly apparent that modernization in China is a much more ambiguous process, and a highly contested one, as different interests assert their claims on what 'modern China' means. The representation of China's non-Han periphery is very much implicated in this burgeoning discourse on Chinese modernity. Tourism development in non-Han regions of Guizhou should thus be viewed through this broader lens of the experience of modernization in China as a whole. The suggestion being made here is that the lingering political economy of internal colonialism provides a framework for tourism development which perpetuates representations of China's non-Han periphery as the antithesis of modernity.

Such a process is occurring for various complex reasons. Despite rural economic reforms, commercial opportunities remain limited for locals to benefit from tourism development in rural ethnic and scenic sites in Guizhou. This is largely due to state-controlled centralization of tourist investment, revenues, and planning, which exacerbates the lack of access to capital, information, and markets which already plague Guizhou's rural economy. At the heart of the issue is a political economy in which the state maintains control over tourism development while simultaneously seeking to promote tourism as a catalyst for autonomous economic growth. The contradictions inherent in this approach result in a continuing internal colonial relationship, particularly between minority nationality groups, such as the Miao, and the state. With few opportunities for local engagement with tourism development, ethnic regions of Guizhou are portrayed for outside tourists according to the dominant images expected of such regions: their remoteness, backwardness, and un-modern primitivism. In their own quest for modernity, local ethnic attractions must perform a delicate balancing act in appearing un-modern for the purposes of modernization. That tourism is channeling the experience of modernization in rural Guizhou in such a way calls into question the kind of economic performance such a contradictory cultural stage is supporting.

Notes

1. Financial support for the author's research in Guizhou was provided by the National Science Foundation and the National Academy of Sciences Committee on Scholarly Communication with China. The author would like to thank Kam-wing Chan, Louisa Schein, and Siu-woo Cheung for helpful comments on earlier drafts of this chapter.

2. Although officials disparaged independent migration for inciting conflicts between settlers and indigenous farmers, government agricultural colonies themselves were probably an even greater cause of indigenous land alienation. Chinese historiography has made much of the 'plundering' of Dong and Miao lands in Guizhou, but the numbers are significant. By the 16th century in Wukai (a garrison near present-day Liping) there were reported to be some 32,261 soldier-settlers tilling 3,251 *qing* (about 21,450 hectares) of land (Qiandongnan G.E.B. 1986: 35).

3. Opium was one of the few products which could generate a profit and, by the late 19th century, poppy was enthusiastically raised by those for whom it was the only source of cash income. But opium producers were also vulnerable to political whims, and poppy production ultimately exacerbated Guizhou's already distorted land tenure situation (see Spencer 1940).

4. As early as the Han Dynasty the Chinese empire had employed a lenient policy of indirect rule over its unstable frontiers. By the Song, this had become institutionalized as the system of native chieftainship (*tusi zhidu*), in which local chieftains were invested with military titles, hereditary offices, private armies, and tax collecting autonomy. During the Ming, the government began to seek the gradual removal of *tusi*, who were antagonistic toward increased central control. The implementation of direct rule intensified during the Qing under a policy known as *gui tu gai liu*.

5. General Zhu De made the following notes in his journal in 1934 (Smedley 1956: 315-6):

Corn with bits of cabbage, chief food of the people. Peasants too poor to eat rice; sell it to pay rent and interest. Rice seized by militarists as 'war rice tax'... Peasants call themselves 'dry men'--sucked dry of everything... People digging rotten rice from ground under landlord's old granary. Monks call this 'Holy rice'--gifts from heaven to the poor. Taoist and Buddhist temples everywhere, Christian churches in cities. Christian converts preach four slogans: "Boycott Japanese goods!" "Buy British and American goods!" "Fight the Reds!" "Believe in God!"

6. This approach to tourism is by no means unique to China. Much research on tourism throughout the world deals with this kind of "demonstration effect."

7. Schein comments that:

As with peak season in any resort, the local guesthouse had doubled its prices for both Chinese and foreign guests for the duration of the festival. Two exhibitions of embroidery and silver jewelry from all over Qiandongnan, advertised in both Chinese and English, had been set up to meet the appetites of tourist shoppers. On the street outside the guesthouse two additional stalls selling handicrafts appeared on the day of the festival. This was particularly noteworthy, because such handicrafts, especially older works, are almost never seen in rural markets frequented only by peasants, thus the target customers were clearly outsiders (1989: 208).

8. In one case, a newly established tourist village along the western route, per capita net peasant income (*nongmin chunshouru*) increased from 110 yuan to 670 yuan in less than two years.

9. The Dong also make up a sizable proportion of Qiandongnan's population, but have not historically been subject to the same attention the Miao have received as some of China's most exotic and primitive 'others.' This, however, is changing with the rapid opening of more accessible Miao regions near Kaili. As this process continues, the Dong regions, still a good day's arduous travel from Kaili, have become the more 'exotic' destinations.

References

Britton, Stephen. 1982. The Political Economy of Tourism in the Third World. *Annals of Tourism Research* 9: 331-58.

Cannon, Terry and Richard Kirkby. 1989. Introduction. In Goodman, David, ed., *China's Regional Development*. London: Routledge, pp.1-19.

Chen Yongli and Wang Jingren. 1990. Guizhou Jingji Diyu Fazhan Zhanlue Chutan (Preliminary Discussion on Guizhou's Regional Economic Development Strategy). *Guizhou Shifan Daxue Xuebao* (Journal of Guizhou Normal University) 63(2): 1-6.

Diamond, Norma. 1988. The Miao and Poison: Interactions Along China's Southwest Frontier, *Ethnology* 27(1): 1-25.

_____. 1993. Defining the Miao: Ming, Qing, and Contemporary Views. In Harrell, Stevan, ed., *China's Civilizing Project*. Seattle: University of Washington Press.

Goodman, David. 1983. Guizhou and the PRC: The Development of an Internal Colony. In David Drakakis-Smith, ed., *Internal Colonialism: Essays Around a Theme*, Developing Areas Research Group: Institute of British Geographers, Monograph #3., pp.107-24.

_____. 1986. *Centre and Province in the PRC; Sichuan and Guizhou, 1955-1965*. Cambridge: Cambridge University Press.

GPRCC (Guizhou Provincial Records Compiling Committee). 1987. *Guizhou Nianjian 1987* (Guizhou Yearbook 1987). Guiyang: Guizhou Renmin Chubanshe (Guizhou People's Press).

_____. 1991. *Guizhou Nianjian 1991*. Guiyang: Guizhou Renmin Chubanshe.

_____. 1993. *Guizhou Nianjian 1993*. Guiyang: Guizhou Renmin Chubanshe.

GPTB (Guizhou Provincial Tourist Bureau). 1988. Gaoyuan Qipai: Xinxing de Guizhou Luyouye (Plateau Attractions: The Emerging Tourism Industry in Guizhou). In *Guizhou Gaige Kaifa de Shinian: 1978-1988* (Ten Years of Reform Development in Guizhou: 1987-1988). Guiyang: Guizhou Renmin Chubanshe, pp. 701-9.

Harrell, Stevan. 1993a. Introduction: Civilizing Projects and Reactions to Them. In Stevan Harrell, ed., *The Civilizing Project: Peripheral Peoples of China Encounter Confucians, Christians, and Communists*. Seattle: University of Washington Press.

_____. 1993b. The History of the History of the Yi. In Stevan Harrell, ed., *The Civilizing Project: Peripheral Peoples of China Encounter Confucians, Christians, and Communists*. Seattle: University of Washington Press.

He Lanchang. 1986. Kaifa Guizhou Shanqu Xianfeng Jingji (Development of the Mountainous Economy in Guizhou). *Zhongguo Nongcun Jingji* (China's Rural Economy) (August): 40-4.

He Renzhong et al, eds. 1988. *Guizhou Jingji Shehui Fazhan Jiaocheng* (Development of an Economic Society in Guizhou). Guiyang: Guizhou Renmin Chubanshe.

Hosie, Alexander. 1890. *Three Years in Western China*. London: George Philip.

Jenks, Robert. 1985. The Miao Rebellion, 1854-1872: Insurgency and Social Disorder in Kweichow During the T'ai P'ing Era. Unpublished Ph.D. Dissertation, Department of History, Harvard University.

Lea, John. 1988. *Tourism and Development in the Third World*. London: Routledge.

Li Wenyan. 1990. Contemporary Spatial Issues. In G.J.R. Linge and D.K. Forbes, eds., *China's Spatial Economy*. Hong Kong: Oxford University Press, pp. 59-84.

Liang Wei. 1990. Lun Wenling Diqu Luyou de Zhanlue Sixiang He Duiceng (On the Strategic Thought and Policy of Regional Tourism in Wenlin). *Guizhou Shifan Daxue Xuebao* (Journal of Guizhou Normal University) 63(2): 7-10.

Liao Zhengshi. 1986. Kaifa Luyou Ziyuan, Zhenxing Minzu Jingji (Development of Tourism Resources: Vitalizing Ethnic Economies). *Minzu Tuanjie* (National Unity) (December).

MacCannell, Dean. 1984. Reconstructed Ethnicity, *Annals of Tourism Research* 11: 375-91.

Naughton, Barry. 1988. The Third Front: Defense Industrialism in the Chinese Interior. *China Quarterly* 115: 351-86.

Oakes, Timothy. 1992. Cultural Geography and Chinese Ethnic Tourism, *Journal of Cultural Geography* 12(2): 3-17.

_____. n.d. Identity and Poverty in Guizhou; A Cultural-Historical Geography. Unpublished manuscript.

Oudiette, Virginie. 1990. International Tourism in China. *Annals of Tourism Research* 17: 123-32.

Prime, Penelope. 1991. China's Economic Reforms in Regional Perspective. In Gregory Veeck, ed., *The Uneven Landscape: Geographical Studies in Post-reform China*. Baton Rouge: Louisiana State University Press, pp. 9-27.

Qiandongnan Gaikuang Editorial Board. 1986. *Qiandongnan Miaozu Dongzu Zizhizhou Gaikuang* (Profile of Qiandongnan Miao Nationality and Dong Nationality Autonomous Prefecture). Guiyang: Guizhou Renmin Chubanshe.

Schein, Louisa. 1989. The Dynamics of Cultural Revival Among the Miao in Guizhou. In Nicholas Tapp and Chen Chao, eds., *Ethnicity and Ethnic Groups in China*. Hong Kong: Chinese University Press, pp. 199-212.

_____. 1993. Popular Culture and the Production of Difference; the Miao and China. Unpublished Ph.D. Dissertation, Department of Anthropology, University of California, Berkeley, California.

Smedley, Agnes. 1956. *The Great Road: The Life and Times of Zhu De*. New York: Monthly Review Press.

Spencer, J.E. 1940. Kueichou: An Internal Chinese Colony. *Pacific Affairs* 13(June): 162-72.

Swain, Margaret B. 1990. Commoditizing Ethnicity in Southwest China. *Cultural Survival* 14(1): 26-30.

TYEC (Tourism Yearbook Editorial Committee). 1991. *Zhongguo Luyou Tongji Nianjian 1991* (China Tourism Statistical Yearbook 1991). Beijing: Renmin Chubanshe (People's Press).

_____. 1993. *Zhongguo Luyou Tongji Nianjian 1993*. Beijing: Renmin Chubanshe.

Wang Changwen. 1985. Lun Shaoshu Minzu Diqu Luyou Shichang de Kaifa. (Exploring Tourism Market Development in Ethnic Minority Areas). *Jingji Wenti Tansuo* (Investigation of Economic Questions) (September): 61-3.

Wu Xiong. 1987. Lun Guizhou Xibu de Wenhua Luyou (The Study of Cultural Tourism in Western Guizhou). *Bijie Shizhuan Xuebao* (Journal of Bijie Teacher's College) (February): 61-6.

Yang, Dali. 1990. Patterns of China's Regional Development Strategy. *China Quarterly* 122 (June): 230-57.

Yi Yunchuang. 1989. Guanyu Pinkun Diqu Jingji Kaifa Wenti de Tantao (The Study of Economic Development in Poor Regions). *Jingji Dili* (Economic Geography) 9(1): 1-5.

13

A Comparison of State and Private Artisan Production for Tourism in Yunnan[1]

Margaret Byrne Swain

Yunnan Province is a major asset in China's domestic and international tourism industry due to its geographic and cultural diversity (Swain 1990). This province, situated in the southwest corner of China, tilts from jungles along the Vietnam border up to snowcapped mountain ranges on the Tibetan Plateau. Complex landform and climate patterns produce distinct environments supporting great variety in animal and plant life and human settlements. Approximately one third of Yunnan's population of 38 million people belong to 25 state recognized minority nationality groups living mainly in mountainous regions. Chinese tourist literature for both domestic and international markets emphasizes this diversity and promotes images of idyllic experiences in places where scenic variation is enhanced by the presence of non-Han Chinese, local peoples living quaint lifestyles.

However, these same characteristics also reflect remote and impoverished indigenous communities. Yunnan, in the early 1990s, is home to some of the most economically underdeveloped people in contemporary China (YINGOS 1993). Efforts to address one of Yunnan's greatest problems, rural poverty, with one of its potentially greatest economic resources, tourism, is a development strategy at both the national and provincial levels. Yunnan became a Special Economic Zone in June, 1992, and tourism has become a heavily promoted industry. Foreign exchange income generated by tourism rose from US$1.75 million in 1980 to US$16.43 million in 1990.

Foreign exchange grew a phenomenal 388 percent in 1991, to US$63.79 million, and stabilized at US$67.51 million in 1992 (Yunnan Sheng Luyouju 1993: 53; Sun 1992).[2]

The huge increase from 1990 to 1991 in Yunnan's tourism receipts was about three to four times higher than any other provincial growth rate in the country (Sun 1992: 104). The province's cultural attractions were clearly an important reason for this growth. Major infrastructure improvements and heavy advertising were already underway by mid-1991 for the February 1992 "Third China Arts Festival," which was held in Kunming and was undoubtedly an important factor in the 1991 increase in Yunnan's tourism. One post-festival report comments that "Curiosity about the culture and arts of the ethnic minorities, added to by the mysterious beauty of Yunnan Province, attracted guests from 27 countries and regions" (Wen 1992: 23).

One source of Yunnan's tourism income is from artisan production of handicraft souvenirs. Handicraft work, as a form of economic development, has not been systematically organized or tracked in Yunnan by government agencies, but statistics on tourism receipts show a huge gain in commodities income from 20 percent of the 1990 total to 71 percent of the 1991 total (Yunnan Sheng Tongjiju 1992: 567). This essay raises questions about the economic significance and benefits of handicraft production by comparing the control over production and income received by producers in government factories, private factories, and household cottage industries. The analysis is based on data drawn from Lunan County in China's Yunnan Province.

The research discussed in this chapter started with the hypothesis that artisans producing for government run factories and government buyers have less control over artistic expression and lower income rates than their colleagues in free market enterprise. This issue is complicated by the degree to which artisans function within a free market economy or a state controlled economy. Factors which impact artisan production for tourism include ethnic group location, organization and gender relations, as well as market demand. Competition for markets at the provincial, national and international levels is expected to continue to grow with the opening of Yunnan to capital development (both foreign and local) and infrastructure improvements.

The selling of the material culture of Yunnan's indigenous peoples and the mass-marketing of pseudo artifacts to tourists can be seen as a "commoditization of ethnicity" (Swain 1990). Rather than the marketing of cultural things per se, there is an added politicized dimension of "otherness," which marks ethnic goods as products traded across ethnic boundaries. As in many other parts of the world, ethnic tourism in Yunnan is built on an us/them dynamic, in this case contrasting the majority Han

Chinese society with the exotic (but now modernizing) minorities. For example, a popular new tourist attraction in Yunnan is the *Minzucun* (Nationalities Village) located on the outskirts of Kunming. In these tourist villages the lifeways of many distinct peoples are presented and ethnic souvenirs are sold.

Lunan County and the Sani Yi

Lunan Yi Nationality Autonomous County (*Lunan Yizu Zizhixian*) is the home of *Shilin* (the Stone Forest), a national park of karst formations near Kunming and extremely popular with domestic and international tourists visiting Yunnan Province. The park is being heavily developed by various government agencies, and there is a comprehensive plan for this and other sites in the county (Kunming Chengshi Kexueyanjiuhui 1990). New roads and hotels are in place and new rail and air facilities are opening. In 1992, there were 1.48 million visitors to Lunan scenic districts, with Shilin alone receiving 1.15 million of these visitors (including 104,800 international tourists). Earning for the park reached RMB¥5.25 million for the year (Wang 1993). Local tourism employment in administration (approximately 100 government agency employees), service, and infrastructure is growing rapidly, but has not been quantified in provincial reports.

Shilin used to be part of the ancestral lands of the Sani Yi people, a Tibeto-Burman group which settled in the region more than 500 years ago. The Sani are one of 28 designated sub-branches of the state constructed "Yi" national minority (*minzu*). The Yi nationality is a macro-linguistic group of over five million people. Sani language, social system and material culture are distinct. Lunan County population in the late twentieth century is about 30 percent Sani (60,000 people) and 70 percent Han Chinese. One of the primary images used to promote the region by the government, and also the logo of the provincial tourism bureau, is the Sani folktale of "Ashima," a heroic maiden who was turned into stone while resisting a rapacious interloper.

Private Free Market Handicraft Production

With the opening of Shilin to international tourism in 1980, Sani Yi free market artisans began to build an informal sector of handicraft souvenir manufacturing. This is primarily a woman's business (Swain 1993), produced and marketed out of the home. The types of handicrafts they began to sell, all based on their embroidered arts, can be chronologically categorized into the following four groups.

a. Indigenous products: own use, handwoven hemp cloth bags, women's clothing, baby pack carriers

b. Tourist goods of their own manufacture using Sani products: pillow cushions from baby packs, simplified shoes, hats and aprons adapted to tourist tastes

c. Invented forms: adapted, non-indigenous goods that are added to the cannon of embroidery motifs, including money belts, table clothes, purses; "Animateur" crafts (Horner 1993) introduced by outside agents, including Latin American-style pulsera bracelets introduced by Japanese tourists, bible markers introduced by Western missionaries, and dolls introduced by a Western anthropologist

d. Mass-produced goods: using machine embroidered ribbons, wholesaled hand embroidery and machine-made children's clothing

This is not so much an evolutionary process ending in debased pseudo-ethnic goods, as it is a range of responses to commercialization conditions (Cohen 1993). In general, new forms of goods have been added to the basic inventory of Sani items. A survey of urban Sani women who were selling baskets in 1992 revealed a high percentages of *b* and *d* products, the quickly produced sure sellers, with a few higher priced unique, "traditional" items and/or self-valued fine embroidery from categories *a* and *c*.

There are two primary sites of Sani ethnic handicraft marketing: in and around Shilin, and in the nearby provincial capital of Kunming, a two hour bus ride from Lunan County. The following section discusses the histories and distinct market conditions of these two sites.

Shilin Free Market

Handicraft marketing at Shilin started from the village of *Wukeshu* (Five Trees) which is located by the present park's main gate. Wukeshu was a nondescript Sani village until the mid-1980s, when the government started to actively administer tourism development. At that time all the village lanes were un-paved, all livestock roamed freely, and most houses were rammed-earth and thatch. The village population of 700 people in 144 households was all Sani, and virtually all adults farmed their adjacent lands, which then included the park itself.

By 1993 numerous changes had taken place: the village lanes were all paved to benefit the locals and wandering tourists; an edict from the Shilin Tourism Bureau enforced with fines the confinement of all livestock, even the pigs; almost all houses had tile roofs; a new house building boom was underway on the village periphery; and non-Sani workers were renting out old buildings in the community. The official village population of 760 people is still almost all Sani, but the number of households has increased to 193, each of which has fewer members than before. Two hundred twenty nine people have been re-classified from peasant (*nongmin*) status to Kunming residents, and the village land base has shrunken from 434 mu (28.95 ha) in 1988 to 191 mu (12.74 ha) in late 1993, as the Tourism Bureau bought up the rights for further park development. These major changes in such a short time are also reflected in Wukeshu's handicraft business.

Three periods of handicraft commoditization in Wukeshu can be seen from 1981 to 1994. The first era, 1981-6, was village family based, marketing indigenous goods mainly to international tourists. Embroidery is generally done by women, but machine sewing construction is often done by Sani men. Sales were usually conducted by local Sani women in the park or by leading tourists into their nearby homes where they ply their guests with sunflower seeds, tea, and a hard-sell.

From 1986-92 during the second era, the Shilin Tourism Bureau become involved in controlling the handicraft trade by forbidding the locals from randomly selling in the park and setting up stalls within the park's gates. All trade must be conducted in these stalls rented, which for RMB¥10 per month in 1990 and RMB¥10 per 10 days in 1993. Rents were collected by the county tax bureau. Up to 125 stalls were rented out, often with 2 to 4 women sharing a stall. While trade had originally been organized mainly around family ties, now some unrelated women from other villages were also renting stalls, and a new marketplace developed outside the park gate specializing in generic manufactured tourist souvenirs. Within the park, purchased manufactured goods, ranging from mass-produced "Sani" style bags and clothes to plastic bead bags emblazoned with "Seattle" or "Jerusalem", were gradually added to the stock as these, rather than indigenous handicrafts, were more often purchased by domestic tourists.

From 1992 on, the third era of Shilin handicraft marketing has continued to develop. Tourism Bureau control has again reshaped the face of handicraft marketing. A 1992 ruling made it possible for only citizens of Wukeshu to sell at stalls within the park, as a compensatory arrangement along with various service work for villagers who are steadily loosing their agricultural base to tourism development. Eighty-eight families officially work as handicraft marketers in Shilin. They rent their stalls by 10 day lottery, as some are much better located than others, and make an average monthly profit of RMB¥400 per woman. They also have a number of expenses, due to extensive purchasing of piecework and manufactured items to sell.

Some of the old rhythms of the pre-1986 days still persist. The seasonality of tourism peaks at Chinese New Year and in July and August, while the busy farming seasons (*nongmang*) for the Sani are in the spring and fall. In Fall 1993, less than 30 of the 88 stalls were regularly occupied. In addition, Sani women still have their social time to sit, embroider, and talk while waiting for the tourists, or to make playful runs into the park for a tourist sale before being caught by the park police and fined. However, the most recent period of Wukeshu handicraft production has been accompanied by a noticeable decline in the general quality of goods, fewer traders, and a pessimism about the future of Sani marketing of handicrafts in Shilin. The Tourism Bureau has constructed a cement and tile shopping plaza just outside the park gates and plans to soon remove the handicraft stalls in the park, forbidding any trade there. They will rent out little shops in the plaza to Wukeshu residents and a number of outsiders who will operate restaurants and competing souvenir shops. Many of the approximately 20 Wukeshu women who are over 50 years old and who have sold in the park have said they will retire rather than compete with the younger, multi-lingual, local women for what trade does continue once Wukeshu's special privileges in the park are removed.

Two other social phenomena related to handicraft production affect Sani traders in both Shilin and Kunming. A secondary, internal wholesale market has become well established within Sani society. Rural, poorer, Sani women sell their personal handicrafts and family heirlooms at country markets to Shilin and urban traders for resale. The impoverishment of these women is a clear example of social stratification in response to free market tourism activities.

The second phenomenon is one of economic competition and cooperation across ethnic boundaries in the production and sale of Sani artifacts. Han Chinese tailors from as far away as Sichuan, most of whom are men, have moved into Wukeshu during the past few years to craft "Sani" goods to sell to tourists or to Sani traders who resell them in the park or on the street. Fourteen Han Chinese families lived in the village in Fall 1993, producing vast quantities of bags and children's Ashima costumes. Small "ribbon bags" which pass for ethnic goods constructed of commercial ribbons are wholesaled for as little as RMB ¥0.50 each, and are popular with domestic and foreign tourists alike. Many Wukeshu women say they have no time to make all the goods they can sell. For a bag they may sell for more than RMB¥15, they have paid a tailor RMB¥1.50 and have purchased the materials for about RMB¥8 to 10. There are also some Han Chinese women who are native to ethnically mixed Sani villages and who also produce and market Sani style goods to tourists in Kunming.

Kunming Free Markets

The history of urban Sani handicraft selling is one of gradually increasing activity. From 1983 to 1986, there were anywhere from a handful to 50 women in the city, depending on the same seasonal constraints found in Shilin. Most of these women make a circular migration from their home villages in Lunan County to one specific guest house in Kunming which has served as a community center for transitory Sani working in the city. This migration began when Sani women followed the tourists back from Shilin and discovered there was another market in core tourist areas around hotels and attractions. Working together in small groups, they would sell their own and family member's handicrafts. They soon also became involved in Kunming's urban money changing black market. This black market was based on the disparity in the exchange rates of China's two currencies. The "soft" RMB yuan was much more susceptible to inflationary devaluation than is the "hard" tourist currency, the FEC yuan, and foreign hard currencies, which were offered for handicrafts purchased by international tourists.

Since 1986 the number of circular migration traders has doubled, with up to 100 sellers coming into the city during the summer, and fewer than 40 in the winter. The women developed distinct "turfs," or selling areas, which included the city's outlying tourist sites. Some women said they made more cash changing money than selling handicrafts. They earned about one percent of the value of US dollars changed into RMB yuan from their Han Chinese bosses. Urban vendors are now also selling Sani handicrafts which they buy wholesale, and some commercial goods, in addition to their own family-made products.

There is considerable diversity among Sani handicraft sellers who range in ideology from Catholics to Communists, come from a number of different communities, and may not even be Sani. Besides the relatively poor, circular migrating farmers, Sani handicraft vendors also include migrants from households in Lunan County towns, headed by salaried workers, and urban residents in Kunming. They may be teenagers or grandmothers, illiterate or high school graduates. They are female and are all trying to make a living from tourism.

These women usually wear their distinctive ethnic dress which shows their handicraft abilities and marks them both as possible money changers and ethnic others. As such, they may be welcomed for their trade or despised for the perceived minority "backwardness" by the local population in the provincial capital.

The issues affecting these Sani handicraft vendors are:

1. the intermittent intervention by the government in the black market, crackdowns on unlicensed vendors; and
2. their fragile niche in urban landscape as unofficial street people tolerated for the foreign currency their trade generates.

Government Handicraft Production Enterprises

In Lunan County there were several government handicraft production enterprises in place in 1993, with plans for other community and work unit (*danwei*) directed enterprises. The Lunan County Women's Federation (*fulian*) Ashima Embroidery Factory was started in 1988 and is affiliated with the Women's Professional Training Center of Lunan County. UNICEF provided three years of technical support, which established an effective production cycle but there was no training in marketing nor any follow-up evaluations. Consequently, the factory now does not have the skills, a catalog, or order forms to market its goods outside of government channels. UNICEF funded a truck, 32 sewing machines, 20 recorders, 1 television and VCR, a copying machine, and 10 bicycles for the factory. The center ran some 65 training sessions for 3,878 women ranging from sewing, cross stitching and other embroidery, to a "civilized work and education" course.

In their 1993 final report to UNICEF, the Training Center states that the motivation for starting the factory was to raise the quality and productivity of embroidery handicrafts done by Yi women in their spare time (when not farming), to bring in more income for their families. In 1993, more than 200 women were reported to be doing piecework for the factory, earning from RMB¥100 to 200 per month. In the five year history of the factory, it has paid out RMB¥500,000 to piece workers. According to the director of the Lunan Women's Federation, the factory pays workers 80 percent of the wholesale price and also provides the materials free of charge. Their profits are usually close to what Sani women make who sell comparable goods on the free market. The Training Center's report, as well as its director, stated that some of their trainees have their own selling stands, in Shilin. When asked about this, the head of the Wukeshu Women's Federation denied that anyone from the village had ever been trained by the Center or worked for the factory. The line between government program trained handicraft workers and self-trained artisans becomes even murkier with the report's statement that there are now more than 8,000 women in Lunan County whose handicrafts are either their profession or a part-time job, earning annual incomes ranging from RMB¥100 to 10,000. There are no trustworthy statistics published on handicraft production by the government, but a *China Daily* (1992) newspaper story makes the interesting assertion that "Yi farmers in Lunan County . . . styled shoes, bags, table clothes and sofa covers have been exported to Japan, the United States, Australia, and Hong Kong, earning the country more than RMB¥700,000 (US$123,000) in the first eight months of this year."

The other government enterprises in Lunan County which produce handicrafts are two clothing and a machine embroidery factories.

Employees (women and men) in these factories construct Sani style items for sale locally, and to the wider national tourism market. The Lunan County Nationalities Clothing Factory (*Lunan Zhen Minzu Yifu Chang*) which opened in 1956 makes and sells hand embroidered bags. They buy piecework from villagers and factory workers, paying 40 percent to the worker and 60 percent to the factory. They make about 1,000 of these bags in a month, selling wholesale for RMB¥10 in Kunming. This factory also makes Sani style women's and men's clothing. Their 140 employees each receives a base annual salary of RMB¥1,000. The Nationalities Embroidery Handicraft Factory (*Minzu Gongyi Xiu Chang*) produces machine embroidered baby carriers wholesaling for RMB¥20 and blue folk fabric clothes. It has about 20 employees, some of whom are part-time. In the past they also made and marketed Sani style embroidered bags but now they do not because there is too much competition.

On the road to Shilin Park outside of Wukeshu, construction was started in 1993 for the Ashima Special Arts Center (*Ashima Yishu Zhuanshang*), a very ambitious joint venture project with a hotel (which was built first), a performance hall, an observatory, a museum, and an artisan handicraft production with an exhibition and sales hall. The chief of the Lunan County Culture Bureau is very enthusiastic about the project for both its economic development potential and as a way to promote ethnic arts and culture. What will be the actual impact of this project, which is named for the Sani heroine but intends to have representatives of some 20 distinct Yi peoples from three provinces, remains to be seen. In Wukeshu, there is another plan being promoted by the Tourism Bureau and local officials to museumize the village, moving all the residents away and setting up a "Sanitized" Sani tourist village with beautiful young people in quaint costumes acting as guides to the past. In a first step toward this goal, the village has been legally transformed into a corporation as of November 1993. One of the proposed functions of the corporation is to regulate handicraft production by its members.

Conclusions

Artisan production of handicrafts is seen by both the government and individuals in Yunnan, China as a valuable asset in tourism development. However, as this brief discussion of handicraft production and marketing in one county illustrates the returns are often small, and issues of control and quality will need to be addressed if many people are to benefit.

As we saw in the case of Lunan, the government's reach is more wide ranging and varied into the informal sector than originally hypothesized in this study. Even though Sani women are free to produce their own goods and buy wholesale, they still must depend on the government to approve the places where they can sell to the tourists. Furthermore, artistic expression is market driven. In China this is often a government controlled market. If the state buying agent is only buying little bags with "Ashima" embroidered in red, it does not pay to innovate. Literally reams of this type of bag are available from Kunming to the Great Wall. In the formal sector, which is controlled even more by government policy, there is the advantage of a known, set income for a given product.

Cooperatives were not discussed because they have not been used for handicraft production in Lunan. However, a quick review of tourism marketing in the Dali and Lijiang regions of Yunnan, indicated that cooperatives are being successfully used in the formal sector to produce and market tourist goods, including indigenous Bai tie-died cloth and Naxi rugs. A Canadian development project is currently working with these coops. In Yunnan it continues to be seen that the government is a powerful arbitrator, determining the range of free markets for artisan production.

The future of China's tourism-based handicraft industries clearly hinges on the success of China's economic and cultural policies. As we have seen among the Sani of Yunnan, promises of a better life through tourism development also brings new problems and old prejudices. The commoditization of Sani culture has resulted in the denigration or loss of art forms and a growing class structure running counter to ethnic group cohesion. The old ethnic stereotype of the Han Chinese majority, which sees a lack of inherent worth in the culture (*wenhua*) of minority traditions, also underlies various attempts to package touristic entertainment in pseudo-authenticity. The very people whose livelihood, lands, and society are appropriated as the basis for this tourism industry may be left out of the decision making process and employment generated by tourism development. Under the Chinese socialist market system, state and private artisan production are contributing to, but not necessarily benefiting a changing Sani society.

Notes

1. Research support by the University of California UREP, 1992 and National Academy of Sciences Committee on Scholarly Communication with China, 1993 is gratefully acknowledged.
2. US dollar and Chinese RMB yuan are quoted in the amounts cited in the original reference sources. For foreign exchange purposes, the Chinese sources used in this essay apparently used an exchange rate of FEC¥4.7 to US$1 for 1990 and FEC¥5.25 to US$1 for 1991.

References

China Daily. 1992. Yunnan Determined to Up Its Exports and Revenue. (December 8.)

Cohen, Erik.1993. Introduction: Investigating Tourist Arts. *Annals of Tourism Research* 20(1): 1-8.

Horner, Alice E. 1993. Tourism Arts in Africa Before Tourism. *Annals of Tourism Research* 20(1): 52-63.

Kunming Chengshi Kexueyanjiuhui. 1990. *Lunan Shilin Fengjing Mingshengqu* (Lunan Shilin Scenic District). Kunming, Yunnan: Kunming City Scientific Research Group.

Sun, Gang, ed. 1992. *The Yearbook of China Tourism Statistics 1992*. Beijing: China Travel and Tourism Press.

Swain, Margaret Byrne. 1990. Commoditizing Ethnicity in Southwest China. *Cultural Survival Quarterly* 14(1): 26-9.

_____. 1993. Women Producers of Ethnic Arts. *Annals of Tourism Research* 20(1): 32-51.

YINGOS. 1993. *Yunnan International Non-Government Organization Society - A Brief Introduction*. Kunming, Yunnan.

Yunnan Sheng Luyouju. 1993. *Yunnan Luyou Tongji Ziliao, 1992* (Yunnan Tourism Statistical Data). Kunming, Yunnan.

Yunnan Sheng Tongjiju. 1992. *Yunnan Tongji Nianjian, 1992* (Yunnan Statistical Yearbook). Kunming, Yunnan.

Wang, Fucheng. 1993. *Guanyu Fazhan Luyoushiye de Qingkuang Baogao* (A Status Report About the Development of Tourism Enterprise). Shilin, Yunnan: Lunan Yizu Autonomous County Tourism Bureau.

PART FIVE

Conclusions and Future Prospects

14

China's Tourism: Opportunities, Challenges, and Strategies

Zhang Guangrui, Lawrence Yu, and Alan A. Lew

Travel and tourism has become a strategic industry in China's development toward a "socialist market economy." A decade of development has yielded both positive experiences and hard lessons. The country is still probing better ways of developing a strong travel and tourism industry which can compete successfully in its regional and global markets. China, therefore, faces both opportunities and challenges in developing its tourism to the next level. China's tourism has a bright future, although it will require arduous efforts to develop it effectively. The opportunities and challenges that China faces are discussed, and the strategies are identified as recommendations for future development.

Opportunities

Opportunities for further tourism development in China are widespread, and much of it is self-evident. An incredible diversity of landscapes and cultures stretch across the vastness of China. There is something for every type of tourist: densely crowded cities with modern skylines and hotels, agricultural villages nestled in lush tropical vegetation, nomadic horse-riders galloping across open grasslands and deserts, and snow covered mountains offering challenging adventures. Most of the many cultures are very old and very traditional. There is great potential in China for specialized tourism, focusing on ethnic groups and environmental adventure. This form of tourism has been growing steadily over the years, but is still comparatively meager. The growing market in *ecotourism* in the developed world will find considerable opportunities in China.

Further deepening of the recent economic reforms and increasing openness to the outside world will help China's economy grow faster. The country's gross domestic product (GDP) is expected to grow at 8 to 9 percent per year through the 1990s. A stronger economy will afford further improvements in infrastructure for tourism development. Wealthy Chinese will increasingly join the army of foreign tourists at international hotels and resorts. Tourism, as an important tertiary industry, may enjoy more preferential government policies in the future, drawing wider attention and support from society.

Internationally, China is situated in the rapidly growing Asia/Pacific realm. Both the economies and tourist travel are expected to grow faster in this region than the rest of the world. According to a World Travel and Tourism Council projection, global tourism growth in both arrivals and expenditures during the 1990s will be less than 6 percent, while the growth in the dynamic Asia/Pacific market is estimated to be between 7 and 10 percent (WTTC 1992: 14). In addition to Japan, which is expected to continue to be a major tourist market for China, the improvement of diplomatic and economic relations with neighboring countries and regions in the Asia/Pacific area is bringing increased numbers of tourists and business travellers. The recent improvement of diplomatic and economic relations with the neighboring countries and regions includes the normalization of diplomatic relations with ASEAN countries and the Republic of Korea, the ice-breaking Wang-Koo Talks between China and Taiwan in April, 1993 in Singapore, the return of Hong Kong and Macao to the mainland by the end of this century, and the official end of the hostilities with Vietnam and the former USSR. China is the largest country in the Asia/Pacific region and an active member of the Pacific Asia Travel Association (PATA). As a unique and interesting destination, China will be a major factor in the future development of tourism in Asia.

Fading memories of the 1989 Tiananmen Square Incident have encouraged increased tourist arrivals from North American and European countries. According to estimates by the National Tourism Administration of China (NTA), Canada joined the United States as the second western country that sent more than 100,000 tourists to China in 1993 (*San Francisco Times* 1993). In the European market, there have been rapid rises in arrivals from Italy, Greece, and Portugal. There are also some emerging tourist generating markets in south America. In 1992, tourists from Columbia, Chile, and Uruguay were doubled from those of 1991. Tourist arrivals from the Latin American markets will continue to grow.

The success of China's market-oriented reforms has drawn attention worldwide, from politicians to business circles and the general public.

Finally given an opportunity, the Chinese people are demonstrating the entrepreneurial skills and ingenuity that have made expatriate Chinese so economically successful the world over. These talents have been long suppressed and will take some time to achieve their full potential. However, there is little doubt that, barring any unpredictable upheavals, China will soon be as successful in the tourism business as any competitor in the international marketplace.

China's rapidly developing business environment is already responsible for a major part of the growth in tourism in recent years. Not only are foreign investments coming into the country, but so are increasing numbers of entrepreneurs, who typically combine pleasure with their business trip. This component of the visitor market will likely increase in the coming years.

In addition, the resumption of member status in GATT provides other opportunities for China's tourism development, including:

- fewer formalities and barriers for cross-border travellers,
- reductions in travelling costs as a result of global competition,
- removal of some protectionist policies, and
- improvement in communication, financial transactions, and information facilities.

The removal of barriers to trade and travel will definitely enhance China's position as a country for financial investment, international business, and business and leisure travel.

The central government in Beijing still maintains great authority over the direction that development takes at the local level. The central governments of very few other large countries have the ability to have such a direct influence at all levels of society. Recent policies allowing the expansion of domestic tourism is one positive example of this influence. The trend in China is toward the decentralization of authority and decision-making. Decentralization, however, has a long way to go and the centralized bodies will likely retain much authority into the near future. If used effectively, this authority can constructively guide China to overcome the many challenges it faces in tourism development in the 1990s, and beyond.

Challenges

Along with the numerous opportunities, however, China will continue to encounter strong challenges. China's tourist industry is not as effective as it could be in the face of powerful international competition. Asia as a whole sees Europe and North America as its main tourist-generating markets. All of the tourist destinations in the region vie with each other for the same markets with similar products. Although China has many advantages in its diversity of tourist resources, these may not be brought into full play due to inadequate facilities, tight transportation, inflexible business operations, ineffective promotion, and undesirable service. Other Asian countries and areas, especially the ASEAN countries, Hong Kong, and Taiwan, are more competitive than China in this region owing to their successful economies, well-developed tourism infrastructure, quick access to information, flexible business operations, wide international connections, and effective promotion with the help of powerful regional tourist associations.

A major barrier to China's development in tourism, and the areas that support tourism, is its large and entrenched bureaucracy. The same centralization that enables China to make tremendous social and political shifts is highly resistant to its own need for institutional changes. Corruption among local officials has been a major impediment to international investment in China. Although considerable efforts are being made to address this problem, they have yet to be effective.

The reputation of China's tourist industry is less than desirable and leaves much room to improve. In fact, a clear and positive tourist image of China has yet to be truly established. Unfortunately, a successful tourist image, which embodies the diversity of tourist resources and attractions, as well as the features of the political and economic systems, cannot be established or manipulated easily. The Han Chinese culture, and the many spectacular natural attractions, should always remain the core of China's tourism development. While this approach is obvious from the standpoint of the international marketplace, it is unclear what the role of ethnic minorities, and the peripheral environment that they occupy, should be in China's tourism development. There is a real threat in China that minority traditions will be lost, or only seen and experienced in museum-like compounds. A greater sensitivity to, and support of, minority difference is sorely needed in the Han Chinese dominated government authorities.

The minority ethnic groups problem reflects the larger image problem of China in the West. The tight control that China's central government exerts over political decent is discussed in the Western media almost as much as is the country's economic miracle. This is an important issue for some potential travelers, particularly from the U.S. and Europe. No matter how many "Visit China" campaigns the NTA plans, they may have less impact on the major international markets than images presented in foreign media outlets of a Chinese government that supresses individual political freedoms. This image problem, however, is created by forces beyond the sway of the tourism industry. Furthermore, the situation is likely to remain unchanged for the foreseeable future.

Of all aspects of the tourism industry, hotel management and operations experienced noticeable improvement thanks to the transfer of management know-how through joint-venture operations and foreign management companies. But, travel service management and aviation operations are still lagging behind. In travel service operations, the lack of service attitude and the low productivity of tour guides are major hindering factors on the improvement of visitor satisfaction (Cai and Woods 1993). The lack of a central reservation system for transportation and accommodations often causes low efficiency in operations and inconvenience to the travelers. Systematic travel service management and operations are badly needed to improve visitor experience and satisfaction.

With the gradual liberalized aviation policy, China now has at least a dozen of domestic airlines. Some of the airlines are poorly staffed and equipped because of the shortage of qualified pilots and air-traffic controllers in the country to meet such dramatic growth. As a result, flight safety has been a major concern for travel in China, which accounted for a fifth of the world's airline passenger fatalities in 1992 (Westlake 1993). In addition, ten airplane hijackings were reported in 1993 alone. There is a lack of experience and proper equipment for effective airport security. Improved airport security and flight safety are vital for China to further promote its tourism industry.

Tourist safety in China has also become a serious concern for the international travel industry. This was highlighted by the March 1994 robbery and murder of 24 Taiwanese tourists and eight Chinese crew members and guides on One-Thousand-Island Lake in Zhejiang Province (Mark 1994a; 1994b). Following this incident the Taiwanese government temporarily halted group travel to China, as well as other types of cultural exchanges and business activities with the mainland. This, and other incidents, has tarnished China's image as a "safe" destination for international tourists. The future success of international tourism to China will require better measures to safeguard the personal safety of international tourists by both the government and private sector.

With increasing disposable income and free time among the Chinese people, growing numbers are participating in tourism. Domestic tourism actually presents a much greater challenge than international tourism for China's transportation systems and the management of tourist attractions. All means of transportation are currently over-burdened, while popular destinations are experiencing severe environmental degradation from heavy usage. Some steps have been taken to control the over use of tourism resources, but more needs to be done, and the sooner the better.

In addition to more frequent and longer domestic trips, greater openness to the outside world is encouraging increasing relaxation of laws regulating cross-border travel for Chinese citizens. This has resulted in a steady increase in outbound international travel by Chinese citizens. Much of this has been in the form of combined business and pleasure trips. Neighboring countries and those of ASEAN are the primary destinations for the Chinese at present. More distant destinations will likely become available to wealthy Chinese individuals in the near future. Although a greater balance between domestic, inbound, and outbound tourism will not be realized in the short term, there will likely be a boom of outbound tourism very soon.

Strategies

Given the highly centralized nature of Chinese society, even under the unprecedented reforms of the 1990s, appropriate government strategies and policies will be key to the future success of the country's tourism industry. China should persist in its economic policy of developing tourism, and more supporting policies favorable to the industry should be formulated. The continued building of transportation infrastructure remains a development priority, including airport facilities, rail systems, and highway development. Only with a well-established transportation network, can China efficiently move its rapidly increasing numbers of international and domestic tourists.

Instead of the current policies which focus on increasing the numbers of international arrivals, greater effort should be made to improve the productivity of the industry. This can be achieved by enhancing human capital through training and education, and by introducing modern methods of management and supervision. In addition, laws, rules, and regulations governing tourism development should be initiated and developed. An industry code of conduct can direct business operations to be more effective and ethical, and a certified travel counselor (CTC) program, as practiced in the U.S., can improve the management effectiveness of the travel services. Communication and education between the government and local populations should also be carried out in order to avoid or reduce the negative impacts of tourism economically, culturally, socially, and environmentally.

Choice and adjustment to target markets should be made according to the changing trends of international tourism, with products being introduced and renovated according to the needs of both international and domestic travelers. China needs to expand its international marketing and promotion efforts. The immediate contact of the NTA with the international market has generally been through its non-profit overseas offices. These overseas offices are primarily liaison offices and their marketing efforts are quite limited. More aggressive marketing, including regional and international cooperative campaigns, should be undertaken. To do this, it is imperative for China to understand international market demands and develop appropriate travel products and services.

One example of a rapidly growing international travel market is nature- and culture-based ecotourism. Ecotourism is one of the most rapidly growing forms of specialized travel in the West, with central American countries, such as Costa Rica, being the principal destinations at present. Ecotourists are often willing to pay a premium to experience cultures and environmental adventures in an authentic manner. The dominant emphasis on mass tourism that pervades most of the development in China is anathema to the interests of ecotourists. Much of China, especially in the more peripheral regions, is still an ecotourism paradise. The Chinese government should act now to preserve the remote and fragile environments and cultures that may prove to be one of their most important tourism resources in the future.

China also needs to pay greater attention to the management and protection of its more accessible tourist resources. The degradation and destruction of tourism resources by careless development or uncontrolled tourist use can destroy the drawing power that pulls the tourists to China at the first place. A demand-based, environmentally sustainable, and culturally sensitive development strategy is needed to guide China's resource assessment and development. These are issues that tourism developers are facing in many developing countries, and China should actively take part in the international discussion on how to best resolve these problems.

It is strongly recommended that China take greater steps to provide better quality guest service to improve the visitor's experience and satisfaction. The concept of service is not well accentuated in China's tourism industry, and visitor discontent and complaints often derive from the poor attitudes and service they encounter. Now that most of service employees regularly expect and accept gratuities from the international tourists, they must begin to provide the level of services acceptable by the international standards. Otherwise unhappy visitors will further tarnish the image of China and the country will lose repeat business, as well as potential new visitors. Service is really an attitude. The teaching and training of service at schools and workplaces needs to focus on developing proper attitudes in tourism workers.

The National Tourism Administration of China (NTA) has an ambitious plan for tourism development into the year 2000 (Li 1993). Its goals include an increase in annual receipts from international tourism to US$5 billion by 1995 and US$10 billion by the year 2000 (with an annual growth rate of 14 percent). The goals for the annual income generated from the domestic tourism is RMB¥50 billion by 1995 and RMB¥120 billion by the year 2000 (with an annual growth rate of 21 percent). If these goals are met, the total contribution of tourism to the national economy would be RMB¥1100 billion in decade from 1990 to 2000. In line with this plan are several large tourism campaigns, including:

- the East Asia and Pacific Year of Travel in 1994,
- the 1997 Visit China Year in celebration of Hong Kong's returning to the mainland, and
- the 1999 celebration of the 50 anniversary of the People's Republic of China and the return of Macao to the motherland.

Other themes for tourism promotion include: natural landscape for 1993, history and antiquity for 1994, folk cultures for 1995, and leisure travel for 1996. These promotions are designed to give full exposure to China's tourism resources, ranging from natural wonders to cultural and historic sites, and modern, man-made attractions. In addition to this advertising approach, tourism authorities and the private and semi-private hospitality industry need to impress upon the government the importance of political stability to their success. As tourism becomes increasingly more important, perhaps its voice on these issues will have greater influence.

A long-term, sustainable development approach supported by adequate infrastructure, well-trained human resource, and aggressive marketing plan could bring international and domestic tourism development in China to the new heights by the year 2000, and beyond.

Reference

Cai, Liping and Robert Woods. 1993. China's Tourism-Service Failure. *The Cornell Hotel and Restaurant Administration Quarterly* 34(4): 30-39.

Li, Xianhui. 1993. Kaituochuangxin, zhenzhuashigan (Report of the National Conference on Tourism). *China Tourism News* (December 1).

Mark, Jeremy. 1994a. Suspicions about Deaths of 24 Tourists Drives Wedge between Taiwan, China. *Wall street Journal* (April 12): A15.

_____. 1994b. Taiwan Curtails Trade with China in Tourist Death. *Wall Street Journal* (April 13): A10.

San Francisco Times. 1993. New Development Patterns in China's Tourism Industry. (July 21): 8.

Westlake, Michael. 1993. Troubled Take-off. *Far Eastern Economic Review* 156(7): 52-3.

World Travel and Tourism Council (WTTC). 1992. *The WTTC Report, 1992 complete edition: Travel & Tourism*. London: WTTC.

Acronyms and Glossary

ASEAN	Association of South East Asian Nations
BTT	Bureau of Travel and Tourism
CA	Air China
CAAC	Civil Aviation Administration of China
CCP	Chinese Communist Party
CIS	Commonwealth of Independent States
CITS	China International Travel Service
CJ	China Northern Airlines
CTC	Certified Travel Counselor
CTS	China Travel Service
CYTS	China Youth Travel Service
CZ	China Southern Airlines
DPLE	Department of Personnel, Labor and Education
FCTA	First Category Travel Service
FEC	Foreign Exchange Certificate
FIT	Foreign Independent Traveler
FYP	Five Year Plan
GATT	General Agreement on Tariffs and Trade
GCR	Great Cultural Revolution
GDP	Gross Domestic Product
GIT	Group Inclusive Tour
GLP	Great Leap Forward
IMF	International Monetary Fund
MU	China Eastern Airlines
NTA	National Tourism Administration (Same as SATT, State Administration for Travel and Tourism; also referred to as CNTA)
NTO	National Tourism Organization
OTS	Overseas Travel Services
PATA	Pacific Asia Travel Association
PLA	People's Liberation Army
PRC	People's Republic of China
PSB	Public Security Bureau
RMB	Renminbi
ROC	Republic of China
SATT	State Administration for Travel and Tourism (same as NTA, National Tourism Administration)
SEZ	Special Economic Zone
SCTA	Second Category Travel Service

SZ	China Southwest Airlines
TCTA	Third Category Travel Service
TIR	Tourism Intensity Rate
VFR	Visiting Friends and Relatives
WH	China Northwest Airlines
WTO	World Tourism Organization
WTTC	World Travel and Tourism Council
XO	Xinjiang Airlines

Ashima. A folk heroin in the Sani Yi culture in Yunnan Province.

Autonomous Region. One of China's administrative divisions, usually designating provinces in which ethnic minority are predominate. There are five autonomous regions in China: Neimenggu (Inner Mongolia) Autonomous Region, Guangxi Zhuang Autonomous Region, Xizang (Tibet) Autonomous Region, Ningxia Hui Autonomous Region, and the Xinjiang Uygur Autonomous Region.

Chan Buddhism. A form of Chinese Buddhism which emphasizes meditation and contemplation. It was influenced by Daoism and formed the basis of Japanese Zen Buddhism.

Compatriots. Ethnic Chinese who are citizens of Hong Kong, Macao, and Taiwan.

Confucius (Kongfuzi, 551-479 B.C.). Classical philosopher who propagated a philosophy of life that established clearly defined rules governing social relationships and behavior.

Daoism (Taoism). A classical school of philosophy founded on the teachings on Lao Zi which focuses on the search for harmony with the Dao (the "way"). It stresses the relativity of values and the smallness of human endeavors within the working of the universe.

Filial piety. Chinese cultural value that emphasizes obedience, respect, and caring for one's parents and grandparents, or in the case of married daughters, parents-in-law.

First Category Travel Services (FCTS). Chinese travel services that are authorized by the China National Tourism Administration to have direct business contact with overseas travel operators and receive foreign visitors, overseas Chinese, and compatriots from Hong Kong, Macao and Taiwan.

Foreign Affairs Office. Local Chinese government department that is in charge of diplomatic relations with foreign governments and official, government sponsored visitors.

Foreign Exchange Certificate (FEC). China has been practicing dual currency system since late 1970s. the FEC yuan (¥) is issued for use by foreign visitors. The Chinese government stopped issuing new FEC¥ in early 1994, with the intention of eventually stopping use of the dual currency system.

Foreigners. Overseas visitors who hold foreign passports. This excludes citizens of Hong Kong, Macao, and Taiwan.

Four Modernizations. Modernization policies initiated in 1978 by Deng Xiaoping, which essentially overturned the approaches emphasized under Mao Zedong. The four areas of modernization were industry, agriculture, science and technology, and national defense.

Grand Canal. A man-made canal initially begun in the fifth century B.C. and completed in the Sui Dynasty (A.D. 581-618). It facilitated travel and trade between north and south China. The southern section of the canal has now become a major tourist attraction.

Great Cultural Revolution (1966-1976). A political ideological campaign launched by the Communist Chairman Mao Zedong to eradicate revisionist and bourgeois capitalist elements in the communist party and Chinese society.

Great Leap Forward. A nation-wide campaign initiated by Mao Zedong in the late 1950s to rapidly collectivize and increase China's industrial and agricultural production in order to move China into a communist society. Failures of the policy resulted in factories and communes making false reports about production levels and many thousands of peasants died of starvation in rural China.

Ground Service. Travel companies that provide the land portion of travel arrangements--air travel arrangement is not included.

Group Inclusive Tours. Packaged tours that include all travel arrangements for a group of tourists, including transportation, accommodations, meals, and local tour services.

Huan Baohai Tourism Circle. Regional tourism development that integrates tourism projects in the three Bohai Bay provinces of Liaoning, Hebei, and Shandong

Inbound Tourism. Foreign tourists coming to visit a host country.

Jinggangshan Revolutionary Base. The base of the Chinese Communist Party in Jiangxi Province. The communist party mobilized hundreds of peasants in this poverty-stricken province prior to the Long March, and defeated four major attacks by the Nationalist Chinese forces. It is now a major historical attraction for domestic tourists.

Joint Ventures Hotels. Hotels built jointly by Chinese and foreign developers. Both parties share the profits and losses according to their proportion of the investment. The Chinese joint venture law stipulates that the investment rate of the foreign partner should not be lower than 25 percent of the hotel's total investment.

Long March (1934-1935). The Chinese Red Army led by the Communist Party escaped the encirclement by the Nationalist forces and took a 6000-mile march from Jinggangshan in Jiangxi Province to Yanan in Shaanxi Province.

Management Contract Agreement. Chinese hotels that are contracted to a foreign hotel management company for operation. It is a form of technology transfer in which the foreign hotel management company introduces new reservation and operation systems and trains the Chinese staff. The Chinese-side maintains complete ownership of the hotel.

Miao Pale. Mountains region of Southwest China and extending into northern Vietnam, Laos, and Thailand in which the Miao ethnic minority group live. The Miao are also known as the Hmong.

Outbound Tourism. Citizens of a country going to visit one or more other countries.

Overseas Chinese. This term has two meanings: (1) Official Chinese government statistics consider "overseas Chinese" to be Chinese nationals reside in foreign countries, but maintain Peoples Republic of China citizenship and a PRC passport; (2) the popular use of "overseas Chinese" refers to ethnic Chinese who are citizens of countries outside of China, Hong Kong, Macao, and Taiwan. These overseas Chinese do not hold PRC passports.

Qingming Festival. A traditional festival celebrated in the Spring to honor the dead.

Renminbi (RMB). The Chinese currency used by Chinese citizens.

Second Category Travel Services (SCTS). Chinese travel services that are not permitted to have direct business contact with overseas travel operators. However, they can conduct sightseeing tours for overseas tourists organized by First Category Travel Services.

Special Economic Zone (SEZ). Cities and region designated by the Chinese central government to experiment free-market economic systems (similar to Hong Kong's economy). The SEZs are mostly on the coast and have experienced tremendous economic growth and international investment in the past ten years.

Special Municipality. Three major Chinese cities, Beijing, Shanghai, and Tianjin, have the administrative status and privileges of a province because of their political and economic importance.

Star-Rated Hotels. The Chinese government's National Tourism Administration introduced the Five-Star Hotel Rating System in 1990 to insure management standards and service quality. Most of the hotels used by foreign visitors participate in this star rating program.

State Council. The administrative body of the People's Republic. It is headed by the Premier and oversees the day-to-day administration of the country.

Third Category Travel Services (TCTS). Travel services in China that are not permitted to receive foreign tourists or provide services to them. They can only handle domestic tourists.

Third Front Policy. An economic development plan initiated by the Chinese government in 1964 that emphasized military defense through state investment in basic industry (agriculture, mining, and heavy industry) over the production of consumer goods, and on relocation of coastal industry to the interior and remote regions.

Tiao Tiao Kui Kui. Vertical and horizontal integration, or fitting closely and nicely-- similar to the English phrase "To fit like a glove."

Tourism and Vacation Zones. A recent tourism plan proposed by China National Tourism Administration to develop approximately a dozen tourist resorts throughout the country.

Zhongqiu Festival (Mid-Autumn Moon Festival). A major Chinese festival to celebrate the Fall harvest. It is popularly known as the Mooncake Festival in the West.

About the Book

Long virtually closed to foreign travelers, the People's Republic of China in the post-Mao era has become a major international tourist destination. Luxurious hotels are reshaping the urban skylines from Beijing to Shanghai, and the number of both foreign and domestic tourists continues to swell. In this first book to offer an objective and comprehensive view of tourism in China, a multidisciplinary group of scholars explores the country's burgeoning tourist industry, a major component of its recent explosive economic growth.

Tracing the historical evolution of Chin'a tourism policies, leading experts examine the development and organization of the industry, including the hotel business and hospitality education. They consider the effects of both international and domestic tourism on China's environment, economy, and society--including on several minority regions. The contributors discuss the little-understood yet strong influence of ethnic overseas Chinese on the PRC's tourism development, as well as the impact of the Tiananmen uprising. The book concludes with an analysis of the prospects for the future of China's tourism development.

Index